TIME TO EXPLAIN

TIME TO EXPLAIN

Christopher Mayhew

Hutchinson
London Melbourne Auckland Johannesburg

First published in 1987 by Hutchinson Ltd, an imprint of
Century Hutchinson, Brookmount House, 62–65 Chandos Place,
London WC2N 4NW

Century Hutchinson Australia Pty Ltd
PO Box 496, 16–22 Church Street, Hawthorn, Victoria 3122, Australia

Century Hutchinson New Zealand Limited
PO Box 40–086, Glenfield, Auckland 10, New Zealand

Century Hutchinson South Africa (Pty) Ltd
PO Box 337, Bergvlei, 2012 South Africa

Phototypeset in Linotron Sabon by
Input Typesetting Ltd, London SW19 8DR
Printed and bound in Great Britain by
Anchor Brendon Ltd, Tiptree, Essex
ISBN 0 09 168440 4

To my granddaughters
Jessica, Nicola and
Hannah

ACKNOWLEDGEMENTS

My warm thanks to my editor, Harold Harris, for his friendly encouragement and much-needed expert guidance; also to my wife Cicely, my stepmother Beryl, my brother Pat, and my old colleagues Norman Reddaway and John Harris for reading the typescript and making helpful suggestions.

I am grateful to Longman's and Century-Hutchinson for allowing me to reuse some material from *Publish It Not . . .* and *Party Games*.

Finally, my thanks to the staff of Word Perfect, especially Shirley Cave, for coping admirably with the typing and word-processing.

'It is time to explain myself – let us stand up'
Walt Whitman, 'Leaves of Grass'.

Contents

ILLUSTRATIONS

1
BOYHOOD

Imagine a brightly-lit room high up in a large house in Kensington. A white-painted dresser lines one wall, filled with toys and books, including picture books of the life of Jesus. There is a coal fire burning behind a heavy brass fender, and over the mantelpiece hangs a reproduction of Botticelli's 'Adoration of the Magi'. My brother Patrick and I are having tea with our governess, Miss Payne. Pat is four and I am five.

Sitting apart, our nanny, Miss Sharp, is surreptitiously writing down our conversation. She sent me her record, dated 20 November 1921, more than sixty years later.

Pat (looking at the Botticelli): Why does Mary wear such a funny hat?
MP: That's a halo. It's a circle of light which painters used to put round the heads of saints and angels in their pictures.
(Pause)
Pat: Is God Jesus' father?
MP: Yes.
Chris: I have heard in a hymn of someone with four fathers.
MP: Forefathers mean a person's grandparents and great-grandparents and so on.
(Pause)
Chris: God can be everywhere at once.
Pat (gazing at the three-quart milk jug): Well, if God is hiding in our milk jug listening to us, can he be in Africa at the same time?
MP: Yes, but he does not hide in odd places. Wherever people are all over the world, he is in their hearts.
Pat: Well if he finds the windows shut, does he fly back to the sky?

MP: He does not come in through windows and doors.
   He comes like a thought comes into our mind.
Pat: Is he only in people?
MP: And in everything beautiful and good which He has
   made, like flowers and the sea and sunsets and music.
(Pause)
Pat: If God has not quite got back to Heaven and is under
   the sky when it starts raining, what happens to him?
MP: Rain and heat and cold make no difference to God.
   What we call the sky is really air, and Heaven is not a
   place, it is really how people can spend time with God.
(Pause)
Chris: Satan hates us when we obey God.
Pat: Why?
MP: Because Satan hates everything which is good.
Pat: Well, I suppose he hates to have chicken for his dinner
   then.
MP: I really meant Satan hates people doing good things.
   And he is a Spirit like God, and does not need food as
   we do.

The search for religious truth, begun so early, and with such
patient and resourceful guidance, preoccupied my brother
and (in more eccentric ways) myself for long periods of our
lives. Pat developed a strong religious faith, which led him
to become a probation officer, then a teacher of handicapped
children and finally the headmaster of a grammar school for
spastic boys. During the war, as I shall recount, he achieved
the extraordinary distinction of winning the Military Medal
while registered as a conscientious objector.

On my mother's side almost all our family were earnest
seekers after Truth. My maternal great-grandfather, Sir
James Paget, was a shy, hard-working person of immense
integrity, a friend of Darwin and Huxley, who rose to
become Surgeon Extraordinary to Queen Victoria. The Paget
family have some very dominant characteristics. They tend
to be tall and stooping, with large noses and high cheekbones. Many of them manage to combine a diffident,
religious temperament with a tendency for getting involved

in fierce public controversy. This was true of all Sir James's three sons. Francis Paget, a quiet scholarly person, Bishop of Oxford and Dean of Christ Church, achieved nationwide fame as the target of a famous undergraduate protest. When he 'sent down' two undergraduates for attending a ball at Blenheim Palace, the two victims had themselves ceremoniously placed in coffins and dragged on a hearse, in the midst of a vast procession, from Tom Quad to the railway station. Traces of the slogan 'D – N THE D – N,' daubed in red paint, can be detected to this day on the ancient walls of the college.

Luke Paget, perhaps the most diffident of the brothers, having been pushed upwards by his parents to become Bishop of Chester, caused a great stir by ridding himself of his episcopal palace – the first bishop ever to do so.

The third son, Stephen, was my grandfather. I remember a bowed, silver-haired, saintly old gentleman, whose presence quietened even the Mayhew grandchildren. A throat defect compelled him to speak in a whisper, but it was hard to imagine him wanting to raise his voice. As a young man, he had followed his father into surgery, but was much too shy and otherworldly to make a success of it, and took up writing instead. About one of his books a *Times* reviewer wrote, 'These essays are proof of the secure charm and value of a sane and active mind.'

Yet Stephen Paget found himself dragged into two of the most virulent controversies of his day. Loyalty to his father and to medical science led him to become the leading opponent of the powerful anti-inoculation and anti-vivisection lobbies. His fearless campaigning exposed him to violent personal attacks and eventually undermined his health. He founded the Research Defence Society, which flourishes to this day. In 1968 I spoke at its centenary dinner, choosing as my subject 'Methods of Misleading Public Opinion.'

The Paget tradition was faithfully upheld by one of Sir James's grandchildren. This was Jim Thompson, a scholarly and orthodox Christian who had been appointed Dean of Divinity at Magdalen. Setting out in the course of duty to demonstrate the authenticity of the New Testament miracles, he found to his dismay that this simply could not be done. With typical Paget integrity, he insisted on publishing his findings, and a tremendous row followed. Magdalen stood by him to a man, but the college chapel was in the diocese of the Bishop of Winchester, and after a bitter public controversy the Bishop forbade him to preach there. In due course, Jim Thompson renounced Christianity, turned to historical research and became a leading authority on the French Revolution.

However, other grandchildren of Sir James were life-long and devout Christian believers, and among these was my mother, Dorothea Mary. Her faith led her to a life of service to the poor and deprived. Beginning at the age of seventeen, when she met and enlisted her first recruit 'under a lamp post in the Portobello Road', she founded and developed a remarkably successful social club for working-class girls in the slums of North Kensington.

Though a typical Paget in many ways – high cheekbones, arched nose, independent mind and resolute otherworldliness – my mother had none of the family's diffidence. I remember her taking me – I must have been about eight at the time – on an outing with her club girls to the seaside near Bognor. In old and shabby clothes, she stood out from the crowd mainly because of her height. I believe she was actually paddling, holding her skirts up, when the forces of darkness struck. Two prosperous-looking citizens appeared on the low cliffs above our heads and one of them waved at us, shouting that the beach was private and we must move on. My mother shouted back, 'How dare you spoil these girls' day at the sea!' Some phrases about legal rights returned faintly from the cliff. 'Legal rights! Go away immediately!'

At the time, this cry of defiance seemed to me partly splendid but also partly embarrassing. Hearing it again in memory, it now seems to me wholly magnificent, an echo of Hampden, Cobbett and Paine, the true sound – missing from so many politicians' speeches – of fearless, angry commitment to the cause of less privileged people. It was also successful: the forces of property and privilege turned tail and departed.

Not long before her death, my mother wrote, 'We believe that the best way to serve those who have had no chance in this life is to try to give them friendship and opportunity and a vision of clean and lovely things.' This, to the full extent of her considerable powers, she did. She died in childbirth, at the tragically early age of forty-one. Her religious convictions had led her, as my father once sadly confided to me, to reject all forms of contraception, and after giving birth to six of us, she became mortally ill in a vain, unwanted attempt to produce a seventh. When she knew she was dying, she arranged for her children to be taken away for a holiday in the country, wanting us to remember her as she had been in happier times. As the end came she asked a devoted friend at her bedside to sing for her a favourite hymn:

'Jesu, Lover of My Soul,
Let Me to Thy Bosom Fly'.

An unusually warm obituary appeared in *The Times*:

She treated her great intellectual and artistic gifts as capital held in trust for the service of others. . . . She had in large measure the gifts of the scholar and mystic, and the rare occasions of rest which she allowed herself she often spent alone in contemplation among the hills of Somerset. . . . In religion, she found a spiritual and intellectual logic which she applied relentlessly to her own life. For her, the world only existed as a school for saints. In the building of the City of God, death did not matter much.

By the highest Christian standards, my mother's character and achievements were beyond challenge; yet it has to be said that they sometimes bore hardly on her children. There were six of us. Dorothea came first, then myself, then Patrick, Paul, Helen and Clare in that order. My mother understood us well, loved us dearly and no doubt prayed for us constantly, but in the struggle for her time and attention we faced intense competition from the girls of the St Francis Club. If challenged about this, my mother would reply that her club girls needed her most – 'The children will be all right.' This was a brave defence, but we did in fact suffer. Defying nannies and governesses, we became noisy and unruly. Nor, for honourable reasons, did our father do much to help. Born into a less distinguished family than the Pagets, the son of an amiable but indolent Ipswich chartered accountant, he devoted himself to earning money to pay for our upkeep and education. This he did most successfully, building up a prosperous firm of chartered accountants, but he neglected his other duties as a father. He did not understand us well and seldom visited us in our nursery or bedrooms.

He was a handsome man of considerable charm, with a fine tenor voice, and he shared my mother's love of music. But in other respects my parents could hardly have differed more – the one imaginative, artistic and otherworldly, the other methodical, conventional and anxious to get ahead. I have often felt this tension within myself, with my mother pulling me in one direction and my father in another. Indeed, I suppose everyone's life is complicated to some extent by this same dilemma. How does one reconcile the urge to pursue what is true, beautiful and/or holy with the urge to get on in the world? My own firm opinion is that they cannot be reconciled, that if we write poetry to make money, or perform good works to win esteem, or preach the Kingdom of God with an eye to a bishopric, our poetry, our charitable work and our sermons will be flawed. Conversely, businessmen, lawyers, politicians and the rest who apply to their careers a deep regard for beauty, truth and selflessness will sleep soundly at nights but on comparatively humble beds.

If my mother had had the worldly ambitions of my father, she could not have founded the St Francis Club, or given spiritual leadership to a wide circle of friends and acquaintances: if my father had been as otherworldly as my mother, he would never have won a knighthood or become High Sheriff of Norfolk.

In 1946, when I was Parliamentary Private Secretary to Herbert Morrison, then Deputy Prime Minister, my father asked him privately what he thought of my political prospects. He replied, disconcertingly, 'I am afraid Chris is too honest.' He may have meant 'too naive' or 'too detached' –

he had a limited vocabulary – but he was a good judge of politics and people.

In 1932, my father remarried, thankfully handing over to his intrepid bride the care of six unruly stepchildren. Fortunately, Beryl Colman was resolute as well as affectionate, and after an initial battle of wills, succeeded admirably in her civilizing mission. She was a daughter of the Lord-Lieutenant of Norfolk, and a member of the famous Norwich family of mustard manufacturers. The wedding reception was held in the grandest style at Crown Point, the Colman family mansion outside Norwich. Returning by train to London next day, I observed my fellow passengers poring over two closely printed pages of the local paper with unconcealed astonishment and amusement. These contained the list of my parents' wedding presents.

My boyhood had been dominated by my intense religious upbringing. Looking back on it now, I think that while it is right to instruct children in Jesus' teachings, it is foolish to tell them that he was born of a virgin and rose from the dead. The teachings need no authentication: they prove themselves by their courage and simplicity, and if told that Jesus was a saintly person who lived in Palestine 2000 years ago and was killed for preaching the truth to people out of love for them, children will become natural believers. But if told in addition that he was born of a virgin and rose from the dead, they will become natural doubters. In my own case, the story of the virgin birth and the resurrection removed Jesus from my grasp. They made him remote and puzzling, and therefore unlovable.

I found it easier, when I became a schoolboy, to love and worship the Sussex and England fast bowler, A. E. R. Gilligan. This god-like person would descend on our playing fields during Horsham Cricket Week and reveal to us the mysteries of the fast out-swinger. I have kept ever since a postcard he sent me, with its celestial heading, 'Lords Cricket Ground, London NW':

Dear Mayhew,
    Well played to you and the team.

So glad your fielding was good, but try and improve the catching.

All good luck.

Yours sincerely,
Arthur Gilligan.

Few postcards can ever have given their recipient more pride and pleasure.

My parents had sent me away to the Manor House, Horsham at the tender age of eight, following the brutal custom of many wealthy families. In my first letter home I put a brave face on it.

May 3rd 1924
Dear everybody,
  I *love* school. I have made three friends at school, Sandy Brown, Richard Medley, and another boy whose name I do not know.
  I am in Class 3.

Love from
Kiffy.

In fact, like any normal small boy, I was desperately home-sick and spent most of the first week of this and subsequent terms in tears.

The Manor House was an admirable Christian school with its own pleasant chapel, and my religious faith should have flourished there. Instead, it wilted before the fires of secular enthusiasms – cricket, football and ephemeral 'crazes' such as yo-yo's, knucklebones, 'conkers', cigarette cards, and expensive clockwork submarines, which we would launch, and sometimes lose, in the school swimming bath.

No doubt the poet Wordsworth would claim that at this time 'God was with us though we knew it not.' Perhaps. Certainly if God was with us, we did not know it. I remember clearly my state of mind during my confirmation service in the school chapel. Even as I knelt at the altar rail, even as the bishop laid his hands on me, I could think of nothing except the outrageously unfashionable straw hat in which my godfather had arrived at the school.

This illustrated a major failing of this otherwise excellent establishment: it made us too conscious of social distinctions. With anxious eyes we would compare our fathers' cars, our mothers' dresses and each others' toys; and, though we never actually met the boys of Horsham Grammar School, we had little doubt that they were in all respects, except perhaps in industriousness, our inferiors. Then, as now, private schools gave their pupils an excellent education at the cost of distancing them from the mass of their fellow-countrymen.

I suppose schoolchildren remember most vividly their most eccentric teachers. The mathematics master at the Manor House, Kenneth Evers-Swindell, brought startling glimpses of the outside world into our cloistered lives. On my last sports day, when I had taken things easily in the half-mile and lost, he strode up to me shouting, 'You bloody boy! You weren't trying. You've cost me a quid!' I was astounded and deeply shocked. However, I also owe to this admirable man the first aesthetic experience I can remember. He had challenged me to prove an algebraic equation without help, and to our mutual astonishment I had succeeded. Deaf to his congratulations, I sat at my desk in a trance. The clarity, economy and certainty of the proof – its obvious, unchallengeable *rightness* – held me spellbound, and I found my eyes unaccountably filling with tears.

Tears, for me, are a reliable measure of truth and beauty – as is the bristling of my skin – and for this reason I prefer reading poetry or listening to music when I am by myself. Tears of this kind, of course, have little to do with sadness, though the two things can get mixed. When we liberated Eindhoven during the war, the Philips radio factory there handed out hundreds of portable wireless sets as presents to the liberating troops. I remember taking my set into a corner and switching on to the BBC. Distantly, through heavy interference, came magic from the Malvern Hills – Elgar's Introduction and Allegro – and I found myself overcome simultaneously by the splendour of Elgar's flowing melodies and by homesickness.

I left the Manor House in 1929, aged thirteen. What kind of a boy was I then? A candid answer was published some

years later in the Oxford undergraduate paper *The Isis*:
' "But I have no sin". Such was the first serious remark ever
made by Christopher, and it gives a very fair indication of
his early life, for he was a perfectly normal example of a
rather horrible child.'

The writer of this trenchant paragraph, surprisingly, was
my much-loved brother Pat. He showed it to me before
publication, and though I thought it a little harsh, I was too
proud, and too much afraid of hurting his feelings, to suggest
any change. I had to admit, moreover, that it was all too
likely that, as soon as I could talk, I should inform people
that I had no sin. From an early age, I held too good an
opinion of myself. I talked too much, pontificating on
subjects I knew nothing about. Adults would tell me not to
be 'superior'. In the nursery conversation which I have
quoted, my contributions strike an unmistakably pious,
know-all note.

I might have learned some humility in my early teens,
when I was persuaded by my mother to start making my
confession to our parish priest, a saintly old man and close
family friend, Father Lester Pinchard. Unfortunately,
however, this well-meant plan backfired. By way of preparation, I was encouraged to write down a list of my sins –
a 'washing list' my mother called it – and to help in this was
given a booklet containing a long list of sins of which a boy
of my age might reasonably be expected to be guilty. I would
run my eye down this list with a genuine desire to find
some shortcoming relevant to myself. Almost by definition,
however, conceit is a sin of which the sinner is unaware, and
I appeared to myself to be innocent of almost all the listed
sins. Had I lied to my father? No. Had I lied to my mother?
No. Had I been idle? No. Had I cheated the bus company?
Certainly not. Had I cheated the railway company? Ridiculous. Had I done impure things with others? Not sure what
that means, but plainly not. Had I done impure things by
myself? Ah, yes, I had. Here at last was a genuine sin,
something to put in my washing list.

'Is that all, Christopher?' 'Yes, Father.' 'Have you no other
sins to confess?' 'No, Father.' 'Well, do not brood on the sin

you have confessed: it cannot always be resisted. Say six Hail Marys.'

And so I would rise from my knees and tiptoe away from the confessional box, ashamed of my sin but strengthened in the illusion that compared with others I was remarkably sinless.

However, I must be fair to myself. A more attractive picture emerges from my school reports and letters home, all of which were carefully kept and filed away by my proud and methodical father. These confirm that I was indeed priggish and self-centred, but also honest, cheerful and intelligent. I must also have had some capacity for leadership, since I became head boy and captain of cricket. I had certainly not yet become a religious sceptic or a rebel. This happened quite suddenly, when I was sent on to a public school, Haileybury, where I had won a scholarship.

2
CLASS WAR AT HAILEYBURY

In later years, when asked why I became a socialist, I was thought to be joking when I replied that it was because I was bullied at school. But this, though I dislike admitting it, is the simple truth; and since the same thing happened to others of my generation, I will explain how it came about.

But first let it be said in defence of my tormentors that when I arrived at Haileybury as a new boy I must have presented a tempting target. I was thin, adenoidal and priggish, and unused to physical violence in any form.

The seeds of rebellion were sown in me in a small ugly room with barred windows called a 'dormitory classroom'. Here were herded together, without effective means of escape, a dozen or more thirteen- and fourteen-year-old boys. We were divided according to custom into two groups – the new boys and the rest. This distinction was all-important. According to tradition, new boys, so far from requiring special help and consideration, needed to be 'licked into shape', to be ground into conformity with a mass of irrational school customs. Normally, this task belonged to the prefects; in practice, however, it was carried out by those members of the dormitory classroom who had been at the school for two or three terms, who had themselves suffered similar torments in their day.

My letters home tell the tale:

> I got a beating (all the five new boys too) for my new boy's exam. It was quite unavoidable and it didn't hurt so I don't mind much. . . . I shall have to do the 'house exam' and the 'clothes exam' which means a couple more beatings (it makes no difference if your clothes are perfect!). . . . I can't say truthfully I am enjoying this term but certainly never expected to!

There were too few of us to fight our tormentors; and we

suspected, perhaps correctly, that if we appealed to the prefects they would reply that our suffering was customary and that they had been through the same thing themselves in their day. A plea for mercy to our housemaster or our parents seemed unthinkable: by every standard of conduct we knew, this would have been the blackest treachery.

In due course, however, rightly overriding my frantic objections, my parents bore down on the school demanding explanations. The authorities were roused from their comfortable sleep. Several boys were interrogated; a few were beaten, one was expelled.

From then on, the physical assaults ended, but the psychological persecution increased and I became extremely unpopular and lonely.

Nevertheless, I refused to let my parents take me away, and so far from encouraging me to 'drop out' my sense of outrage perversely spurred me on to reach the top. Nothing, I felt, could better prove the worthlessness of school traditions and the public school system than to have their bitterest enemy carry off all the prizes.

Pat explained the situation, albeit in rather simplistic terms, in his *Isis* profile:

Christopher's career at Haileybury was an appalling embarrassment to the authorities. . . . He became, perhaps unintentionally, the leader of the opposition – a full-time job in a totalitarian community . . . and yet he achieved almost every available position of responsibility, which he used to try to put his ideas across. As Editor of the School magazine, he waged a ceaseless war against the authorities' censorship of it. In the Debating Society, of which he was Vice-President, he made a brilliant speech, moving that 'The day of the public school is over'. He was in the School Shooting Eight and a senior Company Sergeant Major, but from that vantage point constantly and vigorously criticized the Officers' Training Corps and finally tried to resign. When Head of his House and later Head of the School also, he fought, not always unsuccessfully, against corporal punishment, uniform dress, and the worst features of public school discipline . . . and in all this he had behind him the support of the School, for he was Captain of rugger and hockey, held the

School long-jump record and had been for three years a member
of the Cricket XI.

   The two different aspects of Christopher's life at Haileybury
came to a crisis at the same moment, and it is perfectly true to
say that when one day he was summoned suddenly to see the
Headmaster, he knew he was either going to be asked to leave
or to become Head of the School, without in the least knowing
which.

The school authorities, following the time-honoured stratagem of the British governing class, of loading rebel leaders
with honour and responsibility, made me head boy.
However, I was not to be bought off, and the proletarian
revolution continued. The *Sunday Chronicle* of July 1934
reported:

> Five hundred public school boys may go on strike! The storm
> centre is the famous public school Haileybury College in
> Hertfordshire. . . . The boys have already worked out a plan of
> campaign. They have decided to stage a mass protest. The first
> step will be a refusal to sing in chapel.

It was about this time that the first issue of *Out of Bounds*
was published. This was an outspoken leftist public school
magazine edited by Esmond Romilly, one of Sir Winston
Churchill's nephews, who was then a boy at Wellington. It
showed me that other boys at other public schools were
thinking and feeling the same way as myself, and this was
vastly encouraging. An early issue, I remember, listed on its
cover the names of all the public schools that had banned it.
Haileybury was not in the list and I lost no time in ordering
a number of copies, which sold well. In due course, I was
summoned to the headmaster's house and asked for an explanation. To my fervent oration in support of freedom of
thought, the headmaster replied that he did not object to the
magazine being subversive, though he certainly considered it
that, but to its being obscene. There seemed some truth in
this, and I felt discouraged; and was somewhat relieved when
Esmond Romilly ran away from Wellington, and *Out of
Bounds* collapsed.

After a time I began seeing rebellion against the school as part of a wider struggle, identifying the public school system – hierarchical, authoritarian and philistine – with the new fascist states in Italy and Germany, and with the class-ridden capitalist society of Britain in the thirties. I wrote home:

'The more I think of the public schools the less I wonder at the Englishman's intellectual backwardness, apathetic attitude towards the arts, inferiority complex ("reserve"), tolerance of class distinctions, complacent refusal of progressive ideals, lack of international co-operative spirit, the wrong attitude to sex etc. etc.'

High among the citadels of capitalist–imperialist reaction was, of course, the school chapel; and one of my most strident demands on the headmaster was for the abolition of compulsory attendance there. However, he resisted strongly, and my campaign, which attracted little rank-and-file support, collapsed. Moreover, by a strange paradox – or was it a natural consequence? – I had at this time a simple but unmistakable mystical experience. Walking by myself in the woods near the college, I was suddenly brought to a halt by the amazing appearance of a patch of grass a short way ahead. It was lit by a narrow shaft of sunlight coming through the trees, and had a mysterious, ethereal brightness quite unlike anything I had seen before. I felt strangely drawn towards it and stood there staring at it, spellbound and euphoric, for what seemed a very long time.

Eventually the spell broke and I moved on. But what did it mean? What connection did it have with religion? None, surely, with the prayers and sermons in chapel, still less with the school certificate divinity exams, with their maps of the journeys of St Paul and textual criticisms of the Gospels. Yet it seemed to have something to do with God. If my mother had been alive, I would have asked her. As it was, I kept it carefully to myself. In due course the memory of it became less vivid, and then for long periods I forgot it altogether. It was not until twenty years later, as I shall recount, that curiosity about mystical experience led me to travel, write and broadcast – and even to act as a psychiatrist's guinea pig – in an effort to understand it.

Confrontation – first with the boys, then with the authorities – clouded my time at Haileybury; but there were bright moments as well. In the peace and quiet of his study, George Heywood, my assistant housemaster and future brother-in-law, introduced me to Bach and Mozart. On a tour of Scandinavia with the school dramatic society, I played Rosenkrantz at Elsinore. With my brother Pat, I helped to defeat Cheltenham by an innings in hot sunshine at Lord's. Then there was the excitement of lessons with the school's iconoclast, John Hampden-Jackson. He was a fine teacher, partly because he flattered us, treating us as adults. He lived with his wife and three children in slum-like conditions above the music school. When his fourth child arrived, I stood up as he entered the classroom and offered the congratulations of the sixth form. 'Oh, a mistake, gentlemen, a mistake!' he replied, and began busily cleaning the blackboard.

Strangely, as our confrontation with the authorities proceeded, the school seemed to do better and better. I wrote pompously to my parents,

> I attribute this to the 'Out of Bounds' spirit of the School . . . made possible by the lack of authority at the top. I believe it to be a passing phase, which will vanish when our new Headmaster has settled down sufficiently to 'bring us to heel', dress us in black, close our art exhibitions, ban our magazines, drive us on to the parade ground, teach us to elocute the Lord's Prayer in exact unison (as he is now doing), make us button our coats, cut our hair, talk only to boys of our own age, call masters 'Sir'. Indeed, if he has delayed in thus reforming us so far, it is chiefly through fear of me.

This was arrogant and exaggerated, but there was some truth in it. It may be that a strong dose of rebellion and iconoclasm was just what the school needed at that time.

On my last evening at Haileybury, I called on members of the staff to say goodbye. One of them was the deputy headmaster, R. L. Ashcroft, an elderly, austere man, dedicated to his profession and to the school. He asked me if I had any idea about a future career and I replied that I hadn't. 'Ever thought of politics?' he asked deliberately. I was astounded. Was it possible that Ashcroft, of all people, felt some respect for what I had been trying to do? I felt a sudden surge of conviction. Magically, the road ahead opened up. As it had been at Haileybury, so it would be hereafter. From now on, or at least as soon as the summer holidays were over, I would begin reforming the world.

3

SOCIAL DEMOCRACY AT OXFORD

So now I had an aim in life: I would devote myself to the cause of socialism. The mighty were to be cast down from their seats; inequality, injustice, imperialism, fascism and war were all to be abolished. Such were the conclusions I had drawn from my public school education.

What I failed to foresee was that these convictions, being negative and destructive, would not last me for a lifetime. They could start me off, but not keep me going. Nor, despite outward appearances, was I temperamentally suited to politics. Haileybury had given me strong convictions and some experience of leadership, but I lacked almost all the other attributes of the successful politician – patience, tact, a readiness to compromise, a capacity for dissimulation, gregariousness and a thick skin. Nor had I developed a taste for power. No matter how public-spirited, politicians who hope to succeed must desire personal advancement. I felt inhibited about this: should not socialists, by definition, be disinterested?

Another drawback was that I had no understanding of working-class people. Millions of victims of capitalist oppression did exist, for sure, but I did not know any of them; or at least I did not know any of them well enough to understand how they felt. The working class was an abstraction, a trump card in political debate. My only personal contacts with working-class people had been made at my mother's club in North Kensington or at the holiday camps she organized for them each year at the seaside; and here social class proved an insuperable barrier. It was bad enough that our clothes, incomes, accents, education and social customs should be so widely different: far worse was the fact that we had no subject of conversation in common. I played rugger, golf and tennis: they played soccer, and boxed. We read different newspapers, frequented different parts of London, ate different foods and knew different kinds of people.

The resulting failure of communication made me acutely self-conscious in working-class company. What was a safe subject of conversation with these incomprehensible and fearsome strangers? What were they thinking about me? Were they anxious, resentful? How could one avoid appearing superior?

If I had been a foreigner, unable to speak English, our differences would simply have provided an interesting challenge, and our ignorance and curiosity about each other would have seemed natural. But since we spoke the same language and were nationals of the same country, our failure to communicate made me feel embarrassed and ashamed. It required a long period in the Labour movement – and in the ranks of the British Expeditionary Force in France – before I felt completely at ease in working-class company.

However, as I arrived in Oxford, in 1934, none of these difficulties damped my enthusiasm for the socialist cause. I settled into my handsome, panelled rooms in Christ Church, joined the Oxford University Labour Club and plunged into militant left-wing politics.

I find it easier to understand why I became a socialist at authoritarian Haileybury than why I stayed one at Oxford, where life was breathtakingly free. It would have been so easy simply to have settled in and enjoyed the place. Thirty hours' work a week would have satisfied my tutors and examiners, and for the rest of the time there was golf, rugger, bridge, the finest wines, the best music, the most charming girls. In the event, I enjoyed all of these to some extent but always in a dilettante fashion. They were distractions from the real task – the struggle for socialism. I declined a freshmen's trial at cricket on the grounds that I was now too old for the game, and spoiled my chances in the freshmen's rugger trial by remarking at half-time, when offered a slice of lemon, that it was indeed rather a long time till tea. For every glass of port consumed in the Christ Church buttery, I drank a dozen cups of tea at leftist meetings in somebody's rooms in Ruskin or Wadham. As for music, I remember best

our renderings of 'The Red Flag' and the 'Internationale' in
the Carfax Assembly Rooms or the town hall – and also of
a horrible song which went:

> Blow the bloody bugle!
> Beat the bloody drum!
> Blow the bloody bourgeoisie
> To bloody kingdom come!
> Pile them on the pyre,
> Higher still and higher,
> Burn the bloody bastards up
> One by bloody one!

I always hoped that this song was meant as a joke, but such
was the fervour of some of our meetings that one could never
feel sure.

In those days at Oxford, love affairs called for more
extended preliminaries than they do now, and also for a
measure of mutually agreed deception of the authorities,
which fostered embarrassment. Moreover, the most
charming and beautiful girls tended to be non-political. So
my love-life at Oxford was not very successful. The girls I
knew best were the earnest and intelligent ones, good
comrades with whom I would tramp round the council
houses of Cowley, distributing pamphlets.

It must be admitted that most of us in the Oxford Labour
Club lacked charm and beauty. We were a graceless lot. But
the war was coming, Hitler was in the ascendant, and the
social and economic state of Britain was an affront to all
sensitive people. Our fervent, humourless dedication to
political struggle was ungraceful but not ignoble.

My own obsession with politics is easily explained. It was
a substitute for religion, and a sop to my feelings of guilt
about being rich and privileged. In my subconscious mind I
was perpetually apologizing for my enjoyment of life to a
vast, ghostly audience of hungry and resentful working-class
families.

I also felt a growing intellectual conviction. The more I
studied, argued and travelled, the more the facts seemed to

fit the doctrines of socialism. This was not self-persuasion. Looking back now, after more than fifty years, I can still say with conviction that the social, political and economic facts of those times squared remarkably well with the critique of capitalist society my colleagues and I were preaching. The majority of thoughtful and sensitive people in Britain during the thirties belonged to the left in some form or another, and broadly speaking we were well justified.

Finally, of course, I had chosen socialist politics as a career. I did not see myself then as an MP, still less as a Minister, and cared much more about the Cause than about my personal fortunes; but having joined the Labour Club and Union Society, I wanted to win the arguments and the votes, and was willing in due course to be elected to the leading positions.

So conscience and intellectual conviction drove me in the same direction. I was soon regularly attending the weekly meetings of the Labour Club, intense, crowded affairs in cheerless, smoke-filled halls. The first surprise for a newcomer was the use of the word 'comrade'. This was employed not only as a form of address at public meetings, but in private conversation. In the thirties I used it constantly, in a rather defiant, self-conscious manner, anxious not to breach a well-established, 'progressive', 'anti-fascist' convention.

This was an example of the rather cowardly conformism that affected many of us in the Labour Club at that time. Coming from middle-class families, we had nevertheless joined an organization we ourselves described as 'the working class movement'. We therefore tended to be over-anxious about our own sincerity, and sometimes lapsed into a ridiculous cult of proletarianism, affecting working-class clothes and accents, keeping quiet about our home backgrounds and avoiding the best restaurants.

Our anxiety to conform, to be accepted as 'sincere', was ruthlessly exploited by the 'left' and enabled them for some time to impose on us militant-sounding opinions which in our hearts we knew to be nonsense.

What did we more moderate, orthodox socialists believe at that time?

First and foremost, we held that capitalism – private enterprise – was immoral, unjust and unworkable.

The catastrophic slump of the early thirties was fresh in our minds, and the capitalist system seemed compelled by its very nature to produce cyclical booms and slumps, a permanent army of unemployed and gross social and economic inequality.

The solution was to replace the capitalist system by a socialist system, by nationalizing the means of production, distribution and exchange. From this, all else would flow – full employment, prosperity, equality, democracy, and even (since capitalism was the cause of war) peace.

We also championed public ownership on ethical grounds: cooperation was morally superior to competition. Nationalization would create a new spirit in industry and would produce a fairer distribution of wealth.

We argued endlessly about whether a Labour government would be allowed to build socialism peacefully. Would not the capitalist class resort to violence rather than have the instruments of power snatched from its grasp? I myself thought this most unlikely and on one occasion read a paper to this effect to an earnest study group. My most telling point was a quotation from Marx himself declaring that in Britain, though in no other country, a peaceful transition to socialism might be possible. But other sacred texts were thrown at me from the works of Stalin, Harold Laski, and John Strachey (then a leading communist dialectician) arguing the opposite. Eventually, I was inspired to ask my opponents for the names of three members of the British ruling class who might resort to armed force against an elected Labour government. There was silence at this point, while my Marxist opponents tried, without success, to think of three real, live capitalists who could plausibly be visualized as arresting Attlee and shooting down members of the Christ Church Socialist Study Group.

During my first year at Oxford, though always opposed to the communists, I drifted further 'left' than ever before or since. At the Oxford Union I spoke in favour of a motion 'that this house prefers the Red Flag to the Union Jack'. I cannot recall by what tortured reasoning I came to support such a curious declaration. Possibly it was easier to get called by the president to speak in support of the Red Flag than against it. When the motion was duly passed, with many ex-public school votes cast in its favour, an *Isis* editorial commented perceptively:

> We are forced to the strange conclusion that it is in the interests of Conservatism that the public schools be destroyed before they turn loose too many bitter young Socialists and Communists. If the latter wish to make the country a Communist state, they really should insist that everyone is sent to a public school.

On another page, the *Isis* records: 'Mr Mayhew was not in his best form, and had altogether an unhappy evening.'

To make matters worse, I now allowed myself to be drawn into an international conference 'of all parties and of none' which had been engineered by a Stalinist front organization at Brussels. I was trapped by flattery: 'If people like yourself do not come, your point of view will go by default'; 'As you know, Chris, we strongly disagree with your views, but we must admit that you put them over well, and we want all points of view represented.' The appeal was plausible and I fell for it. Communist techniques at international conferences were then a comparative novelty and I learned a useful lesson. The Stalinists laid on the trappings of democracy thickly, but they controlled all the key committees, including those which drafted the resolutions, the agenda and the speakers' list. My feeble, ingenuous efforts to get some hearing for non-communist opinions were blandly ignored. In the fervent atmosphere created (one high point was the appearance of a masked figure on the platform – 'a member of the German, anti-Nazi underground') – any effective dissent from the Stalinist line was out of the question.

But what was Russia really like? It must surely at least be a better society than ours, being its exact opposite, or so it

seemed to my friend David Nenk* and myself. In the summer
of 1935 we set out on a pilgrimage to the Soviet Union. We
paid £15 each for a fortnight's Intourist trip to Moscow and
Leningrad. David equipped himself, in a phenomenally short
time, with a working knowledge of Russian. We were determined to discover for ourselves the truth about the Soviet
Union, namely that it was a splendid new civilization hitherto
hidden from us by a blanket of capitalist propaganda.

We joined a small Soviet passenger ship at London Bridge,
wearing clothes of a rather proletarian style that we judged
would help us mix easily with the workers of Leningrad
and Moscow. Our first surprise was the state of the ship's
lavatories. By the standards of reactionary capitalist countries, they were so filthy as to be unusable. *Why was this?*
This was a question we should have asked ourselves persist-
ently. We might then have discovered some part of the truth
about the Soviet Union; but we could not bring ourselves to
do it. Since the state of the lavatories was inconsistent with
everything we had read about socialism, it was obviously an
accident, a hangover from a past age, the kind of thing that
would only be of interest to people from sheltered bourgeois
homes such as ourselves. The ship's crew, dedicated to a high
ideal, could not fairly be expected to waste their energies on
such trivialities.

Similar reasons, we felt, also explained the surprising reluc-
tance of the workers of Moscow and Leningrad to talk to
us. Wherever we went, we made earnest efforts to engage the
people of the Soviet Socialist fatherland in conversation. Our
attempts were unsuccessful. Those we accosted would look
at us, note that we were foreigners, and hastily walk away.

At that time, of course, in 1935, with the Stalinist purges
at their height, it was dangerous for a Soviet citizen to be
seen talking to a foreigner. Avoiding contact with David and
myself was a reasonable and necessary act of self-preser-
vation. For our part we knew nothing about the horrors of
Stalinist oppression, which we assumed to be a fiction of

---

* A brilliantly talented Jewish youth, whose promising career in
the civil service was tragically cut short by cancer.

capitalist propaganda. Having carefully studied Stalin's new constitution, our eyes were firmly fixed on the new liberal era it was ushering in. Our failure to communicate with the Soviet workers, peasants and intelligentsia was plainly due to our own shortcomings. Why should they be bothered with ignorant tourists from capitalist countries? Very likely, moreover, they could not understand David's Russian.

Earnestly, eagerly, herded together with other foreign visitors, we followed our guides round the Intourist trail. We visited a collective farm, some factories, a crêche, a school. Some things we saw pleased us: these were proofs that socialism worked. Other things we saw disappointed us: these showed that the vestiges of capitalism could not all be eradicated overnight. Knowing little or nothing of the factories of any other country, we found it particularly easy to wax enthusiastic about Soviet factories, and if some of them did seem below standard, this simply showed that – contrary to the insinuations of capitalist propaganda – Intourist showed the bad side as well as the good.

Apart from our Intourist guides, double-talkers and double-thinkers to a man, only one Soviet citizen deliberately entered into conversation with us during our tour. This was a quiet-spoken man who accosted us in Gorky Street and asked us if we would like to buy roubles at ten times the official rate. At the official rate, the shortest tram-ride cost half-a-crown, and we eagerly agreed to exchange £3 worth. We were given an appointment at a bedroom in the Metropole Hotel. I knocked at the door at the stated time and, when the door was opened, said quite loudly to our new friend, 'I've come for those roubles,' and was astounded by his terrified appeal for silence.

I feel genuinely ashamed about my obtuseness on this Russian visit. Our British system of society seemed so detestable that I simply could not believe that its exact antithesis could be even worse. Though David and I did not know it at the time, several of our colleagues on our package tour were communists or fellow-travellers, and at least one of them later became a Soviet agent. When I leant out of my hotel bedroom window in Moscow to take a forbidden photograph of the Kremlin, the person kindly holding my legs was Anthony Blunt.

I owe a considerable debt to Anthony's brother Wilfrid, who was also in our party. Wilfrid was the art master at Haileybury, and on his return wrote an article in the school magazine describing a Soviet factory we had visited together. An excellent musician and painter, despising politics, he had seen the factory with the eye of truth and wrote about it as it really was. He said it was dirty, overcrowded, noisy, old-fashioned and boring, and that the workers were badly dressed and looked miserably poor and oppressed. This seemed to me heartless treachery, and I was deeply shocked; but I remember forcing myself to read the article again, carefully, and then again, until finally I had to acknowledge that what this political ignoramus had written was probably true and that the opinions of the factory that I myself had formed – I, the expert, the politician, the dedicated student of communism – were almost certainly rubbish. This was an important moment for me.

My visit to Russia was an object-lesson in the dangers of the will-to-believe, of self-persuasion. While I was sleeping and eating comfortably in my Moscow hotel, political prisoners were being tortured and shot in the headquarters of the NKVD a mile or two away. Throughout the Soviet Union hundreds of thousands of innocent people were being arrested, wives and husbands separated and children orphaned by the agents of a paranoid tyrant. And at the same moment of time I sat at a stone-topped table among the ferns and aspidistras in the National Hotel in Moscow, listening to light music played by a quartet in dinner jackets, completely convinced I was visiting a splendid new socialist society. Much of my later bitterness against western communists and fellow-travellers sprang, I am sure, from shame at my own obtuseness during that first visit to Russia.

My political education, begun by Wilfrid Blunt, continued when Frank Pakenham* – then a conservative, and my tutor

---

* Now Lord Longford, later a Cabinet Minister and Leader of the House of Lords in the Wilson governments.

in political history – with characteristic kindness asked me
to dinner to meet Hugh Dalton. Throughout his political
life, Dalton, who was shortly to become Chairman of the
Labour Party, was a source of guidance and encouragement
to young socialists. Our meeting, however, began badly, as
the conversation turned to a sensational book just published
by a mutual friend called *The First Workers' Government*.
This laid down a blueprint for establishing socialism in a
single period of Labour government. An all-embracing
Enabling Act would be passed under which virtually the
entire economy would be nationalized and wealth drastically
redistributed. Unconstitutional opposition would be crushed
by militant action by the organized workers. To my simple
mind it all sounded very practical and satisfactory, and when
Hugh Dalton asked me for my opinion, I said as much.
Observing his incredulity and horror, I took fright and
added, 'I only mean it is good *of its kind*, of course' – thus
showing lack of courage as well as of judgement.

In spite of this bad start, Hugh Dalton persevered with me
and had a great influence on my views. He was the architect
of the party's all-important statement of policy *Labour's
Immediate Programme*, which foreshadowed the achievements of the post-war Labour government, and I duly wrote
a panegyric of it for the university's socialist monthly,
University Forward.

My days were now filled with Labour politics. For a long
period, Labour supporters at Christ Church met in my room
every day for a cooperative lunch. The average attendance
was ten and the meal cost sixpence. I became business
manager of *University Forward* and also founder and editor
of the *Oxford University Labour Club Bulletin*. Despite its
title, this was a lively and irreverent publication. We
announced the accession of Edward VIII with the headline
'Magdalen Man Makes Good'.

Harold Wilson was not a socialist at this time, but our
paths crossed briefly once. On the advice of my tutor, I had
entered for the University economics prize. A friend of mine
told me he thought I was being rather optimistic – 'Haven't

you heard? Harold Wilson's in for it.' The name meant
nothing to me, but Wilson duly won.

Soon after I joined it, the Labour Club merged with the
openly communist October Club. This led to bitter struggles
within the new organization and I soon found myself leading
a small but resolute anti-communist faction. This resulted
from the meeting of the Christ Church Labour Group at
which the news of the merger was announced. In those days
few people in Britain – let alone in expensive Oxford colleges
– knew anything about communist political methods, and
when the announcement of the merger was made I applauded
innocently like everyone else. We had moved on to the next
item on the agenda before a vague suspicion prompted me
to ask the chairman when we had been consulted about the
merger. The reply was friendly but evasive, and I asked
another question. Other members joined in, and it soon
became clear that the merger was simply a communist takeover, fixed up between the open communists of the October
Club and the secret communists of the Labour Club. Three
or four of us thereupon decided to oppose the merger.
Though we were too late to succeed in this, we resolved to
stick together and keep the flag of democratic socialism flying
inside the new club, which was now in fact a large and
powerful communist-dominated organization.

We called ourselves the Oxford University Democratic
Socialist Group, and I was elected the first chairman. We
drafted a constitution and issued membership cards, and
supported each other at meetings and at elections, wearing
a special red-and-white tie to give us courage. This mutual
aid was very necessary, as it needed a strong nerve to stand
up and oppose leftist resolutions at our fervent, crowded
meetings.

I believe there were nearly two hundred members of the
Communist Party at Oxford at this time, including some of
the ablest and most intelligent undergraduates. They dominated the fifteen hundred members of the Labour Club, using
techniques that are familiar enough today but frequently
caught us off our guard at that time.

Our greatest difficulty was to discover which of our social

democratic colleagues were secret communists, and which were not. After a time I began to flatter myself that I had become very good at this, but many years later – long after the war – when I met one of the leading members of our anti-communist group and began reminding him of our campaigning, he sheepishly confessed that he had been a communist all along, having joined our group on party instructions. My vanity was pricked, and I felt extremely annoyed.

We were also handicapped by the communist practice of rigging the Labour Club elections. A friend of mine who took part in this and who left the Communist Party soon afterwards told me how the system worked. The voting was fair, and so was the counting of the votes: all the communists did was to announce the wrong results. After the count, they would meet to decide 'in an atmosphere of considerable hilarity' whom they would declare elected. A particularly engaging point is that they did not always declare the communist candidates elected. On the contrary, in 1936, after the Communist International had called for a 'united front of all progressive forces against fascism', they were so anxious to demonstrate their loyalty to the new tactic that they sometimes declared a non-communist elected when he had been fairly beaten by a communist. Whether my own repeated election to the executive committee was fair or faked I have never been able to discover.

Strangely enough, our bitter struggles did not prevent all factions in the Labour Club from uniting effectively on specific campaigns. Sometimes we would deploy in fleets of buses to London or the home counties for a demonstration or a by-election. We dominated the Oxford Union, consistently winning the arguments and debates and getting our own candidates elected to the various offices; and in 1937, forgetful of our own internal battle, my communist and fellow-travelling colleagues flooded into the polling booths at the Union to get me elected president with a record majority.

Towards the university conservatives we felt a friendly contempt. We quite enjoyed their company, but they were dilettantes, amateurs. In an *Isis* review of Union prospects,

I wrote patronizingly that Mr E. R. G. Heath (Balliol) 'can always be relied upon for a sound speech'.

From time to time we clashed with the British Union of Fascists. I sent my parents a description of one rowdy meeting:

It was an amazing affair. Please don't think I support the tactics adopted by Mosley's opponents. I strongly advised against them before, during and after the meeting – suggesting that we should either go and control ourselves, asking intelligent questions, or stay away altogether. As it was, the town Communist Party, the more excitable and more left-wing members of the Labour Club, and the Oxford busmen (who, since a successful strike, are politically-minded) went 'not to cause trouble or to break the meeting up but to stand by our comrades if rudely treated'. As *someone* was bound to be thrown out, almost certainly with unnecessary violence (no doubt about this), this meant a certain 'rough-house'. However, this in no way exonerates Mosley. I have never heard such a deliberately provocative and offensive speech – sneering at undergraduates, Oxford, the busmen themselves, threatening the audience, and making intolerable remarks about Jews. Finally, when the interruptions became more and more insistent Mosley dramatically ordered one man to be ejected. With great speed a dozen or so stewards bore down on him – a stupid and over-excited busman – and knocked him onto the floor with unbelievable violence. Not a word of 'request to leave the room' or anything like that. This roused the audience to fury – they had already been very well stung up by Mosley's speech – and in a second the whole of the middle of the hall was one colossal fight. I saw my tutor of last term – the Hon. F. A. Pakenham, a pillar of the Conservative Association – attacked by three Blackshirts at once, who were hanging round his neck and hitting him while he swiped about with a chair. Another don from Christ Church, Patrick Gordon-Walker, was fighting hard to defend him, and I saw too Dick Crossman, Vice-Warden of New College and a City Councillor, in the middle of the fight. Chairs – steel ones – were flying about the room: and people were badly hurt, including three non-communist friends of mine. I was in the cowardly position of *Isis* reporter on the press bench by the platform, and the fight was some way away from me. I don't think I should have had the courage to join in anyway. As it was, I rushed to the telephone and sent out reports to the morning papers, and as each man staggered out of the Hall, took his statement.

The Labour Club might have been expected to take a lively interest in the abdication crisis. But not so. We were not republicans, but neither were we loyal or respectful towards the monarchy. The whole issue was felt to be a diversion from the struggle that really mattered – against unemployment, fascism and war. Nevertheless I moved a resolution in the club, urging the Parliamentary Labour Party to come out in support of Edward VIII and, if Baldwin resigned, form a government itself. My resolution was passed unanimously and enthusiastically, and I sent a telegram to Attlee calling upon the Parliamentary Labour Party to conform. I think this was the silliest political initiative I have ever taken; and I remember Clem Attlee telling me many years afterwards that, when he received my telegram, it strengthened his view – which in due course prevailed – that the Parliamentary Labour Party should do exactly the opposite.

For the coronation ceremonies, Oxford's noble High Street was decorated from end to end with what some of us considered to be offensive flamboyance. Returning late one evening, after a cheerful dinner in honour of Oxford's victorious boat race crew, my friend Philip Toynbee and I felt a sudden urge to remove some of the more tasteless streamers and banners. As we turned for home, burdened with loot, we ran into the arms of a policeman and in due course were summoned before the proctors. The senior proctor enquired: 'Was this a political demonstration, gentlemen, or a drunken prank?' As we were wondering how to answer this difficult question, he added: 'I may say that the fine for a political demonstration will be £20 and for a drunken prank £5.' This tipped the balance, and we declared that we had been drunk.

My irreverent and rather silly attitude towards the monarchy also got me into trouble at home. Already upset by the amount of time I was spending on politics – and on left-wing politics at that – my father sent me some angry letters. My replies were unduly aggressive:

I am delighted to agree with you that my views would have infuriated my grandfather. What one's grandfather thinks of one's political views is of no importance whatever; I am concerned with what my grandsons will think of mine.

You flatter me by supposing that my 'immature and egotistical views' are my own private property. They are held by millions of 'decent and sober-minded' people, only they do not write *Times* leaders.

My views are entirely orthodox: they are held by the intellectual leaders of *this generation*. When you dispute them it is as a Conservative against a Progressive, not as a keeper against a recalcitrant lunatic.

I am glad to say that my relations with my father stood the strain – by a small margin – and improved rapidly during the war. In 1945 he sent me a handsome contribution towards my election expenses, expressing the hope that I would be the only socialist candidate elected.

Middle-class socialists were plentiful enough at the universities during the thirties. In the world outside, however, we were still rare birds, objects of some curiosity and derision to our middle-class friends and relations. 'You are too *nice* to be a socialist, Christopher' my aunts would say, meaning that I washed and was reasonably polite. Reacting against this, some of us tended to wash less and to be ruder to rich people.

We were also apt to arouse curiosity and suspicion among working-class members of the Labour Party, who were then far more dominant in constituency parties than they are today. Why had we joined the party? What were we hoping to get out of it? We had to prove ourselves over a long period before we were accepted and trusted.

In return, our attitude towards the 'workers' tended to be rather defensive, and sometimes unrealistic and illogical. They were the victims of injustice and oppression, robbed by society of proper employment, housing and education, but they were also the 'wave of the future' and in some degree, obscurely, *morally* superior to our bourgeois selves.

This last belief was encouraged by the habit of some working-class socialists at Oxford of boasting about their proletarian ancestry, as if this conferred some credit on them. In one sense it did – it meant that they must have done exceptionally well to get to the university. But this was not usually the sense in which they meant it: they meant that an undergraduate whose father was a miner had greater claims to be listened to than an undergraduate whose father was a banker. Boasting about one's lineage was legitimate provided one's ancestors were poor and underprivileged. We middle-class socialists never quite had the courage to challenge this inverted snobbery.

In the summer of 1937, at a routine lunchtime meeting of the Christ Church Labour Group in my rooms, one of our members brought along an unemployed Welsh miner called Llew Davies. He had come to Oxford to try to arrange a concert for his miners' choir from Dowlais, to raise money for the Dowlais social club. Everyone was willing to help and a successful concert was held in Magdalen. As a reward for feeding the choir, I was invited to stay with Llew. I accepted gladly, and a few months later wrote home from his terraced miner's house:

I seem to have met most of the 1,839,000 unemployed already. Everyone is very cheerful and friendly. The town itself is utterly drab and depressing. It used to be very prosperous up till about 1921, but then everything has changed since. The great steel works of Guest, Keen and Nettlefold, the pillar of everyone's life and livelihood, was abruptly shut down in 1930 and has since been dismantled (it would be doing well now!). This was the works visited by Edward VIII on his last public appearance. I was shown the spot where he said, 'Something must be done'. Many in Dowlais believe it was because he really meant to get something done for them that he was sacked. (I don't think so myself.) Anyhow, the remaining furnaces and chimneys and the vast cleared foundations are a tragic sight. A perfectly efficient and extremely expensive steelworks broken up for scrap. As though we couldn't do with any amount of steel and iron if we got down to the job of providing houses and schools in the amount they are needed. Yesterday I accompanied some friends to the ceremony of drawing their dole. The whole town seemed to be there (actually there are 5,000 unemployed) practically all with 'white forms' (holders of white have been out of work for a long continuous period). One of my friends drew £2 2s. 6d., having a wife and four children. He explained how if he worked in a mine nearby he would only be getting 4s. 6d. more, after the deductions of various expenses. There are some financial advantages also in being unemployed – cheaper entrances to football matches, etc. One of the main reasons, for instance, for the satisfactory attendance of Dowlais men at the Government's physical training classes at Merthyr is that threepence is allowed for the return transport fare. The men will walk both ways, slack at the classes, and collect 1s. 3d. per week. Well worth it, too, if you're only getting 16s. otherwise.

A few days later, I wrote:

I have just triumphantly hewn my first chunk of coal. Llew and I (wearing most pro-like overalls) went down to some friends' 'holes' in the outcrops where they collect coal for their own homes. Here and there the seams come up near the surface, and it is possible for a few men to mine down and hack some out. The 'hole' which we went down was about 100 feet deep and 50 yards along the bottom to the coal face. Naturally there are no mine inspectors for this kind of thing, and it was cheerfully explained to me that real mining is much safer, and that men were often killed in the 'holes'. However, I donned my overalls bravely and watched Llew (experienced miner but unemployed now for four years) preparing to climb down a slippery chain (held by two miners at the top) into the shaft. He was out of practice, half lost his grip and *slid* down the chain, hurting his hands and landing rather heavily at the bottom. So, very considerately, they changed the chain for a rope for me, and I struggled to the bottom, using my back and feet together to support me – in a cold sweat I may say, and almost pitch darkness. Having arrived at the bottom, I immediately had to go on hands and knees and crawl painfully along fifty yards to the face. As we passed, they pointed proudly to the home-made pit props (three feet high and five inches thick) of wood, and explained casually how important they were to our well-being. Our light was one naked candle. However, when we got there (the roof here, as in all the tunnels, not being anywhere more than three feet high) I plucked up courage a bit and decided to show them how coal really should be cut. So, armed with a pick, lying professionally on my side, and amid some mirth, I hacked and hacked until an *enormous* chunk of coal fell off, amid loud and prolonged cheers. Eventually we started back, not forgetting to bring a small bit of coal I had knocked off as a token. Getting up was even worse than getting down, especially as my hands were tired now, but all was well and I was dragged to safety in great triumph. There was something of an anti-climax at the top though, as I fished in my pocket for my contribution to Britain's coal output and produced it for admiration. There was a shout of laughter – it wasn't coal at all! However, all agreed it was a very *good* 'piece of muck' and admirably cut.

'This was, of course, an exceptionally unsafe mine but it did make me appreciate how our annual death rate of a thousand miners is possible.

'What a commentary on our economic system that fully trained miners should scrabble about like this (often merely searching for lumps of coal among refuse and 'tips') by the side of perfectly equipped and idle mines. And that they should trundle the stuff home in ancient wheelbarrows along perfectly planned, unused railway lines! No wonder everyone is a socialist here.'

My Dowlais visit was not the first time I had been in South Wales. Two years before, I had toured round it playing rugby for the university, but had learnt nothing about the problems of Wales marking Wilf Wooller at Cardiff Arms Park. It was staying with unemployed miners that taught me how it felt to be destitute, and to have no prospect of work. I was struck by the ingenuity with which my Welsh friends scrimped and scraped, and by the way they filled their hours of idleness in some positive way – with adult education, choral singing, football or political meetings. I hated their worn-out, shabby clothes, the meanness of the streets and the ugliness of the hillsides. Llew Davies's home seemed immeasurably distant from my own. How did the same society produce his grimy terrace house and the spotless luxury of my parents' flat in Hallam Street? How could the native soil of Britain grow the scattered, stunted trees of

Dowlais hillside and also the massed rhododendrons and azaleas of my Norfolk home?

My visit did not make me 'lefter' but it strengthened my socialist convictions; and back at Oxford I plunged still deeper into the political struggle. In practice, however, this meant fighting the communists rather than the conservatives. The Labour Party establishment, shaken by the communist 'unity' campaign, was trying to strengthen its non-communist supporters in the universities, and began taking an interest in our democratic socialist group.

The climate of undergraduate opinion was against them. The climax came at a specially summoned conference of all university socialist groups, addressed by the Labour Party's national agent, Mr George Shepherd. The forces of democratic socialism were hopelessly outnumbered, and our little group from Oxford had to do battle with hordes of fellow-travellers virtually alone. The conference ended on a depressing note of farce. Mr Shepherd was stoutly built, and when he finished his long speech on our behalf and sat down, his chair collapsed beneath him. Our enemies cheered and laughed delightedly, and our rout was complete.

It was left to the next generation of Oxford undergraduates (which included Roy Jenkins and Tony Crosland) to split the Labour Club and found a socialist organization at the university which made some political sense.

Looking back now at my years at Oxford, I feel a touch of sadness. Did life have to be so earnest, so filled with controversy and conflict? In that paradise of freedom and opportunity, could I not have listened to more music, read more books, attended more lectures, pursued more girls, drunk more sherry, played more rugger and golf? Why in particular did I not take my academic work more seriously, and get a first instead of a second? Few students can ever have had tutors of such distinction. I took 'PPE' – politics, philosophy and economics. My tutors in politics were both future Cabinet Ministers – Frank Pakenham and Patrick Gordon-Walker. Huge, untidy, eccentric and well-born, Frank endeared himself to undergraduates by his kindly, penetrating interest in our personal lives. Who was our latest girl-friend? How much exercise were we taking? Did we believe in God? When I first knew him, he was a leading light in the university Conservative Association; but after being assaulted by fascists, as I have described, he joined the Labour Party.

By contrast, Patrick Gordon-Walker was steady-going, reserved, well-organized. He was one of the few left-wing dons brave enough to resist the communist-led 'unity' campaign, and I happily canvassed for him in a parliamentary by-election in 1937.

For economics my tutor was Roy Harrod, already world-famous as the principal collaborator and interpreter of John Maynard Keynes. However, I was not overawed by this. My own economic theories seemed to me much more convincing than his, and I spent much time explaining them to him at my tutorials. He was a patient soul, but eventually wrote me a sharp rebuke:

> The object, I suppose, of a private hour is that you should pick your tutor's brains, for what they are worth, to the best of your ability. Flat contradiction is not the best way of setting about this. . . . You are a sensible man; does it not occur to you that your mental attitude to your subject cannot be quite right if you are prepared on the basis of what is clearly slender reading and slender reflection to be so dogmatic in contradiction to one who has read much more widely and wrestled with these subjects for many years?

I hope my manners improved after this, but cannot feel sure. My equally distinguished philosophy tutor, Michael Foster, suffered almost as much as Roy Harrod. Taciturn, gloomy and inarticulate, he directed me to read the works of Descartes, Locke, Berkeley, Hume and Kant, and I obediently learned off as much as I could stomach of the arguments of these famous thinkers. But what were they arguing *about*? What did 'philosophy' *mean*? What was it *for*? I could make no sense of it, and Michael Foster could not or would not help me. He sucked an empty pipe and looked enigmatic. However, enlightenment was at hand. Browsing one day in Blackwells, I came across a small book in the fashionable new yellow Gollancz jacket called *Language, Truth and Logic*. Excitingly, it was by somebody still alive, a Christ Church don I had actually met, called A. J. Ayer. It only cost 3s. 6d. and I bought it.

It was clear, concise and persuasive, and revealed, to my immense satisfaction, that the works of Descartes, Locke, Berkeley, Hume and Kant – indeed all metaphysics, all theology and all moral philosophy – were a load of rubbish. I was enthralled. The scales fell from my eyes. Now at last I knew the Truth.

The Truth was – as I now recall it (and Freddie Ayer will forgive me if I am wrong) that statements not capable of being tested (at least in principle) were either tautological or meaningless. That is to say, the statement 'two plus two equals four' is tautological because the word 'four' is already implied in the concept 'twice two': nothing new is being stated. At the same time, statements such as 'strawberries are good' or 'God is love' are strictly speaking meaningless since no experimental apparatus can be devised, even in theory, that could prove or disprove them. When we say 'strawberries are good', we are not making a meaningful statement about strawberries but simply exclaiming 'strawberries – hooray!'.

This was liberation indeed. I became an ardent logical positivist and was soon feeling a hearty contempt for Christian and Marxist ideologists, floundering about like dinosaurs in a swamp of generalizations – about transcendence, eternity, goodness, thesis, antithesis, synthesis – all of which were either tautological or meaningless.

What mattered was the specific, observable fact. What was valuable was what worked, or could be made to work. The purpose of politics was simply to help people in practical ways to be free, prosperous and happy. Or so it seemed to me, beyond reasonable doubt, at that time.

Those were good times for youthful politicians. There were major issues at stake, and good causes to be fought for, and we responded with real enthusiasm and conviction. We were absurdly intolerant and dogmatic. We felt we had the key to all political and economic truth: only if our ideas were accepted could catastrophe be averted. We lived the life of large issues, obsessed with ultimate ends rather than immediate possibilities, scorning to count our supporters or feel the pulse of the electorate. We believed in gestures and demonstrations. And since eloquence is mainly a matter of conviction, and we had plenty of that, many of us were genuinely eloquent.

What optimists we were! We had only to eradicate the profit system, to replace private with public ownership, and all problems would be at an end. Not only would booms and slumps disappear and work become available for everyone, but the whole climate of society would be transformed. Since workers would own the fields and factories, there would be no more strikes. Since cooperation would replace competition, personal relationships would improve. Since no one would any longer need to steal to keep his children properly fed, crime would rapidly diminish. Since great literature, music and art would become accessible to all, all would become lovers of Shakespeare, Beethoven and van Gogh. Filled with a glowing consciousness of common purpose, the lives of all of us would have meaning and significance.

Yes, we were wrong, but let no one say we were wrong in an ignoble manner.

After leaving Oxford, there was still another year of peace to go. I got a twelve months' job with the New Fabian Research Bureau doing research work on the Labour Party's financial policies, and wrote a pamphlet for them called 'Planned Investment'. I was also recruited into an unusual and select club, the 'XYZ' Club, in which academic left-wing economists lunched with the few brave City men who sympathized with Labour. The economists included Hugh Dalton, Hugh Gaitskell, Evan Durbin, Douglas Jay and Lord Piercy. The club commissioned me to examine the possibility that the election of a Labour Government might lead to a run on sterling, and to recommend measures for stopping it.

I lived at that time in a social centre in Hoxton, known as the 'Maurice Hostel' after the famous Christian socialist R. D. Maurice. It boasted a canteen, games room and small bedrooms for the part-time 'staff', of whom I was one. I played table tennis with the boys, helped to run the club, and did some after-care visiting in the surrounding slums. The centre was a converted perfume factory, and we ate, worked and slept in a thick odour of talcum powder. From time to time I would escape for a scent-free night in my parents' flat in Hallam Street.

Living in the East End led me to take part in the famous 'Cable Street' demonstration, in which several hundred thousand East Enders came together to prevent Sir Oswald Mosley from marching through at the head of his Blackshirts. I wrote home:

> It was a demonstration of ordinary working men and most of the London Jews against Mosley – and against the Government for allowing him to carry on. I greatly sympathized, having seen Sir Oswald in action . . . 66 people were taken to hospital. I was hit (or rather prodded) with a truncheon: the police were trying to clear the road for the fascists. They are quite different on these occasions from when on traffic duty in Kensington!

In the summer of 1938 the South Norfolk Labour Party was looking round for a new parliamentary candidate. Since my home was in Norfolk, Hugh Dalton put my name forward, and I was in due course selected. Electorally, it seemed a forlorn hope – in 1935 there had been a majority of 12000 against us – but I was flattered and delighted. The South Norfolk Labour Party had about 200 members at this time – mostly farm workers and their wives. We were pioneers, and our spirit was splendid. The farm worker's wage was 35s. 6d. – barely above subsistence level. Many of them lived in tied cottages, resenting the close dependence on their employer and his wife, uncomfortably aware that if their job went, their home went too. Some were deterred from joining the farm workers' union from fear of offending their employer – and victimization was indeed still not unknown.

In the villages, the schools were appalling – old, cold, damp and much too small, and few houses had electricity or piped water. The old-age pension was ten shillings a week.

The farmers themselves were far from prosperous, always at the mercy of wildly fluctuating prices.

The South Norfolk Labour Party was desperately short of money. Our funds came mostly from whist drives, and from selling packets of tea bought wholesale from the Cooperative Wholesale Society. Even today, if I happen to step on some tea-leaves, I am reminded instantly of the floorboards of our old party offices in Wymondham.

In some of the villages we had half a dozen party members, and I would visit them for a whist drive, a dance or a meeting. Elsewhere, with my agent, an old leftist Clydesider called Jock Watson, club-footed and indestructibly good-natured, I would take leaflets round the village publicizing our evening meeting. Alternatively, Jock and I would simply start speaking through a loud-speaker on the village green, in the hope of attracting an audience.

The South Norfolk Labour Party was united and enthusiastic. Our demands seemed to us, and indeed were, incontestably sensible and fair – guaranteed prices for farm products, better schools, a £2 minimum wage for farm workers, a rise in the old-age pension to £1 a week. These were the 'bread and butter' issues: but we also spoke in broader terms about changing the nature of society. Much as I sympathized with the hardships of old-age pensioners and the farm workers and their families, it was this broader vision of a new society which seemed to me to justify our campaigning.

I often spoke at our South Norfolk meetings about the increasing danger of war, partly because I knew more about this than they did (I had visited Poland and Czechoslovakia at the time of the Munich settlement), whereas they knew more than I did about wages, pensions, schools, tied cottages and farming. I remember one windy summer day in 1939, standing on a farm cart on Mulbarton Common, trying desperately to interest the large crowd of farm workers in the problem of the Sudetenland, arguing that appeasement would lead to war. I did not hold their attention, let alone persuade them, but they could have done nothing anyhow. It was much too late.

4
THE SURREY YEOMANRY IN FRANCE

I landed in France with the Surrey Yeomanry on 25 September 1939, surely the worst-trained soldier ever to be sent abroad on active service. My enlistment a year earlier had been simply a political gesture, a response to allegations by the South Norfolk Tories that while I was calling for resistance to Hitler, I had no intention of fighting myself. Stung by this, and convinced that war – and conscription – was inevitable anyhow, I decided to join the Territorials. I boarded a bus bound for the Royal Exchange, where different regiments touted for recruits at open-air stalls. Choice of regiment seemed immaterial, and I decided to enlist in whichever unit first caught my eye as I stepped off the bus.

In due course, we drew up opposite a stall manned by two sergeants in blue uniforms, and I walked up to them.

'What do you do?' I asked.

'Field gunners. Twenty-five pounders.'

'Which regiment?'

'Surrey Yeomanry.'

'What chance would I have of getting a commission?'

'A commission? D'you own a country house?'

'No.'

'Ride to hounds?'

'No.'

'Not a hope, mate.'

'I'll join.'

This was foolish: I ought to have considered carefully which unit would suit me best. But I was only interested in the act of enlistment, which would prove the seriousness of my opposition to the government's policy of appeasement. That was all that mattered. Service anywhere in the armed forces would be unpleasant; no unit would be significantly better or worse than another.

The act of enlistment also seemed to me quite enough personal preparation for war, and from then until I was called up my entire training consisted of two or three evenings spent in a drill hall in Clapham, during which I was weighed and measured and issued with a battle-dress.

My call-up date was 2 September, the last day of peace. However, I coolly decided to report twenty-four hours late. A free day in London would allow me to try on, and get used to, my boots and battle-dress – and also to eat my last meal as a civilian. For this I chose the famous musicians' restaurant, Pagani's, in Great Portland Street, around the corner from the fine old Queen's Hall, where I had heard so many of the classics for the first time. So the last evening of peace saw me sitting alone at a table in Pagani's solemnly consuming a dozen oysters and a steak, and drinking – what seemed to me then the proper wine for the occasion – Chateau d'Yquem.

Pagani's was an early victim of the blitz. Later, in 1941, the Queen's Hall too was destroyed. I was on leave at the time and arrived for a concert there to be confronted with a pile of smoking ruins. A scrawled notice nearby announced, in the fine spirit of those days, that the concert would be held instead in the Royal Academy of Music, an hour later. I walked there sadly. Moura Lympany played the Schumann concerto. I think all of us were close to tears. How much of music, of London, of civilization, would survive the war?

On the fateful morning of 3 September, weighed down by my army boots and prickled all over by my new shirt and battle-dress, I boarded a bus for the Yeomanry's head-quarters in Clapham. Here I was reprimanded briskly for reporting late and dismissed until the evening. Having absolutely nothing to do, I bought a pork pie for my lunch and ate it in leisurely fashion, leaning against a tree on Clapham Common. Surprisingly, I felt happy. I was not weighed down by thoughts of the horrors facing Europe, nor of the possibility – indeed the likelihood, it then seemed – of being killed or wounded myself. Nor did I feel homesick or lonely, in spite of being thrust into a bleak new environment for a seemingly endless period of time. Instead, I made the surprising discovery that to surrender one's personal freedom, to have one's past expunged and one's fate placed in other people's hands, is not to experience humiliation or frustration but an animal-like state of bliss. I tasted something of the euphoria of the new religious or ideological convert. I had surrendered myself. I belonged. I was in the right place at the right time. I would be swept along.

What was missing in my case, however, was the new convert's loyalty to a hierarchy and a faith. I felt little reverence for the army, and no conviction about the war, except that it had to be fought. I had been pushed towards Clapham Common by a sense of obligation, not drawn there by a vision of better things.

The Surrey Yeomanry had been earmarked to be the first territorial regiment to land in France, and we were quickly hustled down to concentration areas on the south coast. Here we were divided into two echelons – trained men to 'A' echelon in Brighton for immediate embarkation, and the rest, myself included, to 'B' echelon in Worthing. However, after an idle fortnight doing foot-drill and press-ups on the Worthing cricket ground, 'B' echelon was suddenly paraded before a sergeant-major from 'A' echelon.

'Hands up all those with driving licences,' shouted the sergeant-major. A sprinkling of hands went up, mine included.

'Fall out those men and report to "A" echelon.'

And so, a few days later, slightly giddy from inoculations, I found myself despatched to Southampton for embarkation, driving the battery quartermaster-sergeant's van.

The manner of my departure was inglorious, an apt prelude to my career in the British Expeditionary Force. As the convoy was assembling, I backed my van with a loud crash into a spotless yellow Alvis sports car to which one of the officers was bidding farewell. In normal circumstances a crowd would have gathered, and I would have felt embarrassed and the car owner angry. As it was, nobody seemed to mind, and when I explained to the officer that I had never driven a van before, we both actually laughed. Fate had cut us off from our families, our careers and our possessions, and might well soon rob us of our lives: what did an Alvis matter now, damaged or otherwise?

After the war, my MP's mailbag would include protests from constituents that their sons had been sent to the Far East after only two or three months' military training. I would forward their complaint to the appropriate Minister, reflecting privately that I had myself been sent overseas with virtually no training at all.

My six months in the BEF did me little credit and ended in anticlimax. Of all the humble jobs entrusted to me, driving this van was the one I performed worst. I disliked driving and found internal combustion engines incomprehensible. My vehicle was a Fuller's confectionery van, specially designed, so I judged, to convey the firm's famous feather-weight iced walnut cakes round the streets of Mayfair. Disguised with a coat of grey-green paint, it was now loaded to the roof with blankets, battle-dress, gas capes, water bottles and iron rations, and was prodigiously under-powered and top-heavy. Disaster was inevitable. It struck as soon as we left Brest for the Belgian frontier. The battery quartermaster-sergeant, my one passenger, was an ex-regular, a copybook 'old soldier', always ready to bend army regulations for profit or pleasure. Unlike myself, he enjoyed driving, and as soon as our van had been checked out and the convoy had started, he told me to move over and let him take the wheel. I pointed out that this was against regulations.

'Fuck the regulations.' he replied. 'Move over.' I objected feebly that at least we should wait until the next halt.

'No need to wait. You stand up, Mayhew, and I'll come across behind you.'

I did as I was told: I stood up and he sidled across behind me. The inevitable moment arrived when I thought he was driving and he thought I was. The road was straight, smooth and dry. The sun was shining. The van turned an imaginary right-hand corner, hit a concrete milestone and overturned. We were unhurt and managed to climb out before the escorting officer drove up on his motorbike.

'What happened, Mayhew?'

'Van's hopelessly overloaded and top-heavy, sir.'

'Were you smoking?'

As it happened I hadn't been, but I judged, sensibly, that confessing to this would land me in less trouble than 'shopping' the sergeant-major. So I confessed, and was duly paraded before the colonel and sentenced to an hour's pack-drill.

Pack-drill meant marching to and fro in full equipment, with rifle and pack, in hot sunshine, under the eye of a sergeant. It was extremely uncomfortable and exhausting. On the other hand, from then on, as we were both silently aware, the sergeant-major owed me a considerable debt, and this brought advantages. The nights were extremely cold – on convoy we slept in the open wherever our lorries stopped – and it became possible to loan oneself and one's friends extra blankets from our van. Also, rations were extremely meagre – one tin of bully beef and twelve army biscuits had to last a whole day – and opportunities now arose for supplementing them.

Like tax evasion in civilian life, scrounging in the army was officially condemned and universally practised. I tried to draw a line between scrounging and stealing, but it was difficult. On one occasion, of which I am ashamed, my sergeant-major persuaded me to interpret for him in negotiations with a parish priest for the exchange of tins of petrol for bottles of wine.

Once we had reached the Belgian frontier, we drivers had less to do, and were given extra duties. One of these was emptying and cleaning out the battery's field latrines. This was rightly considered a lowly and disgusting chore, and my fellow-rankers did their best to avoid it. I took a different view myself. Nausea, I noticed, declined rapidly with familiarity, and with skilful management the whole horrible task could be completed in about ninety minutes. Since this left the rest of the day free, it was an excellent bargain. After ninety harrowing minutes I would spend many hours in my favourite estaminet, drinking cafe-cognac and reading, all by myself. I looked forward to my days as sanitary orderly.

For a time I was attached to an unfortunate junior officer

as a batman. I polished his boots and Sam Browne, cleaned
his revolver, pressed his trousers, cleaned out his room or
tent and woke him in the morning with a cup of tea. I also
waited at table in the officers' mess, and washed up.

Surprisingly, I enjoyed this work. Batmen ate better and
kept warmer than drivers or gunners, and I also felt considerable respect for my officer, Lieutenant Piele. He was – as his
ex-batman I surely have the right to use this term – a real
gentleman. Mild-mannered, fair-minded and of firm purpose,
he miraculously survived all the Yeomanry's gallant actions
throughout the war, ending up as battery commander, with
an MC and bar.

Unfortunately, Lieutenant Piele did not retain my services
for long. Perhaps I was not a good batman. Or perhaps he
thought I could be more useful doing something else. In any
event, I soon found myself with a new job, as a 'GPO Ack'
– a Gun Position Officer's assistant. The work was exacting
and indeed rather glamorous. GPOs were responsible for
siting a troop of four guns, working out their ranges and
angles-of-sight (different for each gun, since each would be
in a slightly different position) and then giving fire orders. I
had to be able to help with this and also to do the whole
job myself if my GPO became disabled. Since we were never
sure from one day to the next that the Germans would not
launch their offensive – and since on exercises my GPO could
be, and sometimes was, declared a casualty – I had to learn
a lot of specialized mathematics and artillery procedures very
quickly.

When an exercise was going well, it was a fine sight to see
the battery going into action. Tractors pounded over rough
ground; guns and limbers swung round into position; teams
melted into their respective guns; GPOs yelled orders through
megaphones; telephones buzzed; gun barrels swung up and
down. It was all very picturesque. Night exercises could be
still more striking. On a quiet night you could hear the guns
moving up many miles away, a low growl coming and going
with the wind, until you could see the long procession
crawling over a moonlit skyline. Few things look as sinister
as a moonlit gun.

However, the picture was often spoiled. Guns would get bogged, telephone wires broken. People would shout and swear. A metal fence would upset your direction-finder. You would drop your india-rubber in a puddle. And, very likely, you were cold, tired and hungry.

It was a very hard winter and it passed slowly. I was billeted with thirty-four men in a stone-floored loft above a cowshed. The snow filtered straight through the roof in a fine mist. Frost gathered on one's blankets, spoons stuck in one's mess tin, damp clothes could be stood upright. Everyone coughed, or talked in hoarse whispers.

At nights, if you went to sleep sober, the cold would wake you in the early hours. The solution was to go to sleep drunk. Drink was easily available and very cheap. Possibly my most useful service to the BEF was the invention of a drink that enabled men to sleep right through the night. It was called 'Mayhew's Bottom Shelf' and consisted of a large glass filled in equal proportions from whatever bottles happened to be on the bottom shelf of the bar in the estaminet. This concoction was very popular.

Our food was abominable. An orderly officer would come round at mealtimes, inviting complaints in the traditional manner, and from time to time I would stand up and complain that we did not get enough food for a hard day's work. This seemed to do no good, and on one occasion, when I was serving in the officers' mess, I overheard a remark to the effect that in any case Mayhew had no right to talk about a hard day's work. So I was gratified to read, many years later, the following description in the regimental history of our feeding arrangements at the time.

Few will forget the stores and kitchen run under the auspices of Bombardier 'Polecat' Parker and Gunner Hornsey. No ill effects were felt by anyone due to the ancient dead horse removed from the next stable before the cookhouse moved in. How Gunner Hornsey managed to produce even the food he did, using as his stove an old iron wheel, will always be a mystery.

In this connection it is worth recording that for the only time in whole war, the food issued by the Army was definitely

inadequate. Breakfast very often consisted of one rasher of bacon
and bread and margarine; margarine which had been produced
for tropical climates did not spread well when the temperature
was well below zero. However, the BEF had been sent over so
hurriedly that it was perhaps only to be expected, and fortunately
local estaminets still had an ample supply of eggs and chips.

My complaints about food had been made on behalf of my
colleagues rather than myself. As the quartermaster's driver,
I could often find reasons for visiting Douai or Lille, and
here I would park my van outside a first-class hotel or
restaurant and wolf down the finest food at absurdly low
prices. In addition, food parcels arrived regularly from my
large and charitable family at home. My parents had
arranged a standing order for me with Fortnum and Mason's,
and from time to time my friends and I would crouch on the
stone floor above our cowshed, swaddled in greatcoats and
blankets, and help ourselves to tinned wild duck, stoneless
dates, pâté, anchovies and liqueur chocolates, washed down
with lobster bisque or real turtle soup.

Christmas was now approaching, and orders came down
from the adjutant's office for 'turns' to be prepared for the
regiment's Christmas concert. A demand arose from my gun
troop that I should write a funny sketch about the battery,
and I agreed readily enough. It would give me something to
think about during the long, silent hours of sentry duty. I
was helped by an intrepid friend, Teddy Stainer (his grandfather was the famous composer of 'The Crucifixion', which
seemed appropriate), who was persuaded to play the part of
the 'Duty Officer', and by Andy Anderson, a gunner of
huge stature and stentorian voice who gallantly agreed to
impersonate 'Sergeant Satan'.

Imagine a large, cold, ill-lit hall, filled to capacity. In the
front rows are the officers of the Surrey Yeomanry and its
sister regiment, the Sussex Yeomanry. Behind come the
serried ranks of NCOs, and at the back – cheerful, raucous,
beating their gloved hands together for warmth – row after
row of my fellow-rankers.

There being no curtains, the sketch begins with the stage

in darkness. When the lights go up, I am revealed facing the audience alone, blindfold, with my hands tied behind me, plainly about to be shot by a firing squad. I begin

> I can't deny it, I'm afraid.
> I did lack smartness on parade.

To my relief, this gets a laugh, in which the officers join. Later, while the hall becomes increasingly uproarious, an uncertain silence descends on the front rows.

> My boots were foul, my cap not straight,
> My gaiters in a dreadful state,
> And daily there grew less and less
> Buttons on my battle-dress.
> If warm the weather, round my throat
> I'd loose the fastening of my coat;
> Or, if it rained, untied the tape
> And smartly donned my gas-proof cape.
> On guard I slept, and if I woke,
> 'Twas only to enjoy a smoke.
> Often without a pass I went
> To neighbouring towns on pleasure bent,
> And managed to escape detection
> Of my consequent infection.
> And now at last, life's pathway trod,
> I face this bloody firing squad;
> And even at this moment grim,
> My boots are foul, my buttons dim.
> One moment now, and my soul flies,
> To do some pack-drill in the skies.

> (*Sounds of rifle fire. Darkness. When the lights go up I am seen backstage carrying and emptying petrol cans, doing sanitary fatigue. I come forward.*)

> Up I flew to heaven's gate,
> But there St Peter told me straight
> 'My man, you've lost your heavenly crown,
> You've got your gaiters upside down.'
> So now you see I've copped a spell

Of sanitary fatigue in hell,
And Christ Almighty does it smell!
(*Looks left.*) But who comes here?
That face severe, that bearing true,
Proclaim a sergeant through and through.
(*Aside.*) So does the smell of cognac too.*
I'll ask him, though.
(*Enter Satan, a sergeant.*)
Sir, who are you?

SS: My regimental number, son,
Is nought-nought-nought-nought-nought-nought-one.
Sergeant Satan is my name,
I know every niggler's† game,
Raw or hardened, fierce or tame,
I give them jankers,‡ just the same.

PRISONER: But tell me, sergeant, on your sleeve,
Three V-shaped stripes, I do perceive.
What mean these strange symbolic Vs?

SS: I've had venereal disease.

PRISONER: Why three, though, if the question's nice?

SS: Because I've had the bastard thrice.
But back to work! – for know this well,
I'll have no niggling here in hell.

PRISONER (*meditates*): The slavish work in Hell, the heat,
The lack of anything to eat,
Are slowly driving me quite barmy.
I might be in the bloody Army!

(*Voice off coming nearer.*): Any complaints?
(*Enter Orderly Officer.*)

PRISONER: Yes, sir – humbly I entreat
I do not get enough to eat.

OO: Who on earth do you think I am?
You've had your daily bread and jam.
(*Writes.*) I'll put your name down in my book
And see you're punished – and the cook! (*Exit.*)

PRISONER (*addressing audience*): With this addition to my woes
Our little play comes to its close;
But ere we reach the very end,
The obvious moral I'll append.

---

*There had been much drunkenness recently in the sergeants' mess.
†Work dodger.
‡Punishment.

Now, fellow gunners, mark me well,
Never risk descent to hell,
Never niggle, don't oppose
Your officers or NCOs,
Unless beyond the slightest doubt,
You know they cannot find you out.

FINIS

So ended my irreverent little sketch, to tumultuous laughter and applause from my fellow-rankers. And so, too, ended my prospects of promotion in the Surrey Yeomanry. The officers were probably puzzled rather than angry. Was the sketch simply meant to be funny, or was it subversive? If they had asked me, I could have replied: irreverent, certainly; irresponsible, perhaps; subversive, no. But it did my military career no good, and when I left the regiment some months later it was without a stripe, let alone the recommendation for a commission.

My firm support for the war had been made clear some weeks earlier, when, on home leave, I had attended the Annual General Meeting of the South Norfolk Labour Party. In my absence, the party had moved to the left, influenced by a handful of local communists, who at that time were opposing the war, following the lead of the Soviet Union. One of the resolutions put forward was: 'That the Parliamentary Labour Party should press the Government to take the lead in calling a conference of all European nations at once, with the object of arriving at a basis on which a firm and lasting peace in the interests of the working classes of the world can be established.' My speech was reported in the *Eastern Daily Press*.

Mr Mayhew opposed the resolution. Familiarity with the weapons of war had brought him to hate war more than ever, he said, but he could see no alternative to standing firm. Calling another conference at this moment would mean calling another Munich conference on a vaster and more tragic scale. It would stop the war, but for how long? Just long enough, he thought, for Hitler to exploit the advantage he would win from us and build a fleet as well – and then war again. When the time came for reconstruction, we must try to avoid the mistakes made last time. Events had shown that peace could never be maintained among completely independent sovereign states. Pacts, alliances, and leagues seemed equally ineffective. He hoped to see Europe rebuilt on federal lines.

However, despite this plea from its candidate, made personally in uniform, the party carried this communist-inspired resolution by a majority vote.

I must now say something about my large, affectionate and supportive family. When the war broke out, my stepmother Beryl devised a simple but ingenious way of keeping us in touch with each other. Wherever we found ourselves, we would write regular letters for family consumption and send them home to her. She would then send us back, in weekly batches, copies of everyone else's letters. This was an inspired idea. The army postal services were efficient and reliable, and copies of the 'Budget', as we called it, reached us regularly throughout the war, often in remote and inhospitable places. I remember reading it in my cowshed in France, in a fly-ridden transit camp in Port Said, under an olive tree in Sicily and in a Gauleiter's castle in Germany. The letters were a warm and vivid reminder that one's war service was an unnatural interruption of civilized life, that one belonged to other people and other places and would return to them when the war was over.

The Budget also kept us well-informed about the war on other fronts and at home. Between us – six young Mayhews and two first cousins, Stephen and David Howarth – we served in the Navy, the Army, the RAF, Special Operations Executive (SOE), the WRENS, the FANYS, the Home Guard and the Auxiliary Fire Service, and at one time or another wrote home from north-east France, Egypt, Tunisia, Sicily, Normandy and Germany – also from an SOE base in the Shetlands, an internment camp in Ireland, the University of Rochester, New York and Biggin Hill airfield.

By the end of the war we had written between us over a thousand letters, and when he retired in 1982, my brother

Pat went through them all and made a book of them, which was published with considerable success.*

My service in the BEF ended in a humiliating anti-climax. On the very day the Germans began their offensive, I succumbed to a severe chill and advanced into Belgium in a field ambulance, running a high temperature. Almost as soon as we arrived, we began retreating, and after some miserable days of confusion and bombing on crowded roads, I was evacuated by ambulance train to Boulogne, and thence by hospital ship home.

By contrast, my brother Pat returned from France in clouds of glory. A conscientious objector, he had enlisted for non-combatant duties in the Royal Army Medical Corps, and in due course found himself near Dunkirk. Here, at a late stage, volunteers were called for from his unit to stay behind to look after the wounded and then surrender. After a certain pause ('during which', he wrote later, 'the cock had time to crow twice') Pat and a few others stepped forward. They stuck to their post under heavy shelling and bombing until there were no allied troops left between them and the advancing Germans. Then, with their officer's permission, four of them, including Pat, decided to make a run for it.

Pat wrote later in the Budget, 'I concentrated all my energies on running – ducking along the shelter of the houses on the front, hurdling over their low stone walls, scrambling over the wreckage and ruin, treading over the dead, swearing and praying.' Escaping bombs and bullets by miracle, the party eventually found and boarded 'an old-fashioned sort of lifeboat in which the propellor is worked by the combined efforts of men pushing a joystick between them'. In this, constantly harassed from the air, they rowed for nine hours, before being spotted by the Fleet Air Arm and picked up.

For his conduct at Dunkirk, Pat was awarded the Military Medal. This was the first – possibly the only – instance of a decoration for gallantry in the field being awarded to a conscientious objector.

*One Family's War (Hutchinson, 1986). A paperback edition was published by Futura in 1987.

5

SOE AND 'PHANTOM'

After Dunkirk, as Britain's finest hour began, I felt an urgent need to redeem myself as a soldier. Pat had won the Military Medal; Paul, a Hurricane pilot at Biggin Hill, was facing perhaps the most perilous and important assignment of any in the war; and at the age of sixty, my father, untrained and in poor health, had been appointed commandant of the Felthorpe Home Guard. Plainly, I must now start taking military service seriously. I must become an efficient, responsible army officer.

This was no time for scruples about pulling strings or jumping queues. The Financial Secretary at the War Office, Kenneth Lyon, was an old friend. I went to see him, explained my situation, and within a few days found myself posted to an officers' training unit at Aldershot.

Here I took myself in hand, worked hard and conformed. Only one unusual incident sticks in my mind. It was a Friday, pay day. Two hundred cadets were lined up on the parade ground in the summer sunshine. An officer and a sergeant sat behind a trestle table, doling out our meagre wages. Far away, I heard the noise of approaching aircraft. There was nothing unusual about that, as the airfield at Farnborough was less than half a mile away; but on this occasion I thought I recognized, from France, the distinctive engine noise of Heinkels. So I broke ranks and ran up to the officer. 'Enemy aircraft approaching, Sir. Shall we take cover?' Surprised, the officer blew his whistle and the parade ground rapidly emptied. Crouched in a ditch, I spent some anxious moments. Had I shown officer-like qualities of initiative? Or had I panicked? The noise of unsynchronized engines grew louder, until, to my considerable relief, nine Heinkels swept low over us and dropped their bombs on the airfield.

I doubt whether this intrepid conduct helped me to get a commission. I was certainly never thanked by the officer concerned. For whatever reason, however, I left the unit with a glowing report. At my leaving interview, I was asked which branch of the Army I wished to join. Having come top in military security, I mentioned this first. 'Not security, Mayhew!' replied the brigadier, instantly and emphatically. I was taken aback. Why not security? I could see no reason, and the brigadier offered none. But now, with hindsight, the answer is clear: MI5 had caught up with me.

I cannot blame them. Indeed, though they got me wrong, I rather admire them for having kept track of me. I doubt if they were influenced by – or even knew about – my career in the Surrey Yeomanry; but they knew I had visited the Soviet Union in bad company and would have opened files, rightly, on all the British delegates to the Comintern-sponsored conference in Brussels in 1934, which I have already described. I was in fact an anti-communist and had become involved in a 'front' operation for the first and last time. But I find it hard to blame MI5 for not knowing this.

In any case, I soon had the last laugh on the security services. From the beginning of the war, I had kept up a lively correspondence with Hugh Dalton, and had gone to see him soon after returning from France. I found him in his element, in a handsome office in Berkeley Square. The war was suiting him. He was now Minister of Economic Warfare, famous and powerful. The old, boisterous, know-all manner, so tiresome in an out-of-office politician, seemed to suit an important Cabinet Minister. He had gathered some highly talented cronies round him, including Hugh Gaitskell and Gladwyn Jebb.*

Dalton had always taken a romantic view of war and the armed forces. A genuine patriot, he had fought bravely on the Italian front in the First World War. He hated the Germans, and now informed me robustly that there was no hope for the world until the young generation in Nazi Germany had been killed off.

He spoke about Churchill with near-reverence. When Churchill was in Cabinet, he said, Britain's glorious past and

*Now Lord Gladwyn, an eminent Liberal peer.

present came together. He described at length, and with legitimate pride, his own part in bringing Churchill to power and in rallying the Labour Party behind the war.

He asked about my future, saying that I could join the Ministry for Economic Warfare if I wished. I replied that I could hardly leave the armed forces for the civil service in the middle of the war. He thought about this for a while, and then took me with him in his official car to 10 Downing Street, where he was to attend a cabinet meeting. I rolled up in my gunner's uniform before the famous doorway, feeling flattered and amused.

Dalton had been deeply distressed by the loss of talented friends, especially the poet Rupert Brooke, in the 1914/18 War; and during the Second World War, as I learned many years afterwards, he arranged for the surreptitious removal from posts of danger of a number of young men he considered to have a promising future. He wrote to me at Aldershot: 'Since you haven't come without being sent for, I have asked that you should be ordered to parade at my Ministry on an early day – I hope this week. I should like to talk to you about the possibility of work for which you would be specially qualified.'

I could hardly turn this invitation down, and in due course went to see him. He explained to my astonishment that besides handling economic warfare he also led a 'black' life as the Minister responsible for organizing resistance and sabotage in occupied Europe. He invited me to join his fledgling organization, Special Operations Executive. I would be attached to the Ministry of Economic Warfare in the guise of an ordinary civil servant, but would familiarize myself with the work of SOE and then act as his personal liaison officer with SOE's Headquarters at 64 Baker Street.

I naturally accepted, stipulating only that I would return to active service in the event of invasion. On this, Dalton remarked that if an invasion looked like succeeding, an underground organization would be set up in Britain, and that a number of young men had already been earmarked for it.

By SOE's standards, little of my subsequent work was

unusual: by my own standards it was fascinating. As far as my family and friends were concerned, I was a temporary civil servant, an economist, working on problems of the blockade and wearing civilian clothes. However, I was in fact an army captain, paid in five-pound notes, tax-free, and known by a code number – LIG.

Before moving to Dalton's office as his 'black' private secretary, I spent short periods in several different jobs at SOE HQ. The assignment which would have worried MI5 most was one which involved handling the famous 'Ultra' wireless intercepts. I would sit alone all day – sometimes far into the night – studying the contents of two in-trays. Into the first came reports of the movement of all our agents in occupied Europe, into the second, up-to-the-minute intercepts of Gestapo wireless traffic. My task was to spot relationships between the two and warn the appropriate department.

Sometimes there would be a let-up in the flow of Gestapo messages, and I could cast an eye on other Ultra decodes, which would arrive on my desk from time to time by mistake. One evening I read some surprising intercepts of Japanese naval traffic. Japan was not at war with us. Why were we intercepting her communications? What was the meaning of these important-sounding messages about fleet movements? I made no effort to find out, assuming that the same intercepts were being read in the Admiralty. Perhaps they were. A few days later, however, achieving complete surprise, the Japanese attacked Pearl Harbor.

I sometimes wonder, Mitty-like, whether from my lonely office in Baker Street I might not have changed the whole course of the war.*

In due time, I was transferred back to Hugh Dalton's Private Office in the Ministry of Economic Warfare, to be his personal secretary/assistant. I would go with him on visits to SOE out-stations, chatting up agents, instruc-

---

*The idea is not as fanciful as it sounds. I have since learned that the admiral commanding the US Pacific Fleet was not informed of these Ultra intercepts by the Pentagon.

tors, explosives experts, Lysander pilots, parachute packers, forgers of ration books and identity cards. When Dalton went for runs before breakfast, I would jog along beside him. Twice I spent weekends at his house at West Leaze in Wiltshire, where, in the evenings, to my secret dismay, he would read aloud some of Swinburne's longer poems.

I was warned at that time, and have since read, that there was a significant element of homosexuality in Dalton's friendships with young men. Although some of his letters – especially to his closest friend, Tony Crosland – are surprisingly intimate, I am not persuaded of this. There was certainly no abnormal warmth in his feelings towards myself, and I was well qualified to judge this, having received and rejected homosexual advances on a number of occasions at Haileybury and Oxford. It may be that Dalton's detractors make too little allowance for the social isolation – even loneliness – of the first generation of middle-class Labour leaders. Estranged by their political convictions from other members of their class, surrounded by working-class colleagues with different tastes and interests, it was natural for them to seek the company of the new, younger generation of socialists with backgrounds similar to their own.

In later years, I found the company of Ernest Bevin and Herbert Morrison interesting and enjoyable; but the talk was almost always about politics and politicians, our only common interest. Clem Attlee, on the other hand, would quickly turn the conversation to other topics. Australia would surely lose the Ashes. Our old school, Haileybury, seemed to have a good fifteen this year. Did I remember those wonderful tries my brother Pat scored in the 'varsity match at Twickenham in 1937? Attlee was notoriously taciturn, but on these occasions he would talk for pleasure instead of making conversation. He seemed to be coming up for air. It was the same with Dalton. Lonely, an exile from his class, he keenly enjoyed the company of people who could talk back at him in his own language on subjects he liked, people who had at least heard of Swinburne, even if they disliked his poetry.

At about this time I became involved in an abortive

attempt to help my brother Paul. After the Battle of Britain, in which he had fought bravely and successfully from Biggin Hill, his squadron was moved to the north-east. Here, after shooting down a Heinkel in an engagement over the Irish Sea, he ran short of fuel and was obliged to force-land in the Irish Republic. Interned, a solitary British prisoner in a wired encampment in the Curragh, he let me know that he would welcome my help in trying to escape. Privately, I would have preferred him kept in internment until the end of the war – about his only chance, I felt, of coming through it alive and uninjured. But the spirit of those times, of patriotism and sacrifice, argued in the opposite direction. Paul had asked me to help, and I was well placed to do so. I decided to do what I could.

He was confined, by himself, in a bungalow inside a wired perimeter, guarded by sentries. Since he was free to leave the camp on parole and meet friends in Dublin or elsewhere, there was no problem about communications. So I had no difficulty in making a large-scale map of the bungalow and its surroundings. I then visited the War Office's escaping department – MI9 – and put forward the following plan. One morning, in the early hours, Paul would move into a specially constructed hideout in the roof of the bungalow, and at the same time an announcement would be made that he had arrived safely in Northern Ireland. After what would hopefully be a cursory search, the sentries would be withdrawn, and the following night Paul would cut through the perimeter wire and walk to a rendezvous with a car.

Neither MI9 nor my SOE superiors disliked the plan, but both objected that they could not operate in a friendly country: they hinted that I would have to do the job myself. I began making preparations, but soon, following a big air battle over the Irish Sea, several more pilots joined Paul in his bungalow and MI9 now warned me off. A major escape operation was carried out, in which several pilots, including Paul, reached Northern Ireland in safety.

Paul was soon again on active service and the long-dreaded tragedy followed. Returning from an operational flight, he crashed his plane and was killed.

He had never expected to survive the war. In 1939, he wrote from his training camp.

> Every officer here seems to picture himself coming out of the war alive. . . . I, on the other hand, am convinced that, if the war lasts more than eighteen months, I shall be a casualty (but really quite unscared by the prospect). But when I suggest that only about ten per cent of us here would survive a five-year war, I am laughed to scorn. They may be right, but I fear that they are only trying to bluff themselves. . . . It's not that I am person-ally afraid of death – I am not, only a bit scared of dying. . . . But I am overwhelmed by the stupidity of man in throwing to the winds everything that might be great and glorious in this world and instead indulging in thoughtless and hopeless self-destruction.

I was still at work, late at night, when my father telephoned me the news. Hugh Dalton overheard our conversation in his adjoining office and came in and offered some kindly, if rather rhetorical, words of sympathy. I went out into a rainswept Berkeley Square and walked to the Great Eastern Hotel in Liverpool Street where my father was staying. He was sitting on his bed, bowed and in tears. The war had already lined his face and whitened his fine head of hair. He talked with difficulty, clinging bravely to a few fragile shreds of comfort. 'They say he must have been killed instantly.' 'They say he was loved by everyone in the squadron.' 'Appar-ently he could not have suffered any pain.'

Try as I might, I could think of nothing to say to comfort him. Perhaps there was in fact nothing to be done except to show affection, to listen and stay. But the long night was bitter proof that in the most important moments of life, affection and goodwill are not enough. I envied my religious friends their well-tested ways of comforting the bereaved.

My father was obsessed by the hope that Paul's ashes could be taken up ceremonially in a Hurricane and scattered from the air. I felt sure that Paul himself would not have wanted this. He would have felt, as I did, that when so many brave men were being killed in the RAF it would be wrong to stage an elaborate ceremony in honour of one of them.

Somehow I should have made this clear to my father, but I could not bring myself even to try. The Air Ministry agreed to make the necessary arrangements, and in due course, on a miserable, cold morning, Paul's family and friends marched with a band in a military parade through the streets of Coventry and endured the scattering of his ashes in the sky.

For some time I had been feeling that my SOE work, however interesting, was unduly sedentary. Now Paul's death, followed soon afterwards by Hugh Dalton's promotion to the Board of Trade, made up my mind for me. I accepted an invitation from an old friend, Norman Reddaway, to join him in an elite 'private army' called 'Phantom'. Organized in squadrons equipped with armoured cars, its role was to report by radio and despatch riders direct to the army commander from the battle front, bypassing slower official channels.

Phantom was based in extreme comfort in a fine period house, Pembroke Lodge, on the top of Richmond Hill. The verandah of the officers' mess offered a majestic view of the Thames and the southern counties. Here we would sit in the evenings, drinking Martinis served by mess waiters in white jackets. The garden was well kept. Richmond Park golf course was a few minutes away by armoured car.

Most Phantom officers had been recruited by personal invitation, as I had been, and quite a few were well-born, wealthy and bibulous. Some were also eccentrics. The best known of these, the actor, David Niven, once sent out his men on an exercise which required them, among other things, to urinate against the winning post at Ascot.

Among its other amenities, Richmond was comparatively bomb-free. In the previous eighteen months, living in a stoutly built block of flats in Chelsea, I had suffered less from the blitz than most Londoners. But the nights were often noisy. Once my windows were blown in, the flying glass slicing up my curtains and my precious butter ration. Then there was an occasion when a stick of bombs fell near a restaurant in Marylebone High Street where I was having lunch. My fellow-lunchers threw themselves on the floor more quickly than I did, and I had time to marvel at the sight of a score of white-topped lunch tables apparently springing up, mushroom-like, from the ground.

Late one evening a score of incendiary bombs fell noisily into the streets round my block of flats. My fellow-residents and I rushed out with sand buckets, some of us in tidy suits or dresses, some in dressing gowns and bedroom slippers. We must have made a strange sight, running about in the erratic orange glow of the incendiaries, amid the din of bombs and ack-ack guns.

On another occasion I was in a crowded cinema when a bomb fell very close, shaking the building unpleasantly. For a moment the audience was quite quiet, waiting to see if the bomb was a singleton or one of a stick. Then it hurriedly made preparations to leave. Hats were retrieved. Handbags clicked. Seats banged as they were tipped up. But then, as though it was a single person, the audience paused, changed its mind, sat down again and saw the film through. Only two people left.

In Richmond, Phantom had been well removed for some time from these excitements, but 'J' Squadron, to which I had now been posted, faced greater dangers. As soon as I joined them, I was mysteriously given command of a miscellaneous collection of other ranks and told to 'get lost' for a fortnight. This was because the rest of the squadron was due to take part in the Dieppe raid, and for security reasons wanted non-participants out of the way.

Typically – since Phantom was a private army, and our squadron commander was Jakie Astor – J Squadron was billeted at the Astor family home at Cliveden, on the Thames. So I decided to requisition rowing boats and camping equipment and take my motley command by leisurely stages up the River Thames. The exercise was a great success. Radiant in the summer sun, empty of civilian traffic and tourists, the upper reaches of the Thames can never have looked more beautiful. Knowing nothing about the Dieppe project, I felt relaxed and cheerful.

However, there was one unfortunate incident, fully recorded in a subsequent court of inquiry. Trooper Jones was sitting in a farmyard cleaning his rifle, when the farmer's small son came up.

'I know how to fire that,' he said. 'Bet you don't,' replied Jones. 'Have a try.'

His rifle butt was on the ground, its barrel leaning against his shoulder. The lad lifted up the butt and pulled the trigger. Nothing happened.

'Told you so,' said Jones. 'You've got the safety catch on.' So the lad released the safety catch, raised the butt, pulled the trigger and shot poor Jones in the shoulder.

My otherwise idyllic holiday ended abruptly. A telephone call instructed me to go immediately to Newhaven to prepare for the return of Phantom personnel from Dieppe.

This was a miserable task. As survivors trickled back, it became clear that the raid had been a shambles. One of our four Phantom officers had been killed. The other three returned considerably shaken. One, an intrepid professional soldier with the MC, had taken a long, cool look at the beaches and then, bravely and rightly, decided not to take his patrol ashore.

I had laid on dinner at the Old Ship at Brighton: it was a dispiriting occasion.

At Cliveden we were billeted in the stables and servants' quarters – very comfortably by army standards. Occasionally, however, a junior officer would be invited up to the big house for dinner, and in due course my turn came round. I let myself in by the heavy front door into an immense darkened hall, where I paused for a moment to get my bearings. At the far end I could see a wood fire burning, and silhouetted against it, unmistakably, the beard and eyebrows of George Bernard Shaw. Other famous faces, dimly illuminated by an ugly standard lamp, were turning towards me, when a shrill voice pierced the gloom.

'Who is that soldier standing there? Hold yourself up, man, hold yourself up!'

I was being welcomed by my hostess, Lady Astor.

I should have shouted back that I was under the absurd impression that I had been invited to dinner, and left. Instead, I straightened up and stepped timidly forward.

No social embarrassment could ever equal that of being the only undistinguished guest at a dinner party hosted by Lady Astor. Ignored, occasionally insulted, my eyes sometimes on my plate and sometimes, furtively, on my wristwatch, I longed to be back in the servants' quarters where I plainly belonged.

From time to time, some bolder, grander guest would interrupt the flow of our hostess's chatter, and once or twice we were rewarded by some Shavian remarks from Shaw ('Of course I read Marx long before Lenin did') but the evening was a torment.

Shaw, however, had been surprisingly gentle and courteous. The following day he arrived with his wife on the banks of the Thames as I was about to start an exercise with my patrol. He asked me what we were doing, and I explained that we were an amphibious assault unit, and were about to swim the Thames and set up a transmitting station on the other side. He was very friendly, so I said I now had a question for him: which of the plays did he and his wife like best? Would it be *Saint Joan*?

'Oh, yes, *Saint Joan*,' they chorused.

Service in Phantom introduced me to another famous writer. Attached for a time to a commando brigade in Sherborne, I had my first and only encounter with Evelyn Waugh. He was deep in an armchair as I entered an otherwise deserted officers' mess. I said good morning, picked up a magazine and sat down to read. He then addressed to me a remark which was so breath-takingly offensive that – such are the strange workings of our psyches – I have never been able to recall what it was. All I can remember is sitting upright in my chair, staring blindly at my *Country Life*, asking myself whether I could possibly have heard him aright. I knew of him only through his splendidly funny prewar novels. No one had warned me that he was also famous for being gratuitously and devastatingly rude to strangers.

Soon afterwards, the assault detachment of Phantom was despatched round the Cape to North Africa, to take part in the invasion of Sicily.

The voyage was a pleasure cruise. HMS *Bulolo* was a

headquarters' ship, equipped with staterooms for important passengers, and as the only two army officers on board, my commanding officer, Alastair Sedgwick, and I were given a stateroom each. Our duties were minimal. The sea was calm. At the wardroom bar a double gin cost a shilling, and cigarettes were 10d. for twenty. Apart from a few submarine alerts, the only unpleasantness occurred one evening at the bridge table in the wardroom. I was partnered by a diminutive Scotsman, and we had just reached a satisfactory contract when a tall, heavily-built naval officer approached us unsteadily from the bar.

'It is Saturday,' he announced in an Australian accent. 'On Saturdays we don't play bridge in the wardroom.' He then overturned our table. Characteristically, I remained seated, feeling helpless. Not so my small partner. He leapt up and floored the intruder with a single, resounding punch in the face. The bleeding victim was helped away and we resumed our game.

When we put in at Durban, a crowd of friendly ladies met the officers on the quayside. How would we like to spend our day ashore? I pointed far up the beautiful green hill that runs down to the harbour: 'Could I play a round of golf on that splendid-looking course?'

'No problem,' they replied, and led me to a car and swept me away and upwards to the Royal Durban Golf Club. And there, in my army boots and with ladies' clubs, I added to the lustre of the British army by playing round in four over par.

Our mission in Sicily was to land with the first wave and send back situation reports by radio direct to the army commander, Montgomery. The task seemed important and dangerous, but turned out to be safe and virtually useless. A storm delayed the arrival of our landing craft on the beaches, and we were too late for the assault, which was in any case largely unopposed.

As though by way of compensation, I was invited a few weeks later to volunteer for a commando assault by night, direct from the sea, into the German-held harbour in Catania. The operation had been mounted hurriedly and was plainly suicidal. But how could I refuse? What would my patrol think of me? What would I think of myself? With a show of casualness, but privately cursing my bad luck, I volunteered.

The operation was scheduled for the same night. I wrote a provisional last letter home, entrusted it to a friend, and boarded a small, open assault craft. It was pitch dark and raining. There was nowhere to sit down. I had no desire to capture the harbour in Catania. I felt nervous and depressed.

Then, suddenly, the heartening message flew round – 'Operation cancelled'.

Nobody in the assault craft said 'Thank God' out loud: everybody, I suspect, did so privately. I certainly did myself. The future suddenly reappeared. There would be tomorrow, and the day after tomorrow, and days after that. There would be beds, dry clothes, drinks, friends, all the more highly prized for having been retrieved unexpectedly and without dishonour.

But my military career was now becoming a farce. Illness had saved me from the shambles in France, a storm from assaulting the Sicilian beaches, and now a last-minute change of plan from being drowned or blown to bits in Catania harbour. Better soldiers than myself would have felt frustrated, even ashamed. A few would even have regretted lost chances of excitement and glory. But that was not how I felt myself. Danger, I thought, was something to be avoided as far as was conscientiously possible. One faced it if obliged to, and not otherwise. If good fortune removed it, so much the better.

Through no fault of ours, the assault detachment's mission had failed, and we were sent home and disbanded, so I joined instead a new 'private army' being formed for the Normandy invasion, in which my SOE experience seemed likely to come in useful. The role of the 'Special Forces' was to liaise between the army in the field and the resistance movements. We were to keep Army HQ informed of resistance activities, especially railway sabotage, that might affect the battle, and if possible coordinate these activities with the Army's plans.

Thus the run-up to D Day, on 6 June, found me under

canvas in a pleasant meadow near Army HQ, which Montgomery had established in the old fort at Portsmouth. I was in charge of a small advance party of SF – four men and a w/t truck. We were scheduled to land on D + 2.

As my dairy records, our main worry was the weather.

4th June. A horrible windy day – surely too bad for D Day tomorrow. Many rumours go round: the Americans sailed from Bristol and had to put back: there was a colossal loading shambles at one of the south coast ports: there is the biggest depression ever coming over from the Azores, battling with an anticyclone somewhere else – and so on. One hard bit of news is that Eisenhower wrote his D Day communiqué well beforehand and Columbia Broadcasting System obliged by broadcasting it yesterday! Today's *Sunday Despatch* confirms this, adding that at a baseball match in New York, the spectators stood, with bared heads, in recognition. Long live America!

5th June. Still windy and overcast – a very grave state of affairs. If D Day has to be postponed again, it will be for a long time.

19.00 hours. The operation is on. H hour, 07.25 tomorrow. Spend evening listening to our BBC action messages going out to our resisters. It is a moving, dramatic business, this sending out of odd, cheery, humorous phrases – 'Nancy est une très belle ville', 'Charles est gros' – which mean so much to the brave chaps hearing them. They have waited four years for this moment, and now, through the enemy's jamming (surprisingly weak this evening) they hear the word 'Go' and spring into action. All over France men will be jumping on bikes, or running round the streets or getting out a hidden car, to warn their comrades, dig up their arms and explosives, and blow up the target we have allotted to them. It is a tribute to the size and efficiency of SOE that the recital of the phrases by the BBC takes thirty-six minutes.

This last comment, I now realize, was surprisingly naive: to keep the Gestapo busy, the SOE would have included many bogus messages among the genuine ones. Nevertheless, there were 100,000 armed resisters in France on D Day.

Typically, I landed in Normandy well behind schedule, my landing craft having been diverted to take a bulldozer to help the hard-pressed Americans on Omaha beach. By the time

Aged eight

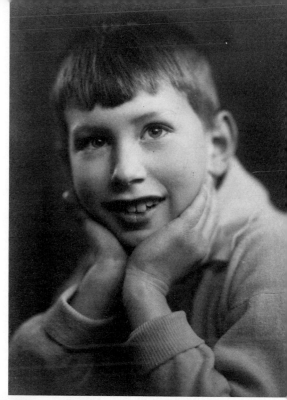

My father as a young man

My mother as a girl

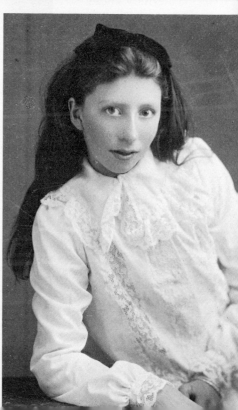

Haileybury's head boy, with fellow prefects

Opposing the Munich settlement at the Oxford Union, 1938

With my father, preparing to defend Felthorpe against the invasion threat, 1940

In Special Forces

Wedding at Felthorpe, 1949   At the Foreign Office, 1946

Felthorpe Hall

we disembarked, the fighting was many miles inland. We settled with the rest of SF near Army HQ at Creully and began supplying the army staff with a flood of sabotage reports. Our staff contacts included two men who were to be friends and parliamentary colleagues in later years – Selwyn Lloyd, the future Foreign Secretary, and Kenneth Younger, who succeeded me in 1950 as a junior minister in the Foreign Office.

Life at Creully was comfortable and comparatively safe. However, shells occasionally landed nearby, so I told my batman to dig a shallow, square hole inside my tent so that I could sleep below ground level. This was a sensible idea and rapidly caught on. However, a directive was quickly issued by Montgomery: the danger from shelling was minimal; staff officers ought to be glad to share a small part of the dangers to which troops of the line were exposed; the practice of digging-down camp beds was to cease immediately. Embarrassed and ashamed, I hastily told my batman to re-elevate my camp bed above ground level. However, many years afterwards I read with amusement, in Nigel Hamilton's splendid biography of Montgomery, that on noisy nights at Creully this strange man would himself take refuge below ground.

In the planning stages for Overlord, Special Forces had assumed that Gestapo activity behind the German lines would be too intense to allow our agents to operate there. But it soon became clear, from agents we had overrun, that the reverse was true, and that there was often so much civilian movement behind the German lines that resisters could operate there without excessive risk. So I began returning one or two of our overrun agents through the lines on tactical intelligence missions. The idea succeeded, and I found myself increasingly occupied on infiltration work. My diary recorded a typical operation, carried out soon after the break-out from the Normandy bridgehead.

2nd August. At the pub, I pay 2,000 francs for the bikes – a huge price – only payable because I have last week's poker winnings on me. Then an exceptionally cordial drink inside the pub before going back to the pre-arranged rendezvous, where we pick up the two agents, Charles and Jean. Everything has gone well with them — they've had a thorough briefing; their clothes and papers are in order; their cover stories seem appropriate; their matches and cigarettes are French; their morale is high.

I take the two men to a deserted looted house. We gingerly collect some furniture, looking for booby-traps, and sit down to wait. I am impatient to get the men off — they have only 2½ hours before curfew time. Jean asks if he can write a letter to his parents for me to deliver. I agree, if he allows me to see it first, which he perfectly understands. Our relations are the friendliest possible. Neither man seems very nervous, though Jean is quiet and Charles yawns a lot. They are delighted with the bicycle idea. I tell them to exchange the bikes immediately they arrive at their first contact.

. . . As our jeep gets nearer the front line, the only noise comes from our own guns and small arms, as far as I can judge. It is remarkably quiet on the whole. The countryside is like Gloucester, and it is a lovely evening.

We start contacting individual armoured cars and getting news about individual German points of resistance. At last, on a main road, we come to a couple of tanks drawn up on either side, guns pointing down it in a business-like fashion. Just over the crest of a rise, two hundred yards away, is a 88 mm and German road block. Here we sit down and eat a short meal, with a generous allowance of whisky for the two heroes. We all feel rather subdued. 25-pounders bang away in a field on our left.

At 2100 hours we go a little further south down a smaller road and find a similar British tank block, and are told that as far as is known there are no Germans ahead. A mile or two over to our left a village is burning fiercely, shells from our guns scream overhead — also towards the left. In front the countryside looks perfectly peaceful. So we decide this is the place. We take the bikes out of the back of the jeep, shake hands with the two agents and watch them go off into the distance. After waiting thirty minutes without hearing a shot we go forward into no-man's-land, partly out of curiosity, partly to retrieve documents and German clothes, of which we are short, from a wrecked German lorry. This done, we get back into the jeep and set off home, leaving our forward troops somewhat respectful and mystified.

The task given to these two agents was to recruit other agents who could return back through the lines with information about enemy dispositions. The plan worked, and the first two 'exfiltrees' arrived within a few days. I sent a pre-arranged message to Charles and Jean through the BBC in London: 'De Paris à Rome. Jean et Eugene vous saluent. Que l'eau deborde' – i.e. 'Your first two men are okay. Send us more.'

However, not all our line crossing operations were as successful. Far from it. An agent might turn back, unable to find a way through, or might get through and be unable to operate his radio, or might be quickly overrun by advancing troops. And all of them had first to be recruited, instructed and briefed. By the end of October I had mounted ten operations, infiltrating eight agents, and failing to infiltrate three. However, all the agents survived, and my seniors decided to develop infiltration on a large scale. I sent them a summary of what I had learned.

1. The infiltrees should be escorted to the bitter end by a SF Officer. It is possible simply to hand them over to a BDE or DIV and ask for them to be put through. If the formation like the purpose of the operation, they will do the job very willingly and probably well, but (a) they cannot easily cope with a last-minute change of plan, e.g. night instead of day, or bike instead of foot, or a decision about postponement, and (b) if the attempt is abortive, they will have the agents left on their hands.

2. The best place for infiltration is in the wake of an armoured push when agents can easily go through on the flanks of the spearhead. In the beachhead breakthrough it was possible to launch two men on bikes down a main road in broad daylight, with a reasonable certainty that they would meet no Germans at all. But these conditions have their drawbacks – (a) planning, briefing and equipment must be a matter of hours rather than days, and (b) if the agents have a tactical mission they will quickly be overrun again by our troops.

3. Even when the front is fairly static there are sometimes sectors with a fair-sized unevacuated no-man's-land between the lines. This again is a good opportunity.

4. When the front is static and the opposing forces are close to each other, patient recce-ing can sometimes find a place where the enemy is sufficiently thin on the ground, at any rate for crossing on foot at night. Patience is essential. The SF officer, without the infiltrees, should go from BDE to BDE, then from BN to BN, and finally COY to COY, until he finds the right place. Sometimes there can be an excellent quiet 'gap' within a mile or two of a tough battle.

5. Very often an entire DIV front, or even a Corps front, is quite impracticable day or night.

6. If required, formations will usually lay on patrols to escort the agents across the lines, or allow agents to follow up their routine patrols. A patrol escort is essential when there is a river or canal to cross, and in any case has the advantage of giving the agents a better chance of escape if Germans are encountered. On the other hand, it increases the infiltrees' chances of being spotted. On the whole, I think patrols should be avoided where possible unless the personal safety of the agent justifies risking a patrol for his protection, e.g. infiltration of a resistance leader.

7. No doubt on occasions use can be made of diversionary patrols, artillery barrages, etc. I have no experience of these.

8. If a local man is being infiltrated, he will want to consult his friends in front line villages before going across. Sometimes this is invaluable, e.g. a civilian may have just gone across the lines and may guide the agent back – but in general it should be discouraged, on security grounds and because front line civilians' views on enemy dispositions are usually inaccurate and exaggerated.

9. There is of course a vital distinction between infiltrees who carry incriminating material and those who don't. The two types should never be sent across together. The latter, if well briefed, is not necessarily lost if picked up and interrogated when crossing the lines (by day).

10. It is worth taking trouble to camouflage incriminating material. If picked up by a front-line soldier, an agent may not be carefully searched until he reaches a formation HQ and during the journey has a period of only mild suspicion and lax custody in which he may be able to escape. For example an infiltree was recently picked up with an S-phone and pistol packed in a muddy sack of potatoes on his bicycle

carrier. The potatoes were not examined and he escaped
without difficulty.

11. The escorting officer should always carry with him stocks
of food, strong drink and spare clothes. If an operation is
abortive he will have to feed the agent – away from formation HQ – and perhaps clothe them as well after they have
swum a river or canal.

Besides infiltration, my duties included picking up
important agents as soon as they had been overrun by our
forces. This sometimes produced strange situations. In the
French town of Evreux, for example, an important resistance
leader, known as 'Compass', had foolishly been infiltrated
(not by myself) without a password or confirmatory BBC
message. The Evreux resistance had consequently taken him
for an agent-provocateur and were about to kill him. He was
saved by the intervention of a Madame Phillipe, a café owner,
whose husband had been shot by the Gestapo. So the Evreux
resisters handed over the wretched 'Compass' to the police
(who were, unbelievably, under their control) and he was
clapped into Evreux prison. As I arrived in the town with
our forward troops, local resisters hurried me off to the
prison, only to find that 'Compass' had already been released.
So we hastened to Madame Phillipe's café, where my diary
records the scene.

I am uproariously welcomed and sat down to eat and drink. It
is a magnificent party. Compass is there, sitting next to the
Inspecteur de Police who clapped him in jail. Madame Phillipe
rushes round with drinks and embraces everyone. People have
come straight out of hiding or out of prison, all flaunting enormous tricolour badges and a vast variety of German, French,
British and American arms. Outside in the little garden a tall,
pale, dark-haired man, suspected of treachery, is being roughly
interrogated by three angry men: he looks absolutely terrified,
as well he may, but inside we take no notice, and I turn a
diplomatic blind eye to an essentially French quarrel.

We drink and drink, and soon I have Compass and the rest
falling on each other's necks. I explain that the local Resistance
had acted with commendable caution in the affair; but Compass
had done everything possible in very difficult circumstances; and

that the British were to blame for faulty briefing, due to the extreme urgency of the mission; and that in spite of everything Evreux had been liberated without heavy loss, and that the local Resistance had done excellent work. So everyone is pleased, and my fellow SF officer will never hear of my making him the scapegoat, so that is all right.

Eventually the party breaks up. Madame Phillipe offers me 1,000 bottles of wine absolutely free, if I care to take them. The Resistance has 10,000 bottles to dispose of, all taken that morning from collaborationist cellars. I accept four bottles under the strongest pressure, and even then have some misgivings. I do not wish to put an official stamp of approval on the other 9996. Having distributed cigarettes, I return to the Prefecture.

Our troops are still not in the town in force, and there is a grave danger of the enemy re-entering Evreux from the west. So I make sure that the prefect and the resistance chief have been warned that if the Germans look like coming back, *every* resister and every possible civilian must evacuate themselves immediately to the south to avoid wholesale reprisals.

My job gave me a great deal of freedom. I could travel wherever I wished on the allied front, with access to anyone, military or civilian, I needed to see. After the breakout in France, I saw that our rapid advance would soon bypass the little mining town of Leforest, where I had been billeted for some months with the Surrey Yeomanry in 1939. The town would be undefended, and I got permission without difficulty to 'liberate' it myself.

I drove in my jeep through the familiar town square, past the *mairie*, up to my favourite estaminet, where Madame Pollet and her two daughters had plied me with food and drink five long years before. My old friends recognized me immediately. There were shouts of delight, embraces, laughter, questions, tears. One of the daughters ran to the cellar and returned with bottles of champagne, hidden away for years for this exact moment. A crowd gathered. For a moment, the whole miserable war seemed to have been worthwhile.

One of SOE's golden security rules was that agents must be segregated from each other as strictly as possible, so that if one was captured he could not betray others, even if tortured. The Germans were less careful about this, and in due course one of their agents gave himself up and presented us with a list of likely line-crossers.

One night I was woken up by a telephone call from a Brigade HQ and told that one of my men had returned. I asked what password he had given and guessed from the answer that he was an enemy agent. So I referred the caller to counter-intelligence and went back to sleep. Soon afterwards the telephone went again: the counter-intelligence officer was away – would I deal with this man myself? I dressed and went over to the security caravan. A sergeant handed me a list of expected enemy line-crossers. The man was brought in, a dark, shortish Frenchman. I asked him his name. 'Duclos, Jacques.' I looked down the list. Yes – Duclos, short, dark hair *en brosse*, signet ring. . . . It all fitted. I put the man under close arrest and went back to bed. He was a traitor, but I felt sorry for him, and angry with my German opposite numbers.

In my unusual job, few of my superiors would have worried overmuch if I had been killed; but if I had been captured, they would have been seriously upset. They would have had to assume that I would tell my interrogators everything. Agents would have had to be recalled, operations cancelled. For this reason, I was careful never to venture too far forward and also specifically instructed my small unit never to confide in a particular officer, Captain Peter Baker, who was operating in our field, building up a line-crossing agency for the Army's escaping organization. Peter was brave and enterprising, and had already won the Military Cross. However, he was also reckless. One night, predictably, he went too far forward and was captured, with fatal results for a number of agents.

He was one of the strangest people I have known. Once, when we were taking refuge in a cellar from some shelling, he told me that after the war he would like to stand for Parliament, like myself. Which party did I think he should join? I thought carefully and advised him, I am sure rightly, to join the Tory Party. Six years later, by an extraordinary coincidence, he was selected as Tory candidate against me in South Norfolk, in the 1950 general election. He fought a brilliant campaign and won comfortably. But then, instead of building up a political career, he forged a signature to a cheque and was sentenced to seven years' imprisonment.

In 1957, when making a film in Wakefield prison for BBC Television, I was accosted by a fierce-looking inmate, a convicted murderer. 'I know somebody you know, sir.'

'Peter Baker, I suppose,' I replied.

'Yes, Captain Baker, sir, a real crook – steals our Mars bars in the canteen.'

I saw Peter occasionally after his release, but he had become an acute alcoholic, beyond help, and died soon afterwards in hospital.

As the Second Army raced across northern France into Belgium and Holland, my work became more varied. When we liberated Brussels, a high-level decision was taken to arm the Belgian resistance, for guarding bridges, escorting prisoners and similar duties, and I was given the task of organizing an air drop of weapons for the resistance from London. The drop turned out to be a festive affair, as my diary records.

9th September. A lovely fine day, just right for the drop. Drive off to our pinpoint. On the way, find three war correspondents in a fast-looking touring saloon. Are they looking for some air operations? Yes they certainly are. Would they care to follow me? Yes they certainly would. When we get to the field – a wide expanse of roots and stubble – half a dozen Belgian resisters are there and the bonfires in triangle are being stoked up. Our w/t section report they have been sending 'okay' to London at the prescribed thirty-minute intervals. Before long, more cars roll up with more Belgians and British officers, including Jack Wolff [a fellow SF officer] with a couple of good-looking female resisters in tow. Numerous civilians swell the throng and soon there is something of the atmosphere of a race meeting. All we need now is binoculars, tweeds and shooting sticks.

Exactly two minutes after zero hour – 17.00 – the first Stirling appears on the horizon, flying low, straight towards us. An extra dollop of hay goes on to each of the bonfires. Then another

Stirling hoves in sight, and another and another, all bearing towards us. The first one makes a circle round and then flies straight in against the wind, about 1000 feet up. Suddenly the whole of her underside seems to give way, and in seconds the sky is filled with vividly coloured parachutes – red, yellow, white, green, brown – and the packages and containers are floating down. Two parachutes fail to open, and the containers hurtle into the ground with great rendings and crashings, but no explosions. Then the second plane flies over, followed by the rest of the twenty. It is an impressive sight, and everyone is delighted.

Suddenly the noise of small-arms fire comes from the other side of the field. German soldiers? No, impossible. British soldiers firing at us, thinking we are Germans? A horrid thought, and I jump into a jeep and race round. But it turns out to be the Belgian resisters themselves, highly excited and using the approach of civilians to the precious containers as an excuse for firing off their weapons, to scare them off. I restrain them with difficulty – one of them fires a shot just past my ear while I am talking to him.

The operation has been a success. Several parachutes failed to open, and one container went slap through the roof of a barn; but that was to be expected. Leaving the resisters with trucks and carts to carry off the booty, we return to Army HQ after sending a message of thanks to London.

On arrival back, we find an Air Intelligence officer – would I kindly find some resisters to guard his squadron's planes from souvenir hunters? Dear me, this was *not* one of the tasks envisaged for the Belgian resistance movement. But why on earth not? I promise to try and lay something on.

At this stage of the war, I began feeling for the first time that I was actually earning my army pay. In the BEF, in North Africa, in Sicily, even in SOE in London, my achievements had been minimal; but now I had work that suited me, which I felt I could do better than other people. However, my growing self-esteem was soon to be somewhat shaken. Despite some marks of official approval – promotion to Major and a mention in despatches – I was summoned to Army HQ in Brussels, for an interview with General

Templer. He was the designate military governor of Germany and responsible for SOE activities there.

'How many agents have you sent over, Mayhew?'

'Twenty-one so far, sir.'

'Why so few?'

I was staggered. I thought I had done well. I began explaining that infiltration needed planning, and that local agents had to be recruited, trained and briefed, but Templer interrupted. 'Not scared, are you, Mayhew? Not afraid of getting killed?' I was furious, and jumped to the conclusion, quite wrongly, that he was referring to a recent abortive infiltration operation. I had enlisted the help of British troops to give covering fire, if necessary, to two agents and myself as we approached a river bank. Since it was essential for the agents to get across undetected, I cancelled the operation as soon as some light small-arms fire came our way. This could have been misconstrued as cowardice.

Templer seemed to accept my explanation, and I learned later that he was in fact simply employing his usual eccentric interviewing technique, and had me in mind for a new and important post. After the war, we met occasionally in friendly fashion. He was widely regarded as a fire-eater, and I am not surprised.

In Holland, infiltration became more difficult. As the Army's advance slowed down and then halted, the front often coincided with waterways and became static and hard to penetrate. I was constantly amazed by the courage and resourcefulness of our agents. A fair number would encounter, and be questioned by, enemy soldiers, but always managed somehow to bluff their way through or fight their way out. By the end of the war I found that, to the best of my knowledge, of the twenty-nine agents I had infiltrated all except one, who died of pneumonia, had survived. But I was always afraid for these gallant men and sometimes felt wretched recruiting them. I remember enlisting a Dutch student, very brave but young and sensitive. I made a mistake in interviewing him at his home, as my diary shows.

While we are talking, his father comes in. A fine, tall, blond man, he makes me feel very miserable with his affection for his son. What are Sebo's chances? Evens? What right have I got to lay this man's son open to a 50/50 chance of death and worse? And yet Heinz [a successful infiltree] has probably already saved dozens of lives by his work. Perhaps his reporting of the German weakness in Tilburg has helped to save hundreds of civilians from death by bombardment. What is my duty? Clearly to carry on with the job. And yet here is the result – explaining to an anxious father over a cup of tea, in a finely furnished drawing room, that because of me his son is to go on this terribly dangerous mission. Because he evidently knows all about it. At first he was ready to be angry: I could see him about to say 'Why don't *you* go instead?' and then checking himself. Then he did say 'Why did you pick Sebo?' I replied that he was one of four resisters selected by the regional resistance chief. 'Why is he not properly trained?' Because no specialist training is needed – only intelligence and courage. I stated that Sebo could withdraw his offer at any time he liked and we should perfectly well understand. The father quietened down and spoke very cordially about other things. But I continued feeling utterly miserable, and cursing the war with all my heart.

In Holland, I had to expose one or two agents to particular danger, asking them to take a special radio transmitter through the lines. This was the 'S-phone', an SOE invention that was small and very simple to operate, and transmitted skywards, so that it would be heard by British aircraft but not by the Gestapo. We managed only one successful S-phone operation mission, but this was particularly fruitful, with the agent on one occasion actually speaking to our Auster aircraft while there were German soldiers below him in the same building.

Occasionally, intrepid Dutchmen would come through the lines on their own initiative, bringing valuable intelligence. One of these was a professional soldier, an artillery officer called Henk Van Leunen. He was particularly intelligent and brave, and it occurred to me that if he could be returned through the lines with an S-phone, he might be able to direct the fire of our medium artillery on to a particular bridge that

was worrying the staff of XII Corps. Henk was delighted
with the idea, and the Corps Commander of Artillery was
enthusiastic and promised full cooperation.

I quickly briefed Henk, helped by my old Surrey Yeomanry
experience as a 'GPO ack'. The difficulty was to get him
safely across the lines. Never had infiltration been so difficult
and dangerous. Henk made four gallant attempts and all of
them failed. I was then in favour of giving up, but Henk and
the XII Corps staff persuaded me that one more attempt
should be made. I agreed to sound out the splendid American
101st Airborne Division, who were holding a particularly
placid sector of the front to the south of us. The Americans
replied readily that they knew a suitable place for infiltration,
and would lay on a patrol for us.

Our party consisted of Henk, two other Dutch agents we
needed to infiltrate, a five-man patrol, led by a captain, and
myself. The plan was to cross, at night, eight hundred yards
of flat country beyond our furthest outpost until we reached
a wide river. Here the three agents would be rowed across
by two of the patrol while the rest of us lined the bank to
give covering fire if necessary.

To begin with, all went well. We met no Germans on our
side of the river, and crept quietly without opposition to a
convenient hollow by the river bank. On a signal from the
captain, the advance party silently picked up the boat and
edged their way forward to the river. We could hear a sound
of scraped rubber as the boat was launched, and soon a
shadow was moving noiselessly down and across the river
in front of us. Ten minutes passed without incident, and the
captain and I, lying prone in the hollow, turned on our sides
and gave each other thumbs up. Neither of us was looking
over the bank at that moment, and this was fortunate. With
fearful suddenness, a machine-gun opened up from straight
across the river, sending a stream of tracer smacking into the
bank, flicking the turf up over our heads. Another machine-
gun joined in from our left, and flares went up all along the
river for miles. This was not what we had been led to expect: the
Germans were present in some strength. We could hear them
calling to each other: 'Have you seen anyone?' 'Who is that?'

Compared with the advance party, our position on the river bank was reasonably safe. Perhaps we should have exposed ourselves and tried to give some covering fire, but this seemed suicidal. The American captain showed courage enough in raising his head above the bank for a brief moment and looking steadily round for the advance party. However, he saw no sign of them. There was nothing we could do except wait.

Our bank was a stout one and, after a time, feeling less frightened, I turned on my back and watched the tracer disappearing behind us into the distance. One of the bullets snapped a strand of wire near a patch of roots, and a whole fence twanged noisily. I saw no clouds to the windward of the moon, which meant that it would be awkward crossing the skyline on the way back. My heart was pounding heavily, and despite a heavy cold my nose and throat had cleared completely.

Long minutes passed in complete silence. Then one of the Americans coughed, loudly, and all of us turned our heads towards him with the same expression of agonized entreaty.

After a time, one of the American privates crawled round and whispered to his chief, 'Say, Cap'n, they'll never be able to come back this way tonight. Why don't we scram?' But the captain decided to wait another ten minutes, rightly, though there was nothing we could do.

When time was up, the captain signed to us to get mobile. We crawled along to a flank and doubled over the skyline singly, at thirty-second intervals. No one fired at us, and after a scramble along a ditch and a rapid crouching walk across meadow land, past some dead and dying cows, we regained the outpost safely.

Here to our astonishment and delight we found Henk and two others of the advance party. They had hidden in the river and then swum back. A fourth had been wounded, but the fifth was safe.

Henk was silent, standing up rigidly in his sodden clothes. He was too cold to move or speak. I tugged his clothes and boots off, covered him with my overcoat and massaged him till my arms ached.

Unbelievably, this was merely the beginning of Henk's ordeals in the Dutch resistance. He insisted on getting back into Holland, and such were his qualities that I sent him to England for parachute training, following him later to brief him for a major resistance role; and in due course he was parachuted by the SOE into Holland. These, however, were the tragic days of the 'Englandspiel', when most of the SOE's activities in the Netherlands were being controlled and manipulated by the Germans. Henk's 'reception committee' was a trap set by the Gestapo. He seemed sure to be killed like other hapless Dutch agents before him, yet somehow shot his way out and escaped. Soon afterwards, unbelievably, he had contacted the resistance on the Canadian Army front and was transmitting intelligence by S-phone and organizing successful parachute receptions. He survived the war.

It was about now that Templer decided to disband Special Forces and attach me to Army HQ as SOE's representative for activities in Germany. This was flattering to myself but absurd, and I refused. I could not speak German, and as a parliamentary candidate would need to go home immediately after the armistice.

However, once Germany was invaded, there was little else for me to do. SOE had no contact with any organized German resistance, and the speed of our advance made infiltration pointless.

However, there remained a final, traumatic war experience. Though I had no business there, I visited Belsen concentration camp soon after it was liberated. The scene of horror has been described by better writers than myself. At the time of my arrival the most urgent need was to separate out the living skeletons from the dead, and bulldoze the dead into pits. The fortitude of the officers and men of the RAMC faced with this dreadful task seemed superhuman. I was not asked to help, and to my shame felt relieved by this. Those moving skeletons were fellow-humans; yet I found to my dismay that I could not feel for them as such. Compassion was blotted out by horror. This was a shameful thing, though those who were at that place at that time may understand.

For many years afterwards I unconsciously repressed the

memory of this visit. I did not refer to Belsen in my letters home, for the sole reason that I did not recall it. It was not until the late fifties that I suddenly remembered that I had been there.

At least the experience should have hardened my heart against the Germans. But which Germans? That was the difficulty. My father wrote to me applauding the Army's policy of non-fraternization: 'The Germans are planning to make fools of us again and to escape the loathing that their actions deserve.'

My reply was unnecessarily combative:

It is much easier to hate people at a distance. If you were out here, would you loathe that old man in the street there with the wheelbarrow with the crockery in? Would you loathe the small girl with long fair hair who brought round some eggs for sale yesterday? Would you loathe the refugee families along the road trundling prams and babies through the mud and rain?

Some people talk as though hating Germany was a shrewd and constructive foreign policy – as though we had only to grind German faces into the dust to secure peace for Europe.

But Germany is only a part – quite a small part now – of the European problem. Not all wars have been caused by Germany, not by any means, and when Germany is dust and ashes, we shall still be shivering in our shoes.

At long last the war ended. One morning I stood in the rain, a casual onlooker, outside a large tent on Lüneburg Heath in which our enemies were signing their instrument of surrender. It was a historic occasion, but my mind was else-where, churning over ideas and phrases for my address to the electors of South Norfolk. As a parliamentary candidate, I qualified for the most envied privilege in the Army – immediate demobilization. A few days later, I joyfully handed in, gave away or threw away all my worn, unloved service gear, and caught a plane home.

6

THE POST-WAR HOUSE OF COMMONS

Unguided by psephologists or public opinion surveys, the British people went to the polls in 1945 expecting to re-elect Churchill and then found to their surprise that their votes had produced a Labour landslide. As my diary shows, my own forecast had been better than most, but I shared the general astonishment at the size of our victory.

25th July 1945. A for Attleborough. Out come the masses of Attleborough ballot forms on the table. I don't think any of us had realized that we were going to get such a good view of the civilian votes before tomorrow's proper count.* We cluster round the counters, checking out the slips with a will. It soon becomes clear that I have won. But probably not by a clear majority, or anyway only a minute one. I am absurdly disappointed, pretend to be enormously pleased. The result is really going to be exactly as I worked out and wrote down before: but subconsciously I had evidently forecast below my real hopes. I think our counters are disappointed too.

26th July. The real count is a formality. The best part is watching the Services postal vote come in. I count a sample – 90 for myself, 25 for Wilson,† 12 for Allen‡ – 70% – well done the Services!

At 11.30 am the count is finished. Self – 16,825; Allen – 10,862; Wilson – 5,761. My written forecast was myself – 18,000; Allen – 13,000; Wilson – 5,500.

A party of us sets off round the constituency, thanking everyone for the victory. Practically everyone smiling and cheering. When they scowl, Jock Watson leans out of the window and makes ribald remarks.

As the news from other constituencies drifts in, a sweeping

---

*For reasons that now escape me the ballot forms in the 1945 election were checked on the day before they were counted.
†Independent Conservative.
‡Official Conservative.

Labour victory is evident. Our spirits rise and rise. In Norfolk
we have won every seat except East.

I remember with pride forecasting a 120 clear majority to
Hugh Dalton, but it really looks like being still more than that.
It is an absolutely unprecedented victory. How utterly astonished
the Tories will be.

The news accumulates. Individual results come in. Ministers
fall like ninepins – Bracken, Grigg – dozens of them.

At dusk cars arrive for a grand evening procession into
Wymondham. We move off, stopping at New Buckenham and
elsewhere for short speeches and general celebration. We pick
up a juvenile brass band. At Attleborough there is a large crowd
in a high state of jubilation. The band plays and I make a speech
which is loudly applauded.

On the outskirts of Wymondham all the magnificent Wymondham workers are waiting. Uproarious cheers as we arrive. Helen*
and I are given bouquets, thrust on the roof of Jock's Austin,
and dragged with ropes through the town. The band goes first,
then the crowd, then the Austin, with me and Helen bowing and
waving like emperors, then a dozen more cars hooting away
behind. Everyone laughing, cheering and shouting.

In the market square several hundreds are already assembled.
Soon the whole square is absolutely packed. Everyone enjoys
themselves hugely, including Helen and myself. Everyone makes
a speech. Everyone gives three cheers for everyone else.

There is a Tory meeting upstairs at the Kings Head. Occasionally, when we are silenter, a sound of mild clapping comes out
across the market place. The Tories shut the windows, then plug
the holes in the windows, to the accompaniment of derisive
cheers from us.

27th July. Out again with the mike, thanking everyone. At
one little village an old woman rushes out wreathed in smiles
and says, 'I *do* hope you get in.'

Can't stop reading the paper. *Everyone* is in – only three
exceptions among my personal friends.

Telegrams come in, including one summoning me to a meeting
of Labour MPs in town tomorrow. Hugh Dalton rings up with
congratulations. He has not got the FO, but is fairly happy
nevertheless – clearly the Exchequer instead, though he won't
tell me over the phone.

---

*My sister Helen had helped me gallantly throughout the campaign
as driver and assistant agent.

28th July. Catch the 6.15 a.m. from Norwich. Edwin Gooch*
jumps on at Wymondham and Sidney Dye† at Thetford. We
have a very cheerful trip up, and arrive just in time at the Beaver
Hall. All the MPs are crowded outside. Shake many hands – a
really great hour for everyone. Clem Attlee gets a tremendous
cheer, makes a nice little speech. Ditto Bevin and Morrison –
cheers about equal. Then Clem disappears for Potsdam, and the
Chief Whip incoherently talks about parliamentary arrangements. Many people get up and ask questions and make suggestions – all very keen to get their own voices heard and faces
seen. Oh dear.

30th July. Dinner with Hugh Dalton. The following are
present – Hugh Gaitskell, Evan Durbin, John Wilmot, Raymond
Blackburn, Dick Crossman, Kenneth Younger, Harold Wilson,
Woodrow Wyatt, John Freeman, William Wells and two others.
There must be many future Ministers and one or two Prime
Ministers among this lot. I was appalled to find how comparatively ignorant and slow-witted I was. The conversation
appeared brilliant to me. We all spoke for a few minutes. I talked
about the possibility of the next two years producing nothing
but blood, sweat and tears, and for the need of warning the
nation now, if possible by forming and publishing an overall
economic plan. But I expressed myself badly, and no one seemed
to agree. Everyone else sparkled brilliantly. Or so it seemed to
me. I should have spoken about agriculture. Go to bed strangely
morose. Why? First, conscious of being heavily outshone by
several persons of my own age. I *must* conquer this desire to
shine and be thought clever. Second, because all the brilliant
talk at the dinner was self-centred and cleverly strategic. Dick
[Crossman], who was irresistibly charming, pointed out the need
for making the party do the propaganda for the Government
instead of the Government itself. Thus a party man would be
put in charge of the Minister's own personal boosting rackets –
and who better than Dick for the job? And what more influential
job could anyone have?

1st August. Enter the Chamber with Hugh Gaitskell at 2.15
p.m. This is half an hour early, but the Chamber is already three-
quarters full. All the rest of the seats have tickets on them with
members' names. But we shuffle in somehow. Conversation with
neighbouring MPs is easy – self-introduction followed by mutual

*Elected MP for North Norfolk.
†Elected MP for South West Norfolk.

congratulations, etc. Everyone highly excited and delighted. Ministers and opposition leaders enter with cheers and counter-cheers. Churchill is given 'For he's a jolly good fellow', while we remain quiet. When it's over, we sing a lusty 'Red Flag' – not very good propaganda perhaps, but much enjoyed by all.

The House looks just a normal gathering of Sunday-suited British citizens. Amazingly quick-witted and responsive by South Norfolk standards.

8th August. Letter from Herbert Morrison – will I ring him and meantime *not* get booked up? This can only mean one thing. I ring him and he says, 'Will you PPS for me?' (be my Parliamentary Private Secretary). I say yes. He says, 'Thank you' – very shyly and humbly it sounded. He mutters over the telephone as though he were using it for the first time and was scared of it.

14th August. HM greets me with references to our 'provisional', 'tentative' agreement, which rather scares me. He tells me to recount the history of my life, which I do. He clinches the deal, saying that if at any time we don't get on, we will 'sack each other'. He has good manners and a sense of humour and has obviously interviewed people before.

Morrison, it appeared, wanted an economist, and my friends must have described me to him as such. Besides being Deputy Prime Minister and Leader of the House, he was responsible for coordinating economic policy, and expected me, besides performing the humbler duties of a PPS, to read and comment on his economic papers and also to write papers myself on subjects – such as the order in which industries should be nationalized – which he was unwilling to entrust to his officials.

One of my first duties was to attend a meeting of all the Ministers concerned with nationalization, to decide which industries should be nationalized first and how shareholders should be compensated. My job was to write the minutes, but I also wrote some private comments on the Ministers:

John Wilmot (Minister of Supply): City-minded but talks to the point.

Hugh Dalton (Chancellor of the Exchequer): Always

striking a pose, and apt to talk with a keener eye for the
figure he is cutting than for the subject under discussion.

Alfred Barnes (Minister of Transport): Rather submerged
– quite the least intelligent of the Ministers but nice and
honest enough.

Stafford Cripps (President of the Board of Trade): Talks
clearly but in rather an academic way – somewhat wintry
humour and cordiality, a slight attitude of superiority and
contempt for the proceedings.

Emmanuel Shinwell (Minister of Fuel and Power): Sensible
and talks a lot – surprisingly 'right-wing'.

H.M.: The best of them all round.

The list of priorities agreed on was exactly the same as in a
paper I had written for Morrison, but the arguments at
the meeting were entirely different, being mainly based on
departmental factors. I noted:

On the whole, I could find among my own contemporaries five
men who would have produced an abler and keener discussion
– but would have probably reached the same decisions. Gaitskell,
Jay, Durbin, Strachey, Younger, Crossman, Fogarty, ? John
Freeman, ? Geoffrey de Freitas. None over forty – just as good
a Cabinet. What fun it would be if we were all there instead.

I had missed out Harold Wilson, whose performance at the
Dalton dinner I had described earlier in a letter home:

It was very humbling to see how knowledgeable and quick-
witted the civilians were compared with us poor dumb ex-
soldiers. In particular there was a pleasant young man called
Harold Wilson, who made me simply gape as he talked. We
knew each other at Oxford – he's a year younger than me, and
beat me up for the Economics Prize the first time I tried. He was
a marvel even in those days but, damn it all, I could at least talk
his language. Not so now. Six years work with Beveridge and
in various Ministries have made him superhuman. I watched his
bulging cranium with anxiety as he talked, expecting the
teeming, boiling brain within to burst out at any moment.

Soon afterwards, I sent my family a description of my maiden speech:

Honourable Members, who had been listening intently to a long and fascinating speech by Jimmy Maxton,* unanimously decided that this was the moment to go out and have a drink. The Speaker had shouted 'Major Mayhew', but if he had shouted 'Fire!' instead, the result would have been about the same, except that Hon. Members would have departed rather more rapidly and without talking quite so loudly to each other as they went out. As the commotion of their departure subsided, I discovered myself saying something about agriculture. Why, it can't think. It certainly wasn't in my carefully prepared speech, and it had nothing whatever to do with the motion. I hastily changed the subject and glued my attention to my notes.

The faithful few who remained were mostly personal pals, and it warmed my heart the way they tried to help me along, laughing whenever they thought I was trying to make a joke, and nodding slowly and wisely when I looked in their direction, as though what I was saying was assuredly of great weight and moment. In about thirteen minutes, it was all over, and I sat down to the accompaniment of polite cheers, and was promptly and mercifully forgotten.

I also chose Wednesday to make my maiden 'interruption'. Or rather I didn't really *choose* at all. Some outside power dragged me to my feet in the middle of Oliver Lyttleton's* speech. It was really astonishing – the House was packed, and right on its toes, and how I had the guts to do it passes my comprehension. Lyttleton was talking about the inflationary effect of payments of compensation in relation to nationalization schemes. We all have our vanities, and one of mine is that I know more about this than anyone else. And so it happened that, as he floundered on and on, I suddenly found myself standing up in the midst of the great assembly. The Speaker called my name, and Lyttleton gave way and sat down.

There was a deathly, expectant hush. For about four seconds

*a colourful Clydesider, leader of the tiny Independent Labour Party.
*Until July 1945, Conservative President of the Board of Trade and Minister of Production. Later Lord Chandos.

I thought very hard indeed. Then in a clear and confident voice I delivered myself of a single long sentence.

To this day I cannot discover what that sentence means. Nor can my economist friends, though we have discussed it at great length. But its effect was overwhelming. Poor Lyttleton blinked, hesitated, and then muttered that he could not follow the honourable and gallant Member's point. And a roar of derision went up from the Labour benches (to show that of course *they* perfectly understood my shattering argument) and the day was won. The House is now firmly convinced that nationalization is *not* inflationary.

All this sounds cheerful enough, and a casual observer might well have concluded that I was settling down well. The reality, however, was very different. I was perilously over-stretched. Living alone in a private hotel in Ebury Street, barely yet adjusted to civilian life, working round the clock on unfamiliar and stressful tasks, I was bending dangerously under the strain. Worries, real and imagined, multiplied. What did Herbert really think about me? Had I misunderstood him over export promotion? How did one write minutes of a ministerial meeting? Was I entitled to use the official typing pool? How did one get a constituent a house? How many parliamentary days did a Bill need before passing? Had I been right to intervene in Herbert's conversation with Cripps?

Soon I was sleeping badly and having nightmares. Then I began being plagued by irrational feelings of anxiety and guilt. I felt that my work was shamefully inadequate, that people were criticizing me behind my back, that without prodigious new efforts disaster was certain.

In considerable distress, I began turning towards religion, reading about the Christian saints and mystics, experimenting with prayer and meditation. Occasionally, in my worst moments, I would feel afraid of going mad. My kind friend, Frank Longford, urged me to seek salvation in the Catholic Church.

20th January. Obedient to my promise to Frank, go to Westminster Cathedral in morning. Am greatly impressed. The feeling that this is the service celebrated by the saints is very forcefully in my mind. I may not believe in God or obey my parents, but I do honour the saints. On way out, buy a three-penny pamphlet called 'What Catholics Believe' and read it in the train. It shows me the hopelessness in present circumstances of my becoming a Catholic. How is it *possible* to believe such nonsense?

Later, Frank invited me to dine with Father D'Arcy at the Carlton Grill, in another attempt to set me on the path to Rome. I liked D'Arcy's quiet manner and saint-like face, but they were offset for me by narrowness of thought and a somewhat arid argumentativeness. He also seemed something of a snob, though lion-hunting for his Church gave him some excuse for that. The dinner was interesting, but left me unpersuaded.

Another kind friend, Evan Durbin,* urged me to see a psychiatrist, and I accepted this advice and arranged a series of sessions with a Freudian analyst in Harley Street. It was not a success. My theory was that I had a fantasy about myself being perfect and immaculate, and that this was associated in some way with my mother. Thus anything that I did that was less than perfect was a humiliation. The analyst's theory, on the other hand, was that my agonizing over writing and making speeches derived from bed-wetting in infancy. This seemed ridiculous to me, even on the assumption that I had been a bed-wetter, which I doubted.

Fortunately, disenchantment with Freudian analysis did not turn me against other forms of treatment, and I consulted instead a modest and sensible psychotherapist, Dr Alan Livie-Noble, who proved more helpful. He told me that my analytical intelligence would not let me experience and feel things as I should, and that my excessive guilt feelings came from some early childhood experience related to my father. At our final session he firmly listed my blind-spots: inconsiderateness, jumping to conclusions, lack of humility, lack of

---

*An exceptionally talented and sensitive Labour MP, son of a miner. Destined for great things, Evan died gallantly saving his daughter from drowning.

outside interests. This sounded convincing, and manageable,
and from then on, for whatever reason, I gradually recovered
my mental balance. However, my dislike of exposing myself
to criticism and ridicule remained: I viewed responsibility,
like danger in war, as something to be avoided as far as
one's conscience permitted.

Meantime, however, I had been presenting a brave front
at Westminster and in South Norfolk, encouraged by genuine
political conviction. I wrote home:

> The best part of all this is feeling in the middle of an adventure.
> We are surely going to be a historic Parliament one way or the
> other. There is our programme, for all to see, laying the basis
> for a complete revolution in our social and economic life, and
> day by day we are hacking away at it. The ideas we have hawked
> round garrets in Bloomsbury, and shouted from street corners
> and on village greens, are being respectably embodied in Bills
> and passed on to the statute book. It is a great thrill, and if we
> fail, no one shall say we haven't tried.

My work for Morrison was very varied. When Leon Blum,
the brave and brilliant Jewish ex-Premier of France, visited
Britain, I was sent to Claridge's to welcome him officially.
Knowing Blum spoke no English, I had prepared some formal
sentences of welcome in French. This was a misjudgement.
As soon as I was shown into his suite, Blum hastened towards
me, hands outstretched – 'Ah! Que vous êtes jeune! Que
vous êtes jeune!'

Few people have made such a strong impression on me as
this great man. Handsome, sensitive, courageous, cultivated
and witty, he seemed to embody all that was best about
European civilization. Miraculously, he had survived a long
period in Buchenwald concentration camp, and his conversation with Morrison, at which I interpreted, began as
follows:

Morrison: 'Congratulations on surviving.'
Blum: 'Ah! The greatest surprise of my life.'

A complicating feature of working for Morrison was his
bitter, long-standing feud with Ernest Bevin, the new Foreign
Secretary. This is best illustrated in my diary.

11th February. Telegram from Palestine says Stern group of terrorists is sending gang over here to assassinate leading members of Government, especially Ernie. I tell HM, who takes it in a humorous spirit. Says Ernie would go off bang.

14th February. On HM's business announcement in the House, including arrangements for Palestine debate next week, Ernie behaves very badly – leaning over indignantly to the PM and inveighing against HM's decision to hold a debate when Ernie had promised Americans not to. He does it in raucous whisper, plus theatrical frowns. Some Tories delightedly notice this plain indication of Bevin/Morrison friction. Chief Whip does his best to shush it up.

20th March. Lunched by chance at same table as Ernie Bevin. He seems to have heard of me and to be interested in me. Lays down the law to Arthur Creech-Jones* and Willie Hall† in the most imperious way. He is enormously vain and domineering, an extraordinary personality. A hopeless man to deal with. I begin to understand some of Herbert's difficulties.

21st March. Herbert goes into a tirade against Ernie, saying that at a recent meeting of Clem, Ernie and himself on the selection of new BBC Governors, Ernie was quite impossible, ruling out all Herbert's suggestions with the utmost rudeness. Clem was apparently very weak. Herbert said he very nearly walked right out. I counselled patience. If Clem is run over by a tram, I say, the only thing which will stop Herbert being PM is the widespread knowledge of his bad relations with Ernie. Eventually he agrees with me, rather reluctantly.

In April, I was asked at the last moment to go to Germany to represent the Labour Party at the annual conference of the German Social Democratic Party. This was an important assignment. The social democrats were faced with a fateful decision – whether or not to join the communist-led Socialist Unity Party – and were looking to their much-admired British colleagues for a lead. After consulting the Labour Party's General Secretary, Morgan Phillips, I decided, boldly, to urge them to break with the communists and strike out on their own.

---

*Secretary of State for the Colonies.
†Financial Secretary to the Treasury.

On my way to the conference, I visited the war crimes trial at Nuremburg, which was stage-managed in an unpleasantly theatrical fashion. I was shown to a comfortable tip-up seat as in a cinema, and a programme was pressed into my hand. Ernst Kaltenbrunner, head of the Sicherheitspolizei, was denying the authenticity of his signature on various papers. He was obviously lying, but I hated the scornful laughter with which his lies were greeted. His crimes were dreadful but he was hopelessly beaten and knew he was about to die.

I recorded my activities at the SPD conference in my diary with much self-congratulation.

13th April. 10.00 a.m. – address SDP women's conference. Make womanly speech, which goes down amid pandemonious applause.

10.45 a.m. – address agricultural conference. Make rustic speech, greeted with uproarious applause.

11.15 a.m. – address academic conference. Give academic speech, greeted with tumultuous applause.

11.45 a.m. – address workers' conference. Give workers speech, greeted with frenzied applause.

As a matter of fact, I spoke really well at all four conferences. It was impossible not to, as my words were interpreted sentence by sentence, and I had hours to think out the most appropriate remarks.

14th April. My speech to the full conference goes down well, which it couldn't help doing. Am given a tremendous ovation.

The SPD Conference decided, for whatever reason, to break with the communists; and on my return I found that my speech had surprised and angered both left-wing and centrist Labour MPs. They complained, with some justice, that I had had no authority for speaking as I did. However, Morrison seemed pleased, and told me that Bevin was delighted. People seemed to smile at me more in the corridors, and I saw my name mentioned in a newspaper as a possible future Minister. However, I felt no desire at all for heavier responsibility.

My diary records a more personal problem.

24th June. I struggle away at speech on death duties for the committee stage of the Finance Bill this evening. It is quite a topical speech for me personally, as Dad discussed his estate with me on Friday night and said he proposed to distribute £10,000 apiece to the five of us immediately – a gift *inter vivos.* Would I accept it? He would not give it to me if I just gave it away. I say how magnificently welcome it would be, yet it could be a bit of an embarrassment to me, and I didn't see how I could accept it. Dad murmurs something about putting it into a trust, but I don't encourage him. The fact is, and I say so, that I have more money already than my conscience will let me make use of.

This was a serious mistake. In a few years' time, without a job and with a family to support, I was to have plenty of financial worries. Moreover, since everyone seemed to assume that, as my father's son, I must be wealthy, my inability to make large donations to charities and good causes was a source of embarrassment.

I was seeing much of my father and stepmother at this time, staying with them at Felthorpe when doing constituency work in South Norfolk. They were very kind and tolerant. Since my socialist views were anathema to most of their Norfolk friends, they could very reasonably have objected to my preaching them from their doorstep. Fortunately, most of my constituency speeches at that time were about day-to-day issues.

In September, Herbert Morrison told me that he and the Chief Whip had been pressing on Attlee my claims to promotion. Surprisingly Attlee had been opposed, and they had asked him what he had against me. Attlee replied ruefully that when he promoted Geoffrey de Freitas* there had been comment in the papers about the old school tie – and I wore the very same tie myself. Morrison said that he and the Chief Whip had battled away against this until the Prime Minister gave in.

My diary records my reactions:

*A fellow-Old Haileyburian, Attlee's PPS.

23rd September. I must say I am amused and pleased at all this – amused at the new sociological significance of the Old School Tie – a barrier to the best jobs – and pleased that I should be worth arguing about at all in connection with government changes.

Herbert has lost his false teeth while bathing off Ireland. They fell out, and sank to the bottom of the ocean. His present set make him look like a horribly ugly nonagenarian. I tell him so, more or less, and he laughs a lot and says a new set is on the way.

I ask him what he thinks about the King. He replied that the King is a decent sort of chap, but really must be told to give Cabinet Ministers an occasional cup of tea or glass of sherry, instead of just letting them stand around.

4th October. Am shown straight into the Cabinet Room. Clem looks very small and displaced, amid a litter of empty chairs. The table is longer, and narrower, the room duller and less elegant than I had expected. Clem says 'Good morning, Chris', and I negotiate the empty chairs and refuse a cigarette. He says he wants me to be Parliamentary Under-Secretary of State for Foreign Affairs. I make the obvious points – that with Herbert I'd had my eyes glued on the home front for the past year, that I was no specialist in foreign affairs and that the first month or two would be an anxious time for me. He agrees cordially enough – says people with economic backgrounds are needed at the Foreign Office. Specialization, he says, is disastrous – look at Eden. Anyway, Ernie had firmly asked for me.

Could I speak languages, he asked? I say I can get on in French. He says he didn't learn much at Haileybury. Dear man, I knew he would bring that in somewhere.

Afterwards tell Herbert, who gives me some fatherly advice: try to be patient with Ernie, he talks all the time and never listens; try and make him detach himself a little more from the Yanks and the Tories; get him to make constructive social democratic speeches. I tell Herbert that there must be no friction in the Bevin/Morrison axis from now on, and he laughs. Shall have to do some heavy thinking on this subject.

I ring various members of the family, who yell with delight and derision, all making the obvious comment that war is now inevitable.

7

THE FOREIGN OFFICE WITH BEVIN

My first months in the Foreign Office were a nightmare. I had no ministerial experience and no knowledge of foreign affairs; yet Britain still ranked as a great power and the cabinet agenda was laden with problems of world import-ance for which we still held a direct responsibility. When and how should India become independent? Must Germany be divided? How can the advance of Stalinism in Europe be halted? Should we form a military alliance with the USA? How, as the mandatory power, can we prevent chaos and war in Palestine? Where can we get the dollars essential for Britain's and Europe's economic recovery? How can we defeat armed communist subversion in Greece?

For handling these and other questions, Bevin had only two ministerial assistants, the Minister of State, Hector McNeil, and myself. One or other of us was usually abroad, and in addition Bevin was sometimes absent ill. On a few occasions – fortunately very few – I actually found myself in charge of the Foreign Office, attending cabinet meetings, receiving high-level visitors, answering in Parliament. The load of work and responsibility was awesome. The worst moments were those spent waiting nervously in the hall of No. 10, outside the cabinet room, for the agenda items for which I had been summoned to be reached. As likely as not, I would have been summoned at the last moment, without time for adequate briefing. Almost certainly I would have had little background knowledge of the subject – less than the Ministers whose opinions I was expected to oppose. Worst of all, if the subject had been discussed in Cabinet before, as was likely, most of those present would be more familiar with Bevin's views on it than I myself. I did not realize then, as I do now, that Bevin's friends in the Cabinet would have understood my vulnerability and would not have allowed other ministers to take advantage of it.

I relied heavily on my officials. On one occasion, I was faced with a parliamentary question asking whether the Government was negotiating with the Egyptian Government about our Suez base. In fact, negotiations were taking place, but if this became known the Egyptian Government would collapse. So I was advised to reply 'I have nothing to add to previous statements made on this subject.' But suppose I was asked in a supplementary whether negotiations were taking place? 'You might like to say that it is the Government's view that there should be no formal negotiations at this time.' And if I am then asked whether informal negotiations are taking place? 'Then you might like to say that the Government is constantly in touch with the Egyptian Government about questions of this kind.'

On this occasion, no dangerous supplementaries were asked, and as time passed I learned to skate on thin ice without official help.

Adding to my worries at this time was the bitter, unrelenting opposition to Bevin from a sizeable proportion of our own back-benchers. A few were secret communists, others were simply victims of Stalinist illusions. One or two, notably Dick Crossman, were able and ambitious troublemakers.

I described to my family my first ministerial appearance in the House:

The worst of many hair-raising events was my first bout of 'questions' in the House. Thirteen of them there were, last Monday, some of them dirty, subtle things about arms for Greece, resettling Polish soldiers, etc. I spent hours and hours working on them beforehand, swatting up the background, redrafting them, trying to think up likely 'supplementaries'. Finally, after lunch on Monday (immediately after the daily prayers, *which I attended*) the Speaker called 'Wing Commander Harvey', who stood up and said 'Question number one, sir', and the race was on, and I was standing up, sitting down, standing up, sitting down, breathlessly answering questions from every direction. Would I confirm . . . ? Would I emphatically deny . . . ? Was I not aware . . . ? Would I give an explicit assurance that without consulting Russia . . . ? And so it went on. One amusing thing was that in concentrating on what to say next, I overlooked the strain I was putting on my right knee each time I got up, so that I was lame for forty-eight hours afterwards! But as far as I know my answers caused no international incidents, and that was the main thing.

Then last night I had to make a speech on the tricky question of the Polish elections. Luckily it was a small 'House' and I just managed to hold my own against the communists and crypto-communists behind me, who are determined to make my life hell. In a few months' time I shall be the British communists' public enemy number two. Also, a very large proportion of the Parliamentary Labour Party will be thirsting for my blood. But I am on the right side, and it can't be helped.

My diary recorded some early contacts with Bevin and Attlee:

22nd October 1946. Take Ernie through his parliamentary questions. He goes through them very quickly, only altering one. He talks a bit, rather rambling and portentous. I don't think he's got at all a disciplined mind. It's all shrewdness, experience and personality.

PM is on bench for debate, and scribbles me a note – 'Glad to see *Punch* gives you a good chit.' This is a reference to a word of praise for my 'front bench manner' in the current *Punch*, and cheers me up.

Ernie's speech is much too long and bores the House enormously. Later in the evening he asks me how it went, and I tell him that it should have been cut. He is a bit surprised at my frankness.

11th November. Tea at No. 10 with the other Junior Ministers to hear the King's Speech. Chat with the PM – he evidently seeks me out and wants to talk. I get the impression of being liked by the little man. The truth is – our old school tie is a very strong link for him. An absolute fact. Years and years of working-class contacts make him feel entitled to this strong, secret loyalty to Haileybury and Oxford. If Geoffrey de Freitas or I ever let him down I think he would feel it more of a blow than if anybody in the Cabinet did. Massigli* whispered dramatically to me the other day, 'Ush! Is it not true you are an 'Aileyburian, too?'!

My diary also records some fearful blunders. There was a huge lunch at the Savoy, given by the Anglo-Uruguayan

*French ambassador.

Society to celebrate the Battle of the River Plate. When called on to speak, I duly recited a rather pompous speech given me by the department, and then, raising my eyes for a moment from my script, proposed the toast of the Republic of Paraguay.

Then there was the disaster of one of my first ministerial minutes.

I had to decide whether or not an entry visa should be granted to an Italian businessman representing Fiat. The Board of Trade was urging admission, but there was a snag: the businessman and his firm had a record of collaboration with the Nazis. After reading the file, I decided to let him in, but at the last moment, as my pen poised to write 'I agree', there welled up inside me an unaccustomed feeling of power. Here I was, like a Roman emperor, deciding a man's fate. And I saw that with a single word I could express this feeling, announce my decision and make a joke. In large letters, I wrote 'Fiat!'

I thought my officials were bound to see the joke: had they not all been educated at Winchester and Balliol? But no. To them, 'Fiat!' was plainly an expression of disgust at the idea of aiding a collaborationist firm. The entry permit was refused.

Then, later, there was a famous gaffe I perpetrated at the UN Economic and Social Council in New York. Replying to a Soviet attack on the British economy, I made a spirited defence of our record of recovery. My peroration began 'It is time to stop talking about the "recovery" of Britain. For us, the social and economic standards of pre-war years are not things to be "recovered" but rather things to be repudiated', and I went on to point out that we no longer had an unemployment problem, that the nation's health was better than ever before, and so on.

It all sounded fine to me, and indeed received some warm applause. But the fat was in the fire. I had forgotten that in Washington at that very moment the Senate was debating Britain's share of Marshall aid, with all our friends arguing that only a huge allocation of aid could save us from economic disaster. My speech was joyfully seized on by Britain's

Bevin supports me in the South Norfolk election, 1949.

Vicky's cartoon. My speech could have cost one and a half million dollars a word

LITTLE BOY STANDS AT THE FOOT OF THE BED,
DROOPS ON THE LITTLE HANDS LITTLE GOLD HEAD.
HUSH! HUSH! WHAT A TERRIBLE TRICK!
CHRISTOPHER MAYHEW'S BEEN DROPPING A BRICK.

At the UN Economic Commission, Geneva, in 1949. Arutiunian is
on the right, Cicely unfortunately obscured by my glass of vodka

In communist Hanoi, 1955, with the BBC star cameraman, 'Tubby'
Englander

Posing for Denis
Healey at Gizeh in
1963

Navy Minister,
1964–66

With Arafat in Beirut, 1975. There was plenty of goodwill, but unfortunately his English was hard to understand

Visiting Palestinian children at a refugee camp

opponents. An emergency session of the Senate Foreign Affairs Committee was summoned to discuss it. Cripps, as Chancellor of the Exchequer, issued a statement ruthlessly repudiating me. I became headline news on both sides of the Atlantic.

Brooding in my lonely hotel room, I calculated morbidly that my eloquent speech might well have cost the nation one and a half million dollars a word.

However, some good men now came to my aid. A Foreign Office friend, Archie Mackenzie,* dragged me from my hotel room and took me to dinner and an ice hockey match. Comforting telegrams arrived from Hector McNeil, Jim Callaghan and Ernest Bevin. Bevin's read: −

Thank you for your very full statement. No harm was done except in the peroration. The thing to do in future is to avoid perorations. Do not worry too much: when you get into a tangle like this we old ones have to get you young ones out of trouble. Anyway, I understand the circs and don't let it daunt you. Good wishes.

The next day, high-ranking US officials persuaded the Senate committee that I had simply overreacted to 'needling' by the Russians and the crisis passed.

On the voyage home in the *Queen Mary*, at a party in the captain's cabin, I was introduced to a charming and intelligent Canadian woman. She opened the conversation: 'I am longing for the bad boy to arrive.' 'Bad boy?' I replied innocently. 'Yes, I am told he is coming − you know − the man who told the Americans we don't need any more Marshall dollars.' 'Oh, I said, you mean *me*.'

On my return, Attlee stoutly defended me in the House, under heavy fire. Churchill, the Leader of the Opposition, did not join in and came up to me afterwards at a reception. 'I think the newspapers have treated you very harshly,' he said, and moved away.

Despite my gaffe, Attlee remained very friendly, and now

*A leader of Moral Rearmament, later our Ambassador in Tunisia.

asked me to join the small cabinet committee handling the transfer of power to India.

In the early part of 1947, three meetings were held, with the Viceroy, Mountbatten, present, to decide the arrangements for the transfer. They were fascinating and dramatic affairs. At the first, Mountbatten told us that both sides in India were now prepared to accept dominion status. He had arrived in England only an hour or two before, and this was completely unknown to all of us. A kind of suppressed excitement became noticeable. The Prime Minister did not raise his head, but became a shade redder in the face. Cripps started doodling intently on a matchbox. He said, 'This is of course our goal,' and everyone murmured assent, and the meeting broke up almost jubilantly.

The second meeting was slightly more sober, but Attlee announced to everyone's pleasure that he now had the Opposition's pledge of cooperation. Apparently Churchill gave Mountbatten a message for Jinnah positively commanding him to support the Mountbatten scheme.

My diary comments on the personalities involved.

Mountbatten is a bit mercurial – sometimes tremendously confident, and then suddenly pessimistic. But his eagerness, frankness and general charm are tremendously impressive.

Lord Addison is simply frightful, holding things up with demands for an explanation of the simplest points.

Among M's more striking remarks are, 'There will be bloodshed whatever we do. It is a question of how many gallons of blood.' When a suggestion was made involving some delay – 'I must remind the committee that while we wait, India is blowing up under our feet,' at which everyone murmured assent.

The question of altering the King's title from 'Rex Imperator' to something else came up. 'I wonder if the King will mind,' said the PM. 'As a matter of fact, I asked him last night when I was dining with him,' replied M. 'He doesn't mind a bit, but asked whether it would mean changing his signature, R.I., of which he is rather proud. He doesn't want to change that, I don't think.' The Cabinet seemed to agree that to keep the signature would add to Britain's store of valued historical anomalies.

I am much impressed by the way that the PM deliberately

snubs his cabinet colleagues when they are long-winded or stupid. Tom Williams is told peremptorily that he ought to have set up his marketing committee many months earlier. Addison is reminded testily that the point he has just raised was settled only a few minutes ago. PM gives impression of irritability and rudeness: his way, I think, of asserting himself against colleagues with naturally stronger personalities. He doesn't talk much, but lets those who know what they are talking about – e.g. Cripps – make the running.

3rd June 1947. The news on India breaks. The Viceroy has reported his meeting with Jinnah and Nehru was 'All I could possibly hope for'. PM makes involved statement in House – incomprehensible, inaudible. Churchill replies, despite well-meaning but untimely efforts of our back-benchers to stop him on points of order – they think he's going to try to wreck things. In fact, of course, he backs the scheme, promises no opposition on legislation and actually ends with a tribute to the PM. Throughout the whole business he has been public-spirited. Some of our boys are mystified, and Willie Gallagher* speaks for all purblind reactionaries everywhere on the left by saying that he did not understand a word of the PM's statement, but that since Churchill supported it, it was probably highly suspect.

Spoke with Ernie about India later. He said he'd been much responsible for the whole policy. When he had met Wavell as Viceroy, he'd gone straight off to the PM and demanded his removal. The man was a hopeless defeatist, he said. Wanted troops for the protection of British citizens. 'I said that a couple of thousand troops had protected British citizens for decades past.' All the same, Ernie added, it gave him some sleepless nights.

I told him that Herbert was worried by all the talk of E.B.'s becoming economic dictator.... Ernie says, 'Why does not Herbert come and see me himself?' I hazard, 'I think he's a bit scared of you,' and Ernie thinks he will have a friendly word with Herbert.

Morrison's suspicions had arisen from widespread and growing doubts about the state of the economy. In the late summer, there was a serious run on sterling and the convert-ibility crisis came to a climax. Attlee's leadership came under

*A communist MP.

challenge. However, as my diary shows, he could rely on
Bevin.

29th July. Long talk with Ernie about the 'crisis'. Several
members of the Parliamentary Party are gunning for Clem and
want Ernie as PM – or at least some big cabinet changes. Ernie
says several people were crowding round him last night, urging
him to go to tomorrow's party meeting, etc. He said Nye Bevan
was behind it – you could always tell Nye was up to something
from his attitudes in the Cabinet. I say I think Clem is admirable
and should stay. Ernie heartily agrees. Clem is not spectacular,
he says, but what is the finest Cabinet we've had for 150 years?
– the 1906 Liberals, in which a group of personalities were kept
together as a team by a rather dull, honest fellow, Campbell-
Bannerman. Take Clem away, and where were you? Who could
succeed Clem, he asks me rhetorically. Only you, I say. 'Me!' he
said. 'When have I ever done an honest man out of a job?'

17th August. Ernie again brings up the question of Clem's
removal – obviously sounding me out. I repeat that, though he
could no doubt make himself PM if he wished, my view was
that he should let Clem stay, as the best means of keeping the
party united. He agrees again – I am sure sincerely. Says Dalton
and Cripps came this morning to try to persuade him to oust
Clem. 'I told them I have never done a man out of his job
before.' 'That alone would not be much of a reason,' I said. 'The
point is, what with Herbert, Bevan, and so on, I doubt if you
would get a united party.' 'Yes, I'd probably get a split party.
It's all this intriguing I won't do. Dalton, Cripps, all of them.
What happened to Lloyd George and Asquith? The public gets
to know you're an intriguer.' 'It's a big decision to take,' I said.
'Not for me it ain't,' he replied with a huge grin and a gleam in
his eye.

8
THE COLD WAR

In October 1947 Hector McNeil and I left for New York to represent Britain at the UN General Assembly. Hector was the delegation leader. He was almost as young and inexperienced as myself, a Scotsman, a former Beaverbrook journalist, courageous, a great mixer.

Our fellow passengers included many other delegates bound for the UN Assembly, including a large Soviet party led by Vyshinsky, the notorious prosecuting counsel in Stalin's show trials. Hector set out to establish a personal relationship with this repellent man. It was a forlorn hope. He sent a bottle of Scotch and a friendly note to Vyshinsky's cabin, but there was no acknowledgement. He then sent some flowers to the cabin of Vyshinsky's daughter, but with no better result.

On board ship, it is difficult to avoid all contacts with one's fellow passengers, but the Soviet delegates' efforts to achieve this were entirely successful. For most delegates, mealtimes in the dining saloon were diplomatic occasions – good opportunities for meeting one's opposite numbers and breaking barriers. But Vyshinsky ate in his cabin, presumably with his daughter, while the rest of the Soviet delegates would appear punctually, all together, at the entrance to the dining saloon, thread their way between the tables, and disappear into a private room. After an appropriate interval they would then reappear, again all together, and make their retreat, speaking to no one on the way.

This self-isolation of the Soviet delegation was a fair warning of the bitter hostility they were to display towards the non-communist delegations in New York. However, Hector had assigned me to Committee 2 of the UN Assembly, dealing with economic affairs, and here the Soviet representative, Amazan Arutiunian, was unusual in several respects. He was not a Russian but an Armenian, and was witty, inquisitive and likeable. I set out to persuade him to have lunch with me alone, and eventually, after many sittings, succeeded. Absurd though it sounds today, this was a diplomatic breakthrough.

Arutiunian's conversation was discreet but lively and gave me some insight into his thought processes. He took the straight Stalinist line on everything, and evidently believed it all. Taken by themselves, his facts were usually correct, but a strange mental conditioning led him to assemble them into grotesque patterns, leading to wildly simplistic conclusions. Since there were conditions attached to our loan from the USA, Britain was an economic vassal of the USA. Since British newspapers were owned by capitalists, there was no freedom of the press. Our withdrawal from Empire was simply a new form of colonialism.

However, this debased form of Marxism was still plausible at that time. It offered a single, easily understood method of analysis, and an explanation of the errors of apparently intelligent bourgeois intellectuals.

At this time, Stalin's worldwide campaign of subversion and propaganda was at its most effective. Orchestrated from Moscow, or indirectly through the Cominform, scores of communist and communist-front organizations maintained a relentless war against western governments and institutions. The Soviet Union was presented as the exact antithesis of the West, that is, as the true enemy of fascism, the champion of colonial peoples against imperialism, the ally of all peace-loving people and the shining example of a workers' state in which capitalism had been abolished and where the workers prospered and were free.

To this flood of propaganda, the western countries made no organized response at all. At the UN, which the Russians and their satellites used without inhibition as a propaganda platform, the convention among western delegates was not to reply to Soviet diatribes but simply to deplore the abuse of UN meetings for propaganda purposes and to urge respect for the agenda.

After a short experience at the UN, I came to the conclusion that this western strategy was seriously mistaken.

Stalinist propaganda was having an influence, especially in the Third World, and needed to be answered; and if the answer was to be effective, it must go beyond self-defence and carry the propaganda war into the enemy's camp.

I also felt, more controversially, that social-democratic Britain was better placed than capitalist America to take the lead; and also that since anti-communist propaganda would be anathema to much of the Labour Party, it would have to be organized secretly.

On my way back from the UN Assembly, I wrote a paper for Bevin to this effect. It proved to be well-timed: Bevin was now finally despairing of reaching agreement with the Soviet Union. In December 1947, the Council of Foreign Ministers, of the USA, the Soviet Union, France and Britain, met for the last time, in London, to decide the future of Germany. Could agreement be reached on a peace treaty or must Germany be divided? My diary records Bevin's low spirits at this time, and his sense of hopelessness.

13th December. The truth is, EB is not doing well at the Council of Foreign Ministers. There is a lack of leadership, initiative and even clear thinking in our delegation. Ernest knows he's below par. He is not at all fit physically: on Saturday he told me, 'I can't go on forever like this . . . it's the pain in my chest. It's terrible. I can't sleep at nights. You know, it gets you down.' But even if he were fit, it would be hard to beat Molotov at this conference. The man's a genius in his own perverted form of diplomacy.

Ernest keeps saying, 'Will anyone tell me what to do next?' at the delegation meetings. He told me yesterday he just had no idea of Molotov's mind and intentions – whether or not he intended agreement after this initial fighting. Our delegation is in no better shape. I feel ashamed at not being able to suggest a thing – but have the excuse that Germany is only a small part of my job, while the others are specialists. No one in the delegation puts a connected, logical case, and no one is constructive or sounds confident.

21st December. Well, the Council of Foreign Ministers is over. We may still get an agreement on Austria – in fact it looks quite possible – but otherwise the conference has been a complete failure. I always knew it would be. Ernest was wrong to expect anything, but right as a politician not to give up trying too soon. Or perhaps he never really hoped for anything? No, I don't think that. He had a feeling right up to the last moment that Molotov might suddenly come clean. Molotov himself batted well for the powers of darkness: couldn't help admiring his quick mind and imperturbable courage. I should place him well above the other three for these qualities. Of course, it's much easier when you can lie like a trooper and don't have to restrain yourself within the confines of good manners.

Predictably, in these circumstances, Bevin approved my proposal for an ideological offensive against Stalinism. He asked me to clear the project first with the Prime Minister. I went down to Chequers, and Attlee raised no objection. He asked me to write a paper for the Cabinet, and this went through without difficulty.

Some lively meetings followed in the Foreign Office, establishing what came to be known as the Information Research Department (IRD). I summoned a conference of our ambassadors from the communist countries. Everyone seemed to support the new project, but there were different degrees of enthusiasm and some disagreement about the priority we should give to different propaganda targets. How much emphasis should we place on the lack of freedom in the communist world? On communist expansion as a menace to peace? On the low living standards of Soviet workers?

I found myself in a minority in urging that living standards should have priority. It seemed to me that we had little to fear from the appeal of Stalinism to the better-off, and should direct our message to the masses of people in all countries for whom destitution was at that time an even worse evil than lack of freedom. This view was resisted by the majority of ambassadors and officials, who felt that the emphasis should be on freedom. They may have been right. In the end, we agreed to give roughly equal emphasis to all three themes. I added that we needed some powerful phrase to describe the Soviet Union's relations with Eastern Europe. I suggested 'communist imperialism', and this new term was warmly approved and was soon in widespread use.

Our overall message was soon afterwards presented – albeit in polite language – by the Prime Minister in a BBC broadcast. He had asked for my comments on his draft script and at my suggestion included the following paragraph:

The history of Soviet Russia provides us with a warning – a warning that without political freedom, collectivism can quickly go astray and lead to new forms of injustice and oppression. For political freedom is not merely a noble thing in itself, essential for the full development of human personality – it is also a means of achieving economic rights and social justice, and of preserving these things when they have been won. Where there is no political freedom, privilege and injustice creep back. In communist Russia 'privilege for the few' is a growing phenomenon and the gap between the highest and lowest incomes is constantly widening. Soviet communism pursues a policy which threatens with a new form of imperialism – ideological, economic and strategic – the welfare and way of life of the other countries of Europe.

At the time – December 1947 – this was strong language, and Attlee delivered it unusually well. The following morning I spent some time with my radio set listening to the message being transmitted by the BBC to different parts of the world.

IRD seemed to have made a good start, but I now made an extraordinary mistake. One day Hector McNeil came into my room, congratulated me on the progress we were making, and said he had someone available who was uniquely qualified for IRD work. I replied that I was now only taking people with exceptional knowledge of Soviet communism. Who was his candidate? 'My personal assistant, Guy Burgess. Just your man.'

I interviewed Burgess. He certainly showed a dazzling insight into communist methods of subversion and propaganda, and I readily took him on. Fortunately, a few months later my alert private secretary, Norman Reddaway,* advised

---

*With some difficulty, I had conscripted my old friend into my private office. He later became a leading light in IRD and our ambassador in Warsaw.

me to look at Burgess's work. I made some inquiries and dismissed Burgess from IRD, minuting on his file 'Burgess is dirty, drunken and idle'. However, it never occurred to me that he was also a Soviet agent, and had joined IRD – as must have been the case – on KGB instructions. Nor did this occur to anyone else in the Foreign Office, or in MI5. After a short period Burgess was appointed to the Far East department and afterwards to the Washington Embassy, where he continued his work for the Russians in close contact with Philby.

Ironically, I was at this time being attacked by left-wing MPs as a 'McCarthyite'. A Clydesider, Emrys Hughes MP, declared at a meeting of the Parliamentary Labour Party, amid applause, 'The trouble with Chris Mayhew is, he sees communists under every bed.'

At that time our knowledge of the Soviet Union, and especially of the blacker aspects of Stalinist oppression, was extremely limited. We had few secret sources of intelligence; defectors were few and far between; the movements of western visitors were strictly controlled, and the Soviet media gave little or nothing away. However, painstaking research by IRD enabled me in the autumn of 1948 to make what I believe was the first official public denunciation of the Soviet slave labour system. My chance came on Committee 3 of the UN General Assembly, which was engaged in drafting the Universal Declaration of Human Rights. The Soviet delegate had made a routine attack on British colonialism and the 'hypocrisy' of Britain's support for human rights, and I replied by challenging the right of any Soviet spokesman to criticize the lack of freedom in any country in view of the scandal of the Soviet Union's slave labour camps. I then spelled out in detail every scrap of evidence we had about what came later to be known as 'the Gulag Archipelago'. I ended:

Mr Chairman, if the great body of evidence on Soviet forced labour that is now available to us has any meaning at all, it means that there exists in Soviet Russia a monstrous system of oppression, which makes a mockery of the claim that that

country is a democratic or a socialist state. It bears out the truth
– that for democrats, socialists and working men and women
the world over Soviet Russia provides not an example but a
deadly warning.

A great deal more could be said about this question, and a
great deal more evidence produced. The free world is asking
questions about the Soviet forced labour camps. We ask – are
all these reports, from so many different sources, wholly false?
Above all, we ask – if there is nothing to hide, why the silence
and secrecy? If we are wrong, let the truth be known. Until then,
we deny the moral right of Soviet propagandists to attack our
freedom and deride our democratic ways. If the Soviet spokesmen wish to persist in their attacks on human rights in the British
Commonwealth and the countries of the West, let them grant
us the same right of access to their country as we grant them to
ours. Let them publish, as we do, all the facts and figures of
success and failure in the field of social advancement. Until then,
Mr Chairman, we deny that they have the moral right to make
their repeated, unprovoked, unsubstantiated allegations against
us.

My speech was as highly charged and sensational as I could
make it; yet ironically it is clear today, from the mass of new
evidence available, that it actually understated the scale and
horror of Stalin's camps. But this did not prevent the communist delegates from protesting fiercely and at enormous length
that there was not a word of truth in what I had said. The
reactions of the non-communist delegates were mixed: most
were delighted, some were shocked. The American delegate,
Mrs Eleanor Roosevelt, was warmly supportive but
complained with some justice that I should have forewarned
her.

However, my aim was not to impress the committee but
to put officially on record anti-Stalinist propaganda material
for worldwide dissemination by IRD. IRD's material, well-
researched and authoritative, was now finding a ready
market. We had representatives in all British embassies and
high commissions abroad, who fed this material into friendly
and receptive hands. At home, our service was offered to,
and accepted by, large numbers of selected MPs, journalists,

trade union leaders and others, and was often used by the BBC's External Services. We also developed close links with a syndication agency and various publishers.

IRD can probably claim a modest share of the credit for stemming and turning back the Soviet ideological offensive. It expanded rapidly until the mid-sixties, but was subsequently cut back before being finally abolished by the Callaghan Government.

Meantime, great strides forward had been made towards uniting the western countries in defence against Stalinism. It began in January 1948, with a paper by Bevin, drafted by Gladwyn Jebb, called 'The Spiritual Unity of the West'. This had been approved by the Cabinet and I expected Bevin to make an important statement in a foreign affairs debate due on 22 January, urging the need for a defence union of the Western European countries. This, it had been agreed, would be the first step towards forming the North Atlantic Treaty.

Bevin spent the weekend before the debate on the Isle of Wight, struggling long hours with his speech. A copy of his draft reached me on the evening before the debate. It was of enormous length, and apart from a long passage about lifting the ban on foreign travel, said nothing new whatever. The idea of bringing the Western European countries together received no mention at all.

Bevin's standing in Parliament was not high at this time, and I was afraid that this speech would do him serious damage. I therefore went to the office early the next morning and assembled all the key passages from his cabinet paper into a majestic declaration of faith in western unity, coupled with a demand for a defence union of the European countries. Hastily clearing this with the Permanent Under-Secretary, Sir Orme Sargent, I burst into Bevin's presence. He was already harassed enough, surrounded on all sides by bits of the first draft of his speech. However, he took my paper cheerfully enough and began reading it in his usual slow manner. After a time, he said, 'This is a good turn you done, Chris,' and when he had finished reading it, he paused, grunting and wheezing in his familiar way. Finally he said, with a shade of doubt in his voice, 'It's a tremendous declaration.'

A few hours later he said it all in his speech, with great conviction, to the applause not only of the Commons but virtually the whole western world.

Sooner or later, I have no doubt, Bevin would have made this declaration anyhow, and would doubtless then have been careful to consult and inform friendly governments beforehand. As it was, not only our friends abroad but our own embassies were taken completely by surprise and the office was flooded with requests for further information. I sent Bevin a rather defensive note the next day urging him to set up a special working party to plan the next steps.

Bevin's declaration led some of our friends in Europe to believe that he had in mind a Western Europe federation, which was certainly not the case. In his memoirs, Paul-Henri Spaak, the great progenitor of European unity, then Belgium's Foreign Minister, remarked:

> In that speech he put forward the idea of organizing the Atlantic powers and proclaimed his desire for European unity. Never again was he to show up again in this light. On the contrary, he seemed surprised and even worried when he saw the ideas, which he himself had pioneered, being put into practice.

Nevertheless, Western European Union was soon formed, and afterwards NATO, and with the failure of the blockade of Berlin, the balance of power slowly swung against Stalin. One day Bevin said to me, with somewhat vindictive gusto, that at last he had some cards to play against Molotov. He had waited three years, three years of humiliation, but Molotov would have to listen to him now.

On such occasions, Bevin seemed to be using me as a guinea-pig audience, waiting for my uninhibited reactions. I did my best, but noted in my diary 'I do wish he explained himself better . . . he puts everything so incoherently and with so little sense of proportion or logical sequence that it is hard to follow and still harder to remember.'

None of this properly reflects my admiration and affection

for Bevin. At our first meeting following my appointment, after describing my duties, he said "It's like this. Anything bad you do, I stand by you. Anything good you do, I take the credit. Get me a drink. Have one yourself." It was this open, human attitude which endeared him to his subordinates. In addition, he was fearless in face of criticism, and did not visit on us the anger and frustration he often felt against his numerous domestic and foreign enemies. Instead, we served as an audience for his colourful tirades – against Nye Bevan, Molotov, Herbert Morrison, Dick Crossman, the communists, the Zionists, the European Federalists, the "Keep Left" group.

In spite of this, Bevin's mind was also strongly creative, as is proved by his part in promoting the Marshall Plan, Western European Union and Nato. He also kept cool at moments of crisis. I recall a meeting in his room at the time of the Berlin blockade. The Russians had cut off road and rail access to West Berlin, and the Americans and British had fallen back on the desperate expedient of supplying the city with food by air. A few hours before our meeting, which was attended by the Chief of Staff, a British plane had been 'buzzed' by a Soviet fighter in one of the air corridors and had crashed with loss of life. The question Bevin had to decide was whether this was the beginning of a Soviet blockade of the air corridors, which would mean abandoning the air-lift, followed almost certainly by war, or whether it was an accident. After much discussion, Bevin concluded, calmly and correctly, that in spite of appearances it must have been an accident.

Many years later I suggested to Gromyko, then Soviet Foreign Minister, that this plane crash marked the most dangerous moment of the entire cold war. He agreed.

9

BEVIN AND PALESTINE

During my time at the Foreign Office, almost all our major worries were concerned in some way with East/West relations. An exception was Palestine. Here, as the mandatory ruler, we were struggling in vain to maintain law and order, and to fulfil the two pledges contained in the Balfour Declaration – to encourage the establishment of a Jewish national home in Palestine and to safeguard the rights of the indigenous Palestinians.

I arrived at the Foreign Office knowing nothing whatever about the subject. However, a letter soon arrived for me from the Jewish terrorist organization, the Stern Gang, sentencing me to death.* I thought it must be a hoax, but the security services thought otherwise and immediately telephoned my friends and relations to warn them against opening suspicious parcels. And soon, by coincidence or otherwise, letter-bombs began arriving through the post for people supposed – sometimes quite wrongly – to be anti-Zionist. One arrived at Sir Anthony Eden's home as he was about to go out. He stuffed it unopened into his overcoat pocket and carried it around with him for some time before being relieved of it by the security services. Another letter-bomb was sent to Roy Farran, a counter-terrorist officer, and killed his brother, who opened it in error. However, no letter-bomb was sent to me, to the best of my knowledge.

I had to receive a number of Zionist deputations at this time. Usually they came to protest against our limits on illegal immigration into Palestine. On short-term, humanitarian grounds, the case for unrestricted immigration was irresistible. Scores of thousands of desperate Jewish people, fleeing from the scene of their wartime nightmare in Europe,

---

*Sent, it must be assumed, with the blessing of Israel's present Prime Minister, Shamir, who was the gang's leader at the time.

were being channelled by Zionist organizations towards Palestine. Most of them were destitute and many were physically or mentally crippled. How could any civilized government, let alone a British Labour government, fail to admit them? How could we use the Navy to board their ships and force them back to Europe? Never before or since have I known a more distressing task than that of defending this policy to outraged deputations of Zionists. The deputations were almost always well-informed, articulate, demanding, passionate and ruthless. The most formidable of their spokesmen, without question, was Sydney Silverman a left-wing Labour MP. He would attack me personally in the most merciless fashion, placing on my own shoulders the responsibility for the deaths and suicides of immigrants we had turned back. But in spite of everything, were we wrong? Was Ernest Bevin mistaken in thinking, as he said so often, that the Jews were asking for more than the Arabs could ever accept peacefully – more than it was in the Jewish people's own long-term interest to demand? I do not think so. I still think that the scale of the Zionist demands and the ruthlessness with which they were pursuing them were bound to prove in the long run to be self-defeating.

Our task was made more difficult by the absence of any counter-pressure from the people whose land, homes and property these Jewish immigrants would soon be seizing. This was not because the Arabs did not feel strongly about Palestine, but because they had virtually no political influence at all.

Partly as a result, I still had at this time only the vaguest understanding of the Palestinian case. My strongest feeling about the whole tragic conflict was a pronounced distaste for Zionist methods of pressure and propaganda.

Typical of this pressure was an adjournment debate in Parliament in the summer of 1948, initiated by an engaging, loquacious young Labour back-bencher, Mr Harold Lever.* With an importunity typical of Zionists at that time, Mr

*Later a Minister in the Wilson and Callaghan governments. Now Lord Lever of Manchester.

Lever had started the debate at eight o'clock in the morning, after an all-night sitting. I had to wind up for the Government, and my reply sounds appropriately tired and irritated:

> I had hoped that my honourable friend would yield to my request that we might be spared a debate on this subject at this moment. It is a bad time politically, diplomatically, psychologically, and, might I add, physically, to discuss the question of Palestine. . . . Quite clearly a change of policy here would in fact discourage the Arabs and encourage the Jews. I do not deny that. Why for that reason is it right? . . . Has my honourable friend ever heard that there is an Arab point of view? . . . The trouble with my honourable friend, as the whole of his speech shows, is that he is not sufficiently in touch with the Arab point of view on the Palestine problem.*

Even at this distance of time, I find it easy to imagine the scene. The floor and the benches of the House would be littered with discarded order papers. Facing me, on the deserted Conservative benches, would be a single lonely figure, the duty Opposition Whip. In the officials' gallery, over to my left, my private secretary, perhaps my sole supporter present, would be silently praying that I would stick to my brief. And behind me, wide awake, well-informed, passionate, articulate and aggressive, would be a group of twenty or thirty pro-Israeli Labour MPs. Most of them would be Jewish. Sydney Silverman, Maurice Edelman and Ian Mikardo would surely be among them, even at eight o'clock in the morning; and also Israel's most brilliant non-Jewish supporter, Dick Crossman.

And I can easily imagine how I myself would be feeling, sitting alone on the government front bench, thumbing the stiff blue official paper on which my careful speech would have been typed. My mind would not have been on Palestine. I had never been there and had no real grasp yet of the issues. I would have been feeling friendless, nervous and extremely tired, but sustained by a belief that Bevin was more likely to be right than the partisan people behind me, and angered by

*Hansard, 10 June 1948, cols. 2265–7.

the manifest unfairness of the situation: that there should be so many powerful pro-Israeli spokesmen in the House and no one at all to speak up for the Arabs.

Ernest Bevin felt this injustice deeply too. But it was the political pressure on the Cabinet from American Zionists, exerted through the US Government, which angered him most, and I shared his feelings about this to the full. At that time, Britain was dependent on American goodwill for her economic survival – bread was still rationed – and President Truman, as he later explained frankly in his memoirs, was dependent on Zionist goodwill for his election campaign funds. As a consequence, the British Government was subjected to ruthless pressure from Washington to get the Arabs to accept the Zionists' demands. It was a disgraceful abuse of power. On one occasion I was exposed to the full brunt of it myself. In Bevin's absence, I had to receive the US ambassador, Mr Lew Douglas, 'with a message from the President about Palestine'. Mr Douglas explained that he had been asked to repeat the President's urgent request to the British Government to admit 100,000 Jewish refugees into Palestine immediately. In line with Bevin's views, I objected that this was simply a prescription for war. The ambassador then replied, deliberately, that the President wished it to be known that if we could help him over this it would enable our friends in Washington to get our Marshall aid appropriation through Congress. In other words, we must do as the Zionists wished – or starve. Bevin surrendered – he had to – but he was understandably bitter and angry. He felt it outrageous that the USA, which had no responsibility for law and order in Palestine (and no intention of permitting similar Jewish immigration into the USA), should, from very questionable motives, impose an impossibly burdensome and dangerous task on Britain.

I did not then share Bevin's emotional commitment on Palestine, but sympathized with his dislike of Zionist methods and, indeed, of the Zionist philosophy itself. He was passionately unshakeably anti-Zionist. He held that Zionism was basically racialist, that it was inevitably wedded to violence and terror, that it demanded far more from the Arabs than they could or should be expected to accept peacefully, that its success would condemn the Middle East to decades of hatred and violence, and above all – this was his immediate concern – that by turning the Arabs against Britain and the western countries, it would open a high road for Stalin into the Middle East. On all these points events have since proved him right – or so I would myself argue – but in the immediate post-war years, so soon after the truth about the Nazis' treatment of the Jews had become widely known, his plain speaking struck many people as prejudiced and harsh.

Then, as now, there was much confusion between anti-Zionism and anti-semitism. Zionism, the idea that Jewish people everywhere should gather together in a state in Palestine – is a controversial political idea that many Jewish people themselves oppose. However, the insistence of Zionists on identifying the Jewish people with the Zionist state makes it dangerously easy for critics of Zionism to attribute its characteristics – violence, deceit and oppression – to the Jewish people itself.

Sadly, this was a mistake Ernest Bevin made. His mind, though powerful, was undisciplined, and he tended to attribute the characteristics of his Zionist enemies to the Jewish people as a whole.

I had forgotten this failing of Bevin's until, working on this book, I came across the following passage in my diary, dated 16 May 1948:

I must make a note about Ernest's anti-semitism, which has come out increasingly sharply these past few weeks, with the appalling crisis in Palestine. There is no doubt, to my mind, that Ernest detests Jews. He makes the odd wisecrack about the 'Chosen People'; explains Shinwell away as a Jew; declares the Old Testament is the most immoral book ever written; and declares publicly – in the House at question time – 'We must also remember the Arabs' side of the case – there are, after all, no Arabs in the House (loud cheers).' I tell him afterwards that this remark is going too far, and we have a general talk about the Jews. He says they taught Hitler the technique of terror – and were even now parallelling the Nazis in Palestine. They were preachers of violence and war – 'What could you expect when

people are brought up from the cradle on the Old Testament?'
I stoutly deny most of it, and tell him that anyway, true or false,
what he says in public on this subject only gives his enemies a
handle against him. He smiles sardonically. I allow him only one
point – that in giving voice to his irrational and indefensible
prejudices he is speaking for millions of British people.

This account of my years at the Foreign Office has made no
reference at all to my private life. For example, I have made
no mention of my friendships with a succession of charming
and beautiful girls. Some of them I loved and wanted to
marry: others loved me and wanted to marry me. It was sad
how often this vexatious situation seemed to occur. The
resultant heartaches were usually nobody's fault. I remember
all these old friends with respect and affection, and hope
they remember me in the same way.

My bachelor days came to an end in June 1949, when I
visited Geneva as the British delegate to the UN Economic
Commission for Europe. One of our diplomatic staff there
was, astonishingly, a girl, Cicely Ludlam. She was only the
second girl ever to be admitted to the diplomatic service.
One morning, during a typically tedious conference session,
Cicely passed forward to me in my delegate's chair, along
with a briefing paper, a large piece of Swiss chocolate. Such
a thoughtful gesture from such an attractive girl made a
strong impression on me; so much so that during the
subsequent nine days, besides making several speeches and
attending a number of official functions, I pursued her,
proposed to her and was accepted by her.

The Soviet delegate, my witty opponent, Arutiunian, had
met Cicely, and on hearing the news of our engagement he
announced to the conference, amid laughter and applause,
that at long last the UK delegate had made a proposal he
could cordially endorse.

Told that I was marrying a member of his Foreign Office
staff, Ernest Bevin remarked: 'What does Chris think we are?
A bloody matrimonial bureau?'

Cicely and I married soon afterwards, and our family now

includes two sons, two daughters, and, at the time of writing, three grandchildren.

Marriage increased my worries about the future. A general election was due soon and my constituency boundaries had been disastrously redrawn. Worse, I now faced a single Tory candidate instead of two as in 1945. Moreover, the candidate was the dynamic Peter Baker. However, I felt hopeful that if and when I left the House, Attlee would help me to get back. He was dependable and markedly friendly, and had invited me privately more than once to Chequers. On one occasion I was required to partner him at tennis. His play was predictably steady and unpretentious. We must have looked a strange pair – one of us short, static and elderly, and the other tall, mobile and young, both wearing colourful Old Haileyburian sweaters.

One evening at Chequers there was a rather large and formal dinner – black ties, long dresses and several famous faces. After we had assembled in the hall and been ushered into the dining room, it became apparent, as we sat down, that someone was missing. Told that this was a young school-friend of his daughter Felicity, Attlee quickly bid us refold our napkins and hurry back to the hall. There we waited for a short while until the little girl came downstairs, unsuspecting, and joined us. We then went into dinner again, as though for the first time.

'A modest man, with plenty to be modest about,' or so Churchill is reported to have said. But this modesty was part of Attlee's strength. It was a reason for the soundness of his judgement and for the warm respect and loyalty so many of us felt for him. He had not reached the top by pushing himself – he would never have succeeded that way – but largely by accident, as a result of the disappearance from Parliament after the 1931 election of almost every possible rival. Thus, by happy chance, the Labour Party found itself with a leader with little personal ambition, vanity or charisma, but with unassailable integrity.

When he was writing his autobiography, Attlee sent me his draft chapter on international affairs and asked for my comments. I had to reply that it seemed to me far too short and matter-of-fact, and not to do justice to his achievements. I suggested, among other things, that he should write about his relationship with Bevin – for example, about the difficulty I have mentioned of understanding Bevin's precise meaning when he was pronouncing on a complicated question. Attlee sent a good-humoured reply (hand-written – he had no personal secretary at this time) in which he declared that there was only one occasion when he failed to understand what Bevin was saying. This was at the end of a meeting he attended with Bevin, Hugh Dalton and Dai Grenfell. Bevin wound up by declaring, 'We'll leave it all to YEWANDEYE.' 'I didn't know', Attlee wrote, 'whether this meant "You and I", "You and Dai", "Hugh and I", or "Hugh and Dai".'

Attlee ignored all my well-meant suggestions for improving his book, and was magnificently unconcerned about its predictable failure.

When the election came, and I duly lost my seat, he absent-mindedly sent me two hand-written letters, expressing sympathy and thanks in almost identical terms. He was still Prime Minister, and his final paragraph suggests that he was preoccupied at the time with ministerial appointments:

'The words that keep coming to my mind are:

"How well could I have spared for thee, young swain,
Enow of such as for their bellies' sake
Creep and intrude and climb into the fold." '

10
EARLY DAYS WITH BBC TV

It was like stepping off a crowded bus at a remote bus stop: some passengers wave good-bye, the doors close, the bus disappears purposefully into the distance and one is left behind in silence and solitude.

The political wilderness is a desolate place. Hardest to adjust to is the loss of contact with old colleagues. Some friendships can withstand any change of circumstances, but most need regular nourishment if they are to survive. Shared work and frequent casual contact provide this easily: meetings which have to be specially arranged don't.

For a short while I kept in touch with my political friends, but though they were kind, they were also busy. I was aware of taking their time, and of having less to talk about when we met than they did.

This was a difficult time, too, for my wife. In exchange for a promising diplomatic career, she now found herself sharing domestic life with a jobless and impecunious politician.

However, we set our hopes on my early return to Parliament at a by-election, and meanwhile I had no doubt as to what I should do next. At the UN, helping to draft the Declaration of Human Rights, I had become fascinated by the contrast between the Soviet delegates' glorification of freedom under communism and the close control of their personal lives by their secret police. I now felt a strong urge to write a play about this, a political thriller which portrayed the chief Soviet delegate (modelled on Arutiunian) with sympathy while ridiculing Stalinist tyranny. The setting would be the UN. Arutiunian, falsely suspected of being about to defect, would be liquidated by the KGB after an eloquent speech eulogizing freedom under communism.

The BBC liked the play and accepted it for television, and in due course I was invited to what was called a 'first

reading'. This was an eye-opener. The actors, who included
Andrew Cruikshank, Arthur Young and Peter Cushing,
simply sat around in a circle reading their parts aloud. But
I could hardly believe my ears. Was this what I had written?
My most banal lines now sparkled; my cardboard characters
sprang to life, with accents, mannerisms and personalities of
their own. So this was what actors did! They were magicians.
Had I really written this marvellous play? I must write
another one, and then another.

However, my urge to become a playwright was short-
lived. Some weeks before, desperately tired and ill, sacked
by his old friend Attlee from the Foreign Office against his
dearest wishes, Ernest Bevin had died. His constituency party
now invited me to succeed him in the safe Labour seat
of Woolwich East, and I was plunged into a by-election
campaign.

As it happened, my eve-of-poll meeting coincided with
the filming at Alexandra Palace, at night, of the murder of
Arutiunian. It had been agreed that I should play the part of
the killer – the driver of the car which crushed the poor man
to death. So I hurried from my crowded meeting in Woolwich
and raced to Alexandra Palace to perform the assassination.
In the floodlit car park, two large limousines, borrowed from
the American embassy, had been positioned with their backs
to a wall, with a gap between them. The producer explained
that my job was to wait until Arutiunian (played by Arthur
Young) walked between the two cars as though to enter one
of them, and then reverse my own car rapidly into the gap,
stopping just short of the wall. Understandably Arthur
Young had some reservations about this scenario, pointing
out that I might well not stop in time and carry realism too
far. So the shooting script was amended and Arthur Young
survived. Instead, in a trial run, to the anguish of the
producer, I backed my car with a resounding crash into one
of the American limousines.

The count in Woolwich next day was a formality, and I
now found myself with two jobs instead of none. Besides
being an MP, I was under contract with BBC Television, for
a minimum of two years, to make documentary programmes

on current affairs. This had been fixed up by the corporation's leading TV producer, Grace Wyndham-Goldie, for whom I had recently scripted and presented a programme on the Korean war.

Grace was a strong administrator and a producer of genius. If the BBC had not been shamefully prejudiced against women at that time, she would certainly have become Controller of Television, if not Director-General. Our partnership lasted throughout the 1950s and into the 1960s, and I think we both enjoyed it, though we were both difficult to work with, argumentative and demanding, sure that we knew best, determined to have our own way.

On questions of taste, style and presentation, Grace's judgement was fierce and faultless. I remember, for example, beginning to record a commentary over some shots of a Buddhist religious ceremony. A loud cry came from behind me. 'No, Christopher, no! Not reverent – informative! We are not in church!'

Grace would never let me record statements to camera. They were often quite long and there were no teleprompters in those days, but I had to do them 'live', from memory, for the sake of a marginal gain in vitality.

However, on the content and balance of a programme, though we often argued hotly about them, Grace would usually let me have my way.

In those early days, almost every programme we did we broke new ground. We would present new subjects – Apartheid, Titoism, Stalinist propaganda, Britain's industrial decline, social class, Islam – and would often use new techniques, experimenting with animating maps and charts, telephoning Moscow live, illustrating an argument by counterposing contrasted film sequences. In choosing subjects for programmes, I was given extraordinary freedom. During the 1950s my series – usually five or six programmes each – dealt with race relations, class, crime, the cold war, 'the decline of Britain' and mental health.

Perhaps the strangest feature of my BBC contract was that for some years it gave a Labour MP a virtual monopoly of current affairs on television. At that time, *Newsnight* and

Panorama had not yet begun, and there was still only one television channel. In effect, I was Britain's only television commentator.

This strange situation highlighted the problem of objectivity. How was it to be achieved? The conventional solution was to interview experts of different opinions, add some illustrative film and then simply sum up. I disagreed with this strongly: it made everything depend on which experts were selected, which questions were put to them and what precisely was illustrated by the illustrative film. The margin for error was enormous. I argued that the integrity of a programme depended on the thoroughness of the preliminary research (which would include consulting a wide range of experts) and the honesty with which the conclusions were drawn from it. Once these conclusions had been reached, the content of the programme should be deliberately selected to lead up to them.

Rightly or wrongly this was the basis on which I made all my programmes. It was certainly controversial, and led to some fierce arguments; but in the event, although the programmes were monitored by the political parties, there were no complaints of bias.

Television technology was primitive in those days. Almost everything was 'live' and all statements to camera were either improvised or memorized. The studio lights were uncomfortably hot, and the studios themselves cold and draughty. Film sequences often broke, leaving one suddenly facing the camera, without warning, for long periods of time. A 'cue-in' to film lasted ten seconds: this meant giving a cue word and then speaking to camera for exactly ten seconds, no more and no less, before the film came on. This is more difficult than it sounds.

Though popular at the time, our programmes would strike viewers today as very slow-moving and didactic. However, most of our audience were as new to television as we were and shared our excitement in breaking new ground; and the simplicity of our programmes meant that a single commentator could do all the script-writing and presentation, and thus give them unity and clarity, and a personal style.

We suffered from a chronic shortage of film, which often led to difficulties with film editors. Their job was to produce well-shot, well-composed film sequences; mine was to use film to illustrate a point of view, usually political. The two aims seldom coincided. I remember trying to illustrate the problem of communist insurgency in Burma with the BBC's only Burmese film material – a long, finely shot sequence of elephants handling heavy tree trunks. Conversely, I once rescued from an editor's rubbish bin a scrappy but telling shot of an Iranian policeman putting his hand over the lens of our film camera.

Conventional wisdom at this time insisted that television programmes must at all costs be 'visual'. 'Talking heads' were considered suitable only for sound radio. I disagreed with this, and on one occasion circulated a cautionary tale round the department. This told how, once upon a time, a BBC television crew visiting Palestine shot some picturesque coverage of a religious assembly, but ignored, as sound radio material, a sermon being delivered nearby by a speaker on a mount.

I was always agonizingly sensitive about the success or failure of our programmes. Though the audience was not large by modern standards – perhaps 4 or 5 million – it was likely to include all my friends and relations, all the TV critics, most MPs and a large proportion of my Woolwich constituents. The rewards of success and the penalties of failure were thus formidable, and although I was brave enough about experimenting in the programme, I was also extremely nervous about viewers' reactions. Absurdly, I always expected the programmes to have been either very good or very bad, and was never sure which. Our yardstick of success was the BBC audience research department's 'appreciation index', which told us how much our programme had been liked or disliked by those who saw it. Discounting, sensibly enough, the reaction of friends and relations, I lived on tenterhooks until these reports arrived.

The appreciation indices showed clearly that TV programmes such as ours, which attracted smaller, rather specialized, audiences, tended to be the ones most keenly enjoyed by those who did watch them. This finding had some political importance, as it effectively undermined the principal argument being put forward at that time – the early fifties – by those who were lobbying for the introduction of commercial television. This argument was that a broadcasting system motivated to get the biggest audiences would automatically give the public what it wanted. But the audience research reports showed that, on the contrary, such a system would deprive the public of the minority programmes it enjoyed most. For this and other reasons I decided to campaign against commercial broadcasting. In a polemical pamphlet, which sold over 40,000 copies, I wrote:

> For creating large audiences, pride of place must go not to the enjoyability of a programme, but to the universality of its appeal. . . . To get a maximum audience, a TV programme must appeal to everyone at once. . . . That is to say, it must appeal to no particular age, no particular taste and no particular intellectual level.

I had already had a brush with commercial television, when a leading American network company, ABC, bought the rights of my television play. I had specified in the contract that there should be no important changes to the script without agreement. In the event, however, ABC changed all the British characters in the play into Americans (without altering the dialogue) and replaced all references to Britain with references to the USA. ABC also cut the play by twenty-four minutes, changed its ending, and broke it up arbitrarily into four parts to make room for commercials for Lucky Strike cigarettes ('Let's go Lucky . . . Let's go Lucky . . . *Strike*').

I withdrew permission for the play to be broadcast, but ABC took no notice and calmly went ahead, no doubt calculating, correctly, that I had neither the time nor the money to take them to court.

I expected the campaign against commercial television to be a walkover. Opinion polls revealed overwhelming opposition to it. The Labour and Liberal parties were both against it, and so were the churches, the universities, the teachers, the parents' organizations and the trade unions. The Cabinet and the governing Conservative Party were split.

The best strategy seemed to be to launch the campaign from inside the Conservative Party. So I drafted a letter to the *Times* and persuaded a number of influential Conservatives, including Lord Halifax and Lord Waverley, to sign it. I did not sign it myself. The *Times* published it prominently and supported it with a leading article. Hundreds of pledges of support flowed in, often from influential Conservatives, and we quickly formed a heavyweight all-party National Television Council, with Lord Waverley as president.

The launching of our campaign coincided with the Queen's coronation, and this was a stroke of luck for us. When it became known that American broadcasts of that noble ceremony had been interrupted by commercials the public was outraged. Loyal citizens were particularly incensed by a commercial which featured a live chimpanzee called 'J. Fred Muggs'. This animal became instantly famous; and it hit the headlines just as I was about to visit the Oxford Union Society for a debate on commercial broadcasting. It occurred to me, remembering my Union days, that the surest way of winning the vote would be to deliver my speech holding a chimpanzee in my arms.

My instinct was right. As I entered the crowded debating chamber in the president's procession, a live chimpanzee nuzzling into my white waistcoat, the storm of cheers and laughter told me that victory was already won. And so it turned out: J. Fred Muggs won the vote by a vast majority. He was a docile creature, very soft and warm to the touch. I explained to the audience that he was greedy and could only gibber, and was thus admirably qualified for a career in commercial broadcasting.

My closest colleague in the campaign was Lady Violet Bonham-Carter. A daughter of the Liberal Prime Minister, Asquith, she had not lost the grand style and manners of the Edwardian aristocracy. Though a fine platform speaker, possibly her most effective contribution to our campaign was a series of passionate hand-written letters to high-placed

personal friends, including 'Rab' Butler and Winston Churchill. Though we worked closely together for some years,
she never thought to call me by my Christian name. To the
end I was 'Mr Mayhew' and happily adjusted myself to the
role of valued and trusted retainer.

I once accompanied Lady Violet to a conference in
Germany, one of the famous gatherings of British and
German journalists and politicians at Königswinter on the
Rhine. As we stepped from the bus on arrival, Lady Violet
whispered 'Mr Mayhew, I believe there is a journalist among
us called Mr Henry Fairlie. I wonder if you know him?' I
replied that I did. 'Would you mind very much pointing him
out to me?' she whispered. 'I don't know which he is, and I
have to cut him.'

The Cabinet eventually came down in favour of commercialization. Our old-time Tory supporters proved no match for
their upstart business-orientated colleagues. A professional
campaign conducted by an interested pressure group defeated
a traditional campaign run by volunteers.*

It is natural, I suppose, that a 'lobby' should reflect the
characteristics of the cause it supports. Certainly the commercial lobby had all the merits and defects of commercial
television. It was populist, mendacious, mercenary and rich,
whereas its adversary, the National Television Council, like
much public service broadcasting, was weighty, honest,
public-spirited and poor.

The results of commercialization have been as we
predicted. On the one hand, breaking the BBC's monopoly
blew away some cobwebs, but on the other Britain's viewers,
young and old, have since fed increasingly on violence, sex,
crime and soap, interspersed with commercials extolling the
virtues of Mammon. Nowadays, moreover, it all seems quite
natural and acceptable. As my pamphlet had explained:

> After a time many of us will come to like the programmes which
> result. No one has described this process better than the great

---

*The rival campaigns are well described in *Pressure Group* by
Professor H. H. Wilson (Secker & Warburg, London).

philosopher John Stuart Mill. 'Men lose their high aspirations, as they lose their intellectual tastes, because they have no time or opportunity for indulging them; and they addict themselves to inferior pleasures, not because they deliberately prefer them but because they are either the only ones to which they have access or the only ones which they are any longer capable of enjoying.'

In 1962, the Pilkington Committee on Broadcasting recommended, as I and others had urged, that the non-profit-making Independent Television Authority (ITA) should sell the advertising, buy the programmes from programme companies and decide the schedules itself. This would have raised standards, and was fully in line with Labour's policy. So, as the party's spokesman on broadcasting – we were in opposition – I made ready to announce officially – with Hugh Gaitskell's approval – that we supported the recommendation. However, there was now an unexpected intervention from George Brown: he argued passionately against me in the Shadow Cabinet and won the day.

At this time, George was competing against Harold Wilson for the Deputy Leadership of the Labour Party, and after this shadow cabinet meeting Wilson came up to me and remarked 'I don't mind people opposing party policy, but I do think, when they do so, they should declare their interests.' 'What interests?' I asked. 'Well you must know, surely, that George is on Cecil King's payroll.'

I was astonished. Cecil King, boss of the Mirror newspaper group, was campaigning virulently for commercialization. Surely, if George was employed by this arch-enemy of public service television, he would have let the Shadow Cabinet know? I sent him a cable – he was abroad – asking if Wilson's accusation was true. This led to a summons from Hugh Gaitskell. 'What on earth have you been telling George? He says you are accusing him of corruption.'

'I simply asked him if he was employed by Cecil King.'

'Don't be absurd. He would have told us if he had been.'

'Does he deny it?'

'I've no doubt he will clear that up when he gets back.'

And then, after a pause, 'Of course, I know who's put you up to this.'

But Harold Wilson was right: George was being paid by Cecil King as a consultant. Gaitskell thereupon insisted that he should make this public, and he did so. But it was too late. George probably lost a few votes for the deputy leadership, but I could not get the Shadow Cabinet to reverse its decision.

This was not my first or last quarrel with George. But he was warm-hearted and very skilful in repairing friendships. Once, when he had drunk too much and been particularly rude to me, I took the unusual step of writing to him afterwards to remonstrate. He wrote back, 'I've done it again! Why, oh, why do I have to offend the people I really like?' – and so on. I found it hard to resist.

On a similar occasion, he said to me, 'The one thing I envy about you public schoolboys is, you always know how far you can go.' But it was not his class background but his temperament that prevented him from knowing when to stop. He suffered from a fatal lack of inhibitions, over-reacting to every stimulus that came his way, an insult, a chance of glory, a joke, a drink. It made him outgoing, fearless and creative, but also volatile and unpredictable.

He showed both sides of his character one afternoon in Paris, shortly after he had resigned as Foreign Secretary. He was due to make a keynote speech to an important meeting of the European Movement, but had lingered over lunch in the British embassy, drinking too much, becoming obstreperous, refusing to hurry.

Eventually, we managed to shepherd him as far as the terrace in front of the embassy, but then he disappeared. Somebody called up to the ambassadress from a waiting car, 'Isn't George ready *yet*?'; and from Lady Soames, at the top of the embassy steps, came a loud, memorable cry of exasperation: 'George has now gone to pee.'

And then, when he eventually got to the meeting, George captivated his audience with a marvellous speech, made without notes, straight from his heart.

Inevitably, campaigning against commercial broadcasting

led me to make enemies of powerful people. Looking back, however, I think I was needlessly aggressive. In 1970, for example, when the leaders of the ITV appealed to the Government for a reduction in the levy on television advertising, I wrote in *The Times*:

> Sir,
> At the risk of seeming uncharitable (and it is a hard, cold winter), I recommend that we taxpayers reject the piteous appeal for financial assistance being made to us by Sir Lew Grade, Lord Shawcross and other independent television shareholders.
> Nobody likes to see these unfortunate people suffer, and the value of their shares has certainly declined sharply. But before we add their claims for relief to those of the teachers, nurses, old age pensioners, holders of War Loan and taxpayers in general, we should be told:
>
> 1. What has happened to the vast profits made by shareholders in the past?

And so on. A little later, Cecil King caused a sensation by publishing in his memoirs insulting descriptions of famous people he had invited privately to lunch. Still resenting his part in the battle over commercial television, I wrote in *The Times*:

> Sir,
> Those who have been traduced by Mr King should not issue disclaimers. Instead, I feel, we should record for posterity our own impressions of Mr King, and the conversations we have had with him which do not appear in his book.
> My first meeting with Mr King was at a Royal Academy banquet in the late 50s. We were seated next to each other, and Mr King opened the conversation, as the soup was being served, by asking me how my campaign against commercial television was going. I told him. He then said that if, which he doubted, my views ever carried weight with my party leaders, it would be necessary to start a 'Mayhew must go' campaign in the *Mirror*. I replied that he could say what he liked about me in his bloody papers.
> From then on, we sat in silence, while the fish, meat, sweet

and savoury courses were served; and I have never spoken to Mr. King again – wisely, as I now think. He made a most unfavourable impression on me, an arrogant and stupid man, I thought, quite unfit for power in a civilized society.

Yours, etc.

Unfortunately, the media in Britain have since become increasingly controlled by men unfit for power. So much so that on my last visit to the Soviet Union, I found myself wondering whether a culture corrupted by politics is really much worse than a culture corrupted by greed. Would I rather see my grandchildren brought up on *Pravda* or on the *Sun*? The *Sun*, perhaps, but only by a narrow margin.

We British threw out our slops into the streets until science proved that this produced typhus. One day, science will prove that the cultural slops thrown out by our media are a psychological poison of similar virulence.

11
THE CULTURAL COLD WAR

When Stalin died, in 1953, hopes rose that his successors would allow a broadening of Soviet contacts with the outside world. The following year I revisited the Soviet Union as a member of a parliamentary delegation, meeting scores of people of different backgrounds, including the Prime Minister, Malenkov, and the Foreign Minister, Molotov. I wanted to discover how the Russians pictured the West, and what their intentions were towards us.

At that time the West seemed even stranger to the Russians than it does now. As we toured round a factory or a housing estate we would stop and ask questions, and weigh up the replies. But I also asked one of our embassy interpreters to eavesdrop on the comments of bystanders, and these were more revealing. 'Here are the English fascists.' 'How clean they are – you can tell they are not ours.' 'How equal of them, coming to Gorki market on foot.'

When I asked people how they felt about Britain, they all gave the same, obviously sincere, answers. Their feelings towards the British people, they declared, were of the warmest friendship. In particular they admired their struggle for peace, led by their courageous peace fighters – and here they would name British communists and fellow travellers, such as the Dean of Canterbury (Dr Hewlett Johnson), Konni Zilliacus, D. N. Pritt, and Pat Sloan. They explained that they wished the British people well in their heroic fight against the forces of American and British capitalism.

The feelings of friendship were real enough: what was not real was the British people towards whom they were felt. That army of pro-Soviet, class-conscious proletarians never existed outside the daydream of Marxists. Nevertheless, I began to realize that the tiny band of British Stalinists were, after all, politically important. They were important because they helped to sustain in Soviet minds the Marxist myths about Britain. They were the only British people who had easy access to the Soviet media and were generously reported by them. They were also featured, far beyond their deserts, in the only British newspaper, the *Daily Worker*, to which the Russians had easy access. They provided the leadership of the pro-communist 'friendship' societies, and when a party of Russians visited Britain, they would be the heart and soul of the reception committee, feeding back to the visitors their own Marxist misconceptions about this country.

Even the sophisticated people I talked to in the Soviet Union had an absurdly inflated view of the pro-Soviet left in Britain. As one senior official put it, 'You say there are only a few communists in your country, Mr Mayhew, and you are right; but once there were only a few communists in the Soviet Union.'

At a farewell reception, Richard Law MP and I had an informal talk with Gromyko, in which Molotov later joined. I made a record of it afterwards. Law had raised the subject of international communism.

> *Gromyko*: We do not support foreign communist parties.
> *CM*: The parties themselves plainly say that they look to Russia for leadership.
> *Gromyko*: We just give them moral support, that is all. You think all communist parties are agents of the Soviet Union, but they arise out of objective conditions.
> *CM*: On the average, they are 70 per cent natural growths, 30 per cent Soviet creations, and the 30 per cent is a great cause of international friction.
> *Gromyko*: I think you have your mathematical proportions wrong.
> *Molotov* (coming up): I see that Gromyko is one against two.
> *Law*: He is well able to look after himself.
> *Molotov*: So are you two, I believe.
> *Gromyko*: As usual, the strongest attacks have come from the left.
> *Molotov*: Have you seen everything you wanted?
> *CM*: Everything except one thing.

Molotov: What is that?

CM: A communist party.

Molotov (laughing): We are all communists.

CM: We have visited the headquarters of trade unions, city councils – but never the headquarters of a communist party. We find the communist parties very shy.

Molotov (laughing): We are all communists – there is no point in meeting the Communist Party.

Law: We have been discussing the question of your support for foreign communist parties.

Molotov: What do you mean?

CM: Your leadership of these parties through the Cominform, the circulation of unfriendly literature printed in Russia –

Molotov: What literature?

CM: *New Times*, for example.

Molotov (laughing): But that is bought openly by people. It is perfectly legitimate.

CM: The award of a Lenin peace prize to the Dean of Canterbury –

Molotov: The Dean is a fighter for peace.

CM: Should we not define our terms? Your fighters for peace supported North Korea's invasion of South Korea. They are a very warlike crew. Might I offer a definition of peace?

(Molotov nodded.)

CM: Peace is any state of affairs, including war, which forwards Mr Molotov's foreign policy.

Molotov (laughing): The Soviet Union is so strong that no attacks on her can succeed. Equally, she has no cause to attack others. We must learn to talk a common language and conduct our affairs in a friendly and sensible manner.

Law: But Britain and the United States are separated by a common language.

Molotov: The United States is conducting subversive operations in Eastern Europe.

CM: Do the Americans have a right to do this, just as you support communist activities?

Molotov: We are not doing in the western world what the Americans are attempting in Eastern Europe. The Cominform is simply an information bureau, not the same as the old Comintern. It exists to carry out certain ties between communist parties in Europe. There are similar ties between socialist parties. We consider this to be quite natural. The Cominform and its ties are designed to secure peace in Europe. It is a matter for the parties which form it. The Soviet Government is not part of the Cominform.

(Molotov and Law then moved away, but Gromyko continued.)

Gromyko: But you can see for yourself how Marxism has proved itself in history.

CM: Isn't it a question of definitions? For example the hypothesis that Russia is a democratic workers' state, opposed by world capitalism. You maintain this only by defining those who support Russia as democrats and workers, and those who oppose it as capitalists. Thus Tito was a worker one day and a capitalist the next.

Gromyko: But see how Marxism has spread and is spreading throughout the world. And what other philosophy are you putting against it? Who are the philosophers in Britain?

I should have replied that there were many different schools of philosophy in Britain, but instead mentioned Russell and Ayer, and said they seemed to be concerned with the meaning of words. What philosophical work had been done in the Soviet Union since Lenin?

Gromyko: Lenin was right – we apply his teachings. What is your philosophy? Is this glass I am holding 'real' or not?

CM: My grandparents felt sure it was 'real'. Now, modern science has led us to have doubts. Our minds and senses have more to do with the creation of what we call the natural world than we thought.

Gromyko: That is interesting – the way in which the

findings of modern science can lead to two totally
different interpretations.

Marxism insists that certain historical developments are
inevitable and predictable, and as a result Marxist intellectuals tend to confuse what they are sure is coming into being
with what actually exists. I found my insistence that the
British working class was not pro-Soviet and class-conscious
put down to my undialectical approach, my failure to grasp
the underlying dynamic of British capitalist society.

Marxist misconceptions of this kind naturally encouraged
the belief that the Soviet Union had more to gain by fostering
the struggle of the British working class against capitalism
than by cooperating with Britain's capitalist governments,
and on my return home, I decided to try to do something to
dispel this illusion. One way, I felt, would be to promote
contacts between representative British and Soviet organizations, while at the same time choking off Soviet contacts
with the left-wing 'friendship' societies.

The British Council, of which I was an executive
committee member, (representing the Labour Party, which
was in opposition) readily agreed to set up a Soviet Relations
Committee to pursue these two aims, and I became its
Chairman. The Foreign Office promised active support, as
did the numerous bodies who were faced with the problem
of handling Soviet visits in conjunction with the 'friendship'
societies. Sir Ian Jacob, the Director-General of the BBC,
wrote, 'I very strongly agree with your general thesis. It is an
impossible situation that we should deal with these visitors
through the medium of "front" organizations.' Soon I was
able to issue an invitation to the Soviet Minister of Culture,
Mr Mikhailov, on behalf of a dazzling array of leading
cultural and educational establishments, to visit Britain to
arrange a programme of British-Soviet cultural exchanges.

Mr Mikhailov accepted my invitation, and this marked
the beginning of a bizarre cultural cold war. Both sides
genuinely wanted to increase cultural contacts, but both
disagreed sharply about their nature and purpose. The
Russians valued organized contacts as a means of promoting

Soviet communism and as a cover-up for their ruthless
suppression of genuinely free communications. In the Soviet
Union, foreign newspapers, unless communist, were banned.
Foreign broadcasts were jammed. Foreign books were vetted.
Foreign travel, where permitted at all, was tightly controlled.
When Mr Mikhailov or some other Soviet cultural bureau-
crat raised his glass to 'the removal of barriers between our
two peoples' no one supposed for a moment that he meant
it seriously.

But there was humbug on the British side too. We spoke
warmly about Tolstoy and Burns, Oistrakh and Britten, but
our aims were political: we wanted to break down the
isolation of the Soviet people from the West and to disrupt
their ties with British communists and fellow-travellers.

Neither side had any illusions about the other. I regarded
Mr Mikhailov, Mr Surkov, and Mr Zhukov, rightly, as
friends of the British 'left' and enemies of cultural freedom.
They saw me, rightly, as a hardened cold warrior. They did
business with me only because they had to, because otherwise
their cultural and educational delegations were likely to be
cold-shouldered by their British equivalents and ignored by
the media. At one time they entreated the Foreign Office,
without success, to have me removed as chairman of the
Soviet Relations Committee.

Mr Mikhailov's arrival at Heathrow was an apt presage
of things to come. Predictably he made a speech calling
for the removal of barriers to friendship and understanding
between Britain and the Soviet Union. Anticipating this, I
had arranged for the BBC external services to record the
speech and broadcast it to the Soviet Union, where, of course,
it was jammed. So the next day, at our first formal meeting,
I asked Mr Mikhailov whether he approved of his eloquent
appeal for free contacts being jammed by his government.
He replied with a smile that this was a matter for another
department. He took my provocation in good part, and may
even have taken some action afterwards: jamming of the BBC
was temporarily suspended when Khrushchev and Bulganin
visited Britain the following year.

It proved easier to persuade the Russians to develop new

contacts than to give up their old ties with the 'friendship' societies, and eventually I asked Selwyn Lloyd, then Foreign Secretary, to raise this question with Bulganin and Khrushchev on their visit. I urged him to insert the following formula into the official communiqué: 'The two governments accept the need for organizing these exchanges in a manner acceptable to them both.'

I described the fate of this formula in my diary:

'At the Speaker's lunch for Bulganin and Khrushchev, Mikhailov hurried up to me and explained anxiously that every word of the communiqué had been agreed except one point. The point was, of course, my formula. He said he had discussed this with Bulganin and Khrushchev, and both had urged that it should be dropped from the communiqué. I said on the contrary this was the most important part of the communiqué and was an essential condition for future cooperation on cultural relations.'

When lunch was over, the Prime Minister, Anthony Eden, himself came up to me and said that he had spent a good deal of the morning with Bulganin and Khrushchev on my formula. He thought it was very toughly worded. I said it was not tough at all but plain common sense. If the Russians would not accept it, it showed it was all the more important to insist on it. He said I must speak to Bulganin myself about it and led me over to the Marshal. I put the case to Bulganin and after reflection he said, in the Prime Minister's hearing, 'I accept'.

I heard no more until a special performance at Covent Garden for Bulganin and Khrushchev. As I entered the foyer, the Prime Minister came up and began talking earnestly about my formula, saying that he and Bulganin and Khrushchev had again spent considerable time on it that afternoon. He said that Bulganin had given some important assurances. I said, 'You mean you've dropped the formula.' He said rather shamefacedly that he had, but that the assurances were important. I said I didn't trust Bulganin and Khrushchev an inch. He warmly agreed with this but said, 'There was really nothing else we could do.' Then, seeing that I was pretty adamant, he said, 'If they do let us down again, then we shall be in a good position to start denying visas when they use these communist societies.' When I remained unmoved, he said, 'Well you must talk to them yourself over dinner.'

'I waited until the second interval, when we were at supper behind the royal box, and then tackled Bulganin. I was feeling just like Walter Mitty in one of his daydreams, with these powerful figures notably anxious about what was, after all, only my own personal opinion. I began by referring to the constructive work we had done in the cultural field in the past twelve months. However, it was quite inadmissible that the Soviet authorities should use communist-controlled organizations to forward cultural relations between our countries. For this reason a formula had been suggested which Marshal Bulganin would probably know as Clause 7. I understood that this formula had been conceded by the Government in return for certain assurances from Marshal Bulganin. Both the Opposition and my committee felt even more strongly in favour of the principle behind the formula than the Government itself. I felt sure that if the Opposition raised this question in Parliament, they would get unusually wide parliamentary support. (This was for Eden and Selwyn Lloyd, who were listening keenly.) I would like to be able to assure the Opposition and the Committee about the nature of Marshal Bulganin's assurances.

Bulganin said he would very readily explain it to me exactly. He said that he recognized that they had not a sufficient understanding of this problem before. He undertook that when he returned to Moscow he would look into the question with a view to making possible changes.

I said, 'To take a specific example, though, I believe you have been discussing the question of the Moscow Circus* this afternoon. This surely would be a good point of departure.' Bulganin made the hopeful reply, 'When is the Circus due?' I told him 12th May, and he nodded. I then said, 'Let us enlist the animals in the cause of British–Soviet friendship,' at which he laughed. After a pause he then said to me, with flattering earnestness, 'Do you accept my assurances?'

I had worked it out that his assurances were not worth very much. Moreover our parliamentary position, if we attacked the Government for its utter feebleness, would be extraordinarily strong. On the other hand Eden's assurance about visas was important, and we were in any case gaining the ascendancy in this cultural cold war. Finally, if I resigned the constructive work we had been achieving would be largely wasted. So I replied, 'I

---

*Due to visit Britain shortly under the auspices of the British–Soviet Friendship Society.

am sure that when Marshal Bulganin returns to Moscow he will lay the foundation for future cooperation in this cultural field.' The evident relief of Khrushchev, Bulganin, Selwyn Lloyd and Eden was extremely flattering.

A few days after this, the Moscow Circus abruptly tore up its contract to visit Britain, and although the Soviet Government has never completely severed its ties with the 'friendship' organizations, it has given them little support, and they have ceased to be a significant obstacle to British–Soviet understanding.

My diary note about the Covent Garden dinner said nothing about Khrushchev, yet the occasion was entirely dominated by him. He reminded me of Ernest Bevin – burly, coarse-featured, boisterous, humorous, outgoing, shrewd. At one moment during supper he put down his knife and fork and said, 'I will now tell an anti-Soviet story.' After waiting until he saw we were all listening, he went on,

> There were once two friends who shared a flat in Moscow. One was a Professor of Literature and the other a Secret Police Chief. One evening the Professor came home and said to his friend, 'My friend, this has been the worst day of my life: I asked one of my pupils, "Who wrote *War and Peace*?" and he replied, "Honestly, Professor, I didn't." ' Away went the Police Chief (Mr Khrushchev continued) and came back a fortnight later. 'It's all right,' he said to his friend, 'I found that student. He has confessed. He *did* write *War and Peace*.'

As a leaving gift, Khrushchev presented me with, among other things, five albums of Soviet gramophone records. I knew nothing about Soviet records, and was saddened, but not surprised, when the sound quality of the first one I tried turned out to be extremely poor. I assumed that this was another example of the notoriously low standard of Soviet consumer goods. A few days later, however, when I put on a British record, the same sound distortion resulted. It was the British radiogram and not the Soviet record that was at fault. I felt I had been taught a lesson about prejudice.

As chairman of the Soviet Relations Committee I suffered

one moment of fearful embarrassment. It was in 1957. I was in Moscow, leading a British cultural delegation that included Sir Arthur Bliss, Master of the Queen's Music, Sir Philip Hendy, Director of the British Museum and Sir Paul Sinker, Director-General of the British Council. We had just signed with the Russians an agreement on a programme of cultural exchanges, and after a magnificent banquet they had transported us to the front row of the stalls at the Bolshoi, for a performance of *Figaro*.

Music-lovers will agree that the plot of this incomparable opera is complicated enough even for those who can understand the language in which it is sung, and who have not been stupefied by food, drink, and long hours of negotiating with Russians. So when the curtain came down, to a storm of cheers, on the famous ensemble in Act Three, I signalled to my colleagues and we stood up and started moving towards the exit. But then, half-way up the aisle, I noticed people still sitting down and looking at us strangely. The fearful truth dawned: there is a fourth act in *Figaro*. What was to be done? Could we pretend that we were tired, or ill, or had another engagement? No, we couldn't. There was nothing for it. I turned round. 'Back we go. Sorry!' I whispered, and to widespread Soviet titters the cream of British culture about-turned and slunk back to their seats.

At the beginning, my interest in British–Soviet cultural exchanges had been entirely political. I had wanted to do something to weaken Soviet misconceptions about the West. But as time went on, as I made the acquaintance of leading British and Soviet actors, writers and musicians, my motivation began changing. I saw how easily great music, drama and literature leap national and ideological frontiers. Once, I witnessed a British audience acclaiming with genuine enthusiasm a performance of *The Cherry Orchard* by the Moscow State Theatre *in Russian*. On that occasion, in a speech of thanks backstage, I said,

'How can an English audience respond so warmly to a play in Russian? It is because Chekhov and Shakespeare speak the same language. It is because great drama, literature, art and music reflect values which hold good for all peoples at all times.'

These words plainly stirred the Russians. I think they felt, as I myself did increasingly, that the value of cultural exchanges was not for bringing people together, or for displaying goodwill, or for spreading communism or for advertising a nation's talents. *The Cherry Orchard* and *Hamlet*, the War Requiem and Shostakovich's tenth symphony were forces for peace because of the magic in them, and for no other reason. To use them for political purposes, however noble, was to demean them.

12

MESCALIN AND MYSTICISM

Of all my TV series, the one which interested and influenced me most was about the world religions, called 'Men Seeking God', which was broadcast in 1954. After surrendering to the allurement of logical positivism at Oxford, I had become steadily more sceptical about the arguments for the existence of God. On leave during the war, I wrote down, somewhat presumptuously, and at excessive length, the truth about religion as I saw it. These extracts are typical:

> There is no God. When men want badly to understand and influence things and can't, they postulate a deity. They have done this at various times in respect of fire, flood, fertility, madness, mysticism, creation, war, the destiny of man, the orderedness of nature, goodness, beauty and love. As soon as a more reasonable hypothesis has been found, the idea of God has begun to lapse.
>
> The idea of God is a psychological projection of human minds. It has often brought comfort and reassurance and still does. But it is no advance towards truth. Rather, it impedes truth by choking off scientific enquiry. It is a wall built on the limits of man's knowledge, often broken through but always building itself up further on.
>
> We are still, and always shall be, surrounded by mysteries. But we must not be mugs again. They are evidence of our lack of knowledge, not of the existence of deity. Theology is rationalization, full of special pleading, self-contradiction and obscurity.
>
> Saintliness is not inherently mysterious, nor does it necessarily imply the existence of God. The attribution to it of the idea of God has retarded its scientific analysis.
>
> The constituent parts of a spiritual person seem to be the following: he has an integrated personality, at peace with itself. In psychological terms, his instincts are harmonized, sublimated or expressed in ways approved by his reason and will. He has, partly as the result and partly as a cause of this, a lively perception of the goodness in things, leading to an apprehension of,

and love for, an abstract idea of goodness. This induces in him self-forgetfulness and often, in a wicked world, other-worldliness.

Some outstanding personalities can be saintly in the worst of circumstances. Many can be saintly in fine weather. But the vast mass of people are prevented from thus realizing themselves fully by their nature and circumstances. For people born in slums or inheriting mental or physical weaknesses, or prevented by circumstances from experiencing things of goodness and beauty, saintliness is as difficult to attain as the beauty of music to someone born deaf. Preaching 'only believe' to these people is cant.

But how then did one account for the indisputable fact of religious experience? That was the puzzle. When devout religious people felt aware of the presence of God, were they simply deceiving themselves – victims perhaps of some neurotic delusion? If God did not exist, what was the source of religious experience? Confident that other people would share my curiosity about this, I asked Grace Wyndham-Goldie to let me make six thirty-minute film portraits of devout adherents of different world religions. I then visited Rome, Jerusalem, Benares, Calcutta, Lahore and Rangoon, selecting and interviewing representative and devout believers – a Catholic, a Jew, a Hindu, a Christian Methodist, a Moslem and a Buddhist, asking them about their religious experience rather than the doctrines and observances of their faiths.

My first conclusion was that my friends' religious beliefs, if taken at all literally, hopelessly contradicted each other. For the Christian, God was a loving personality, for the Hindu, a much less personal 'inner self of you, of me, of everything else that exists', for the Buddhist, God did not exist. God was a Trinity for the Christians, but for the Moslem and the Jew, one and indivisible. For the Christians, God revealed himself uniquely in the person of Jesus Christ, for the Moslem, not only in Jesus Christ but in a long line of prophets of whom Muhammad was the last and greatest. In fundamentals, as well as in countless matters of detail, the beliefs of these devout people were mutually irreconcilable.

Then was one set of beliefs right and the other wrong? This seemed unthinkable. It would be a strange God who revealed himself truly in one geographical area and falsely, or not at all, in others. Moreover if one conception of God was true and another false, one would expect this to be reflected in the moral and spiritual stature of the believers. Yet I returned from my journey with the impression that the depth of a person's spiritual life depended less on which religion he belonged to than on his own inner qualities and the devotion with which he followed the religion of his choice.

But perhaps there was some common truth underlying all the different beliefs? This too was untenable. Subtract from the world religions their diverging doctrines and nothing important would be left. If the Jew was right and Christ was not divine, Christian doctrine became meaningless. If the Christian was right, and God revealed himself to Christ but not to Muhammad, what was left of Islam?

So I returned from my voyage more sceptical than ever about the arguments for God's existence.

However, when it came to my friends' religious experience, a different picture emerged. Admittedly, they interpreted their experience differently, each in the idiom of his own religion. The Christian spoke of a 'sense of the presence of God', the Hindu of 'unity with Brahma', the Moslem of 'peace through submission to the will of Allah', the Jew of the feeling of 'being at one' with God in the sense that we are performing his will, and the Buddhist of 'enlightenment', 'Nirvana' and 'the absolute detachment which comes at the last stage of perfection'. In every case, there were important differences – in the language in which the experience was expressed, in the manner and intensity with which it was felt, and in the methods by which it was achieved; and yet it was impossible to doubt that the experience itself was basically the same in all cases. All agreed that it could not be defined exactly, that it was extremely precious, that it was accompanied by joy and a sense of peace and unity, and that it was associated in some way with moral goodness – with unselfishness and detachment from material values and desires. Finally there was a striking similarity in the descriptions they gave of the occasions when they tried to achieve it and failed.

In short, when my friends talked of their religious beliefs, they talked with different voices, and they also differed when they talked of their religious experiences in religious terms. But when they spoke of their religious experience in everyday language, they came together.

What then was the source of this common religious experience? Was it, as my friends believed, some outside power or spirit? Or did it simply come from within themselves, the product of particular physical or psychological conditions?

At the time, I inclined to the latter view, and this opinion was now to be strengthened in a curious manner. Dr Humphry Osmond, Medical Superintendent of a highly-regarded mental hospital in Saskatchewan, was an old schoolfriend of mine. In his search for a cure for his schizophrenic patients, he had for some years past been experimenting with a particular range of drugs known as 'psychotomimetics', which produced in those who took them some of the symptoms of insanity. He had recently administered one of these drugs – mescalin – to Aldous Huxley in the fascinating experiment described in Huxley's *The Doors of Perception*.

In anticipation of a visit to Britain, Humphry asked me to approach the BBC about the possibility of his broadcasting on the Third Programme about his work. I replied by suggesting that we should make a television film together about mescalin, in the course of which he would explain his research ideas and give me the drug, and I would describe my reactions.

The year was 1955, long before the 'drug scene'. There was little awareness of the dangers of addiction, and except to a few specialists, hallucinogens like mescalin and LSD were unknown. The term 'psychedelic' had only just been invented, by Humphry himself. In these circumstances the BBC approved my idea, and in due course a BBC producer and film team arrived at my home and filmed me drinking down 400 mg of mescalin hydrochloride before Humphry's watchful eye.

Even today, after hundreds of thousands of people have taken drugs of this kind, often with bizarre or ridiculous or disastrous results, I still look on this mescalin experiment, professionally supervised and filmed, as the most interesting experience of my life.

In particular, the drug totally changed my experience of time. At irregular intervals – perhaps once every five minutes at the peak of the experiment – I would find myself withdrawn from my surroundings in a state of euphoria, quite rational and conscious, for a period of time which – for me – simply did not end at all. It did not last for minutes or hours but apparently for years. During this period I would be aware of a pervasive, radiant light.

On the first occasion when I 'came back' from one of these excursions, I exclaimed to the film team in astonishment, 'Are you still there!' From my standpoint, they had been waiting, with fantastic patience, for years. From their standpoint, however, no time had elapsed and they had not been waiting at all. From my standpoint, I had spent years in paradise: from theirs, I was deranged.

On one occasion I made a time excursion in the middle of an intelligence test.

Dr Osmond: Will you subtract seven from a hundred and go on subtracting until nothing is left?

Myself: Ninety-three, eighty-six, seventy-nine, seventy-two, sixty-three – whatever it is – fifty-eight, fifty-one, forty-four, thirty-seven, thirty, twenty-three – I'm off again for a long period. But you won't notice that I've gone away at all.

Dr Osmond: When are you coming back?

Myself: I am now in your time.

For several days afterwards, I remembered that afternoon not as so many hours spent in my drawing room interrupted by these strange 'excursions', but as years of heavenly bliss, interrupted by short spells in my drawing room.

Common sense would say that I had simply taken a hallu-
cinogenic drug and had a hallucination, a dream-like episode
lasting a fraction of a second during which I had been
deluded into thinking that I had been conscious for a long
period. Psychiatrists would – and indeed did – explain the
experience in terms of depersonalization, time distortion,
light hallucinations and the disintegration of the ego. But I
thought then, and still think now, that a truer explanation
is that I had had an experience that had taken place outside
time, that I had visited, by a short cut, the timeless world
known to mystics and to some schizophrenics.

I understand very well the feelings which Dostoevsky –
himself an epileptic – attributed to Prince Muishkin in *The
Idiot*.

When his attack was over, and the Prince reflected on his symptoms, he used to say to himself – 'These moments, short as
they are, when I feel such extreme consciousness of myself, and
consequently more of life than at other times, are due only to
the disease – to the sudden rupture of normal conditions. Therefore they are not really a higher kind of life, but a lower.'

This reasoning, however, seemed to end in a paradox, and
lead to the further consideration 'What matter though it be only
a disease, an abnormal tension of the brain, if when I recall and
analyse the moment, it seems to be in one of harmony and
beauty in the highest degree?'

What more unanswerable than a fact? And this fact had
occurred. The Prince had confessed unreservedly to himself that
the intense beatitude in that crowded moment made the moment
worth a lifetime. 'I feel then', he said one day to Rogojin in
Moscow, 'I feel then as though I understood those amazing
words "There shall be no more time".'

Is there then no dividing line between sacred and psychotic
mystical experiences? Given that its causes and results are so
vastly different, how could the end-product of sanctity and
insanity be substantially the same?

Determined to solve this mystery, I began studying the life
and work of perhaps the greatest and most articulate mystic
of all times, St Teresa of Avila. I paid special attention to

her attempts to define the difference between mystical experience and insanity. About 'inner voices' for example, she wrote:

> It will be a good thing, I think, to explain the nature of the voices God bestows upon the soul. The words are perfectly formed, but are not heard by the physical ear. You can't shut them out, however hard you try. But when our understanding invents voices, no matter how subtly, we are aware of the intellect actually ordering the words and speaking them. And the soul knows they are the ravings of the mind and takes no more notice of them than of someone it knows to be a lunatic.

Sadly, however, this explanation, characteristically brave and thoughtful, conflicts with what we now know about schizophrenics. Their auditory hallucinations would often slip through St Teresa's test. They too are not heard by the physical ear, cannot be shut out, and include perfectly formed words. I could find no criterion put forward by the saint that clearly marked off sacred from psychotic mystical experiences.

Did this mean that her exemplary life and work, her voices and visions and the reverence paid her by religious people over many centuries were all based on an illusion? I found this hard to accept, and decided to look deeper.

Once again, television came to my aid: the BBC agreed to my visiting Spain and making a documentary portrait of the great saint.

The film began taking shape in my mind during a visit to the USA on a different television project. I came across this diary note, written in a New York hotel:

> Strange how the idea of the Teresa programme develops and increasingly overwhelms me.
>
> Reach T's account (in her autobiography) of her leaving her home: 'I do not believe that I shall ever suffer more when I come to die than when I left my father's house . . .'
>
> The sound of this spoken, as it will be spoken, over the sight of the road to the Convent of the Incarnation, as it will be filmed! I heard these words spoken, in the most beautiful, clear, determined voice of a radio actress, over the most lovely shots

by Tubby Englander of the road; and then I suddenly realized that we hear the bells of Avila too, and found myself saying aloud, 'The bells! The bells!' in my hotel bedroom.

Before leaving for Avila, I called on the Papal Nuncio in London, and asked for the Vatican's permission to film inside St Teresa's foundations. It emerged that, apart from an occasional doctor, no man had ever crossed the threshold of these convents since they had been built. However, the Vatican approved our project, and attached a Dutch Franciscan friar to our party, to help us obtain the permissions we needed.

Each day of filming would begin at a grille near the entrance to one of St Teresa's convents. Here, tense negotiations would be conducted between the friar and the mother superior. Though not understanding Spanish, I could guess the arguments on both sides, and my better self sided with the mother superior. Why should she allow this quiet and holy place to resound to the tramping feet of my Spanish film crew? How could she be expected to set aside the rules of her Order, decreed by St Teresa herself, kept inviolate for centuries?

However, the Vatican's wishes could not be set aside, and in the end a compromise would be reached. We would be allowed, for example, to film for a set time in one part of the convent, while the mother superior and the nuns – none of whom were on any account to be filmed – took refuge in another part.

Our producer was an old friend, a member of the BBC's religious affairs department, the Rev. Peter Hamilton, and the chief cameraman was Gerry Pullen. Their sequences of Avila and the foundations were strikingly beautiful, and we persuaded Flora Robson to record passages over them from St Teresa's autobiography, including her fervent descriptions of her strange, powerful, visions and voices.

I was tempted to let this wonderful film stand by itself; but stuck grimly to my original purpose. The finished version suggested that the world the saint visited in her trances was real, and that we must try to understand and serve the spiritual power that dominated her life, but that sacred and psychotic mystical experiences were hard to differentiate, and that at times during the early part of her life St Teresa could, by modern definitions, be held to have been mentally ill.

To my sorrow, this conclusion was disliked by the BBC's religious affairs department, and led to the programme being shown only once, and then very late at night.

The mescalin experiment naturally also increased my interest in mental sickness. It had helped me to understand what it must feel like to be insane, and given me a fellow-feeling for sufferers from schizophrenia. Their bizarre behaviour, I thought, was a natural, desperate, human reaction to wildly unnatural sense-data. And their illness must surely have a simple physical origin. How could my symptoms have been caused by environmental stress, or genetic make-up, or some traumatic childhood experience? They could only have been caused by what I had drunk. All that was needed, therefore, was to isolate and neutralize whatever chemical substance in the bloodstream of schizophrenics was distorting their perceptions, as mescalin had distorted mine.

Later, I realized that schizophrenia takes many different forms, that my symptoms may not have been typical, and that research along the lines I hoped for had already been attempted without producing decisive results. But at the time my convictions were simple and strong, and led me to think about ways of helping the mentally sick.

For most people in those days, mental patients were objects of fear and shame. Herded into locked wards behind high hospital walls, they were widely seen as unpredictable and uncontrollable, at best embarrassing, at worst frightening. I thought television could be used to soften and civilize these attitudes, and persuaded the BBC and the Ministry of Health to allow, for the first time, a mental hospital to be filmed from the inside. They also agreed to my interviewing some of the patients, provided their faces were not shown. To help bridge the gulf between patients and viewers, I stayed in one of the hospital wards myself, as a 'patient', for some days before the filming.

If shown today, the programme that resulted, the first of a series called 'The Hurt Mind', would arouse little interest; but in those days it was startlingly original. It attracted a large audience, and according to an elaborate opinion survey helped to lessen the stigma surrounding mental illness. My work on it led me into many years of campaigning for the mentally sick, including a seven-year spell as Chairman of MIND, the National Association for Mental Health.

13

SUPPORTING THE PALESTINIANS

I have described earlier my turbulent introduction to the Palestine problem, as Bevin's parliamentary secretary in the Attlee Government. Though not personally committed at that time to one side or the other, Zionists had browbeaten me in my office, shouted me down in the House, and even threatened me with assassination.

Imagine my surprise, therefore, when soon afterwards a determined and skilful attempt was made to lure me on to the pro-Israeli pay-roll. It happened in 1951, when I was earning a living as a journalist and television commentator. The political director of the World Jewish Congress, Mr A. L. Easterman, invited me to become an adviser to the congress. Whenever I was asked for advice and gave it, I would be paid a substantial honorarium. The appointment would be a purely personal arrangement between the two of us, and nothing would be set down about it in writing.

The proposition was put to me so delicately that I found it hard to take offence. But acceptance would obviously have exposed me to pressure, prejudicing my freedom of speech where Israel was concerned.

Some years later, Mr Easterman published his own version of the incident:

> At no point of our talk did I offer Mr Mayhew, directly or indirectly, to become a 'political adviser' and it is nothing short of preposterous that I offered him 'a very large salary'. All I did say to him about finance was that, naturally, we would reimburse him for any expenditure he might incur on our behalf.*

This was untrue, and I wondered at the time, whether I was the only broadcaster or journalist to be approached in this way, and, if not, whether all the others had turned down the

Jewish Chronicle, 16 October 1960.

offer as I had. This seemed unlikely, and thereafter I would sometimes ask myself whether this or that influential supporter of Israel was a paid adviser to the World Jewish Congress.

At that time, I still knew nothing about Palestine at first hand, and it was not until 1953, on my first visit to a refugee camp, that the tragedy of the Palestinian people became real for me. I was visiting Jordan as a member of a parliamentary delegation sent out by the Foreign Office to show support for King Hussein. The camp was near Amman. It was very crowded and I soon found myself separated from my parliamentary colleagues in a large, mud-floored hut, filled with ragged, thin-faced refugees, including many children. There were no windows, and the only light came through an open doorway. One or two of the refugees began asking me questions, translating the answers for the rest of the audience. What was the British Government going to do for the refugees? I explained what we had done to initiate and support the relief and rehabilitation work of the UN. I hoped this answer would be well received, as Britain's record had been a good one, compared at least with that of other countries. But to my dismay my reply only made my audience more angry and suspicious. What was Britain doing to get their land back? I explained that we supported their right to choose between returning to their homes in Israel, or being compensated and resettled. But what were we *doing* apart from talking? Did I not realize that it was we who were responsible for the Jews taking their land? What crime had they and their children committed that they should be driven from their homes and robbed of all their possessions?

The intensity of their bitterness and anger dismayed me, but their case seemed unanswerable. Listening to their stories, it was impossible to believe, as the Israelis insisted, that they had left their homes voluntarily. And even if they had, why were they not allowed to return? If the Israelis had been willing to let the refugees stay, why had they slammed the door behind them so quickly after they had left? I felt that these proud, innocent people were suffering an intolerable injustice, and saw these refugee camps not as relics of a war but as seedbeds of future vengeance.

I wish I could record that on my return I began campaigning for the Palestinians, but my heavy commitments to the BBC and to the Labour Party made this impossible. Ten years passed, until 1963, before I became actively committed to their cause. This resulted, paradoxically, from a meeting with Mrs Golda Meir and other Israeli leaders during a visit to Jerusalem.

I was part of an official Labour Party delegation, which had arrived in Israel after an extensive tour of Arab countries. Confident, friendly and sophisticated, our Israeli hosts welcomed us at the frontier as though we were returning home from exile in some alien, barbarous land. They did not argue with us about the Arabs or attempt to persuade us: they simply assumed from the start that we were on their side, that we agreed that the refugee camps were an artificial problem, kept alive for political purposes by the Arab states; that the Palestinians had left their homes of their own free will and could and should now resettle elsewhere; that they had brought their miseries on themselves and had no claims on Israel.

I was already familiar with this line of talk, but the bland assumption that I agreed with it was irritating. Why did these Israeli leaders assume that they knew the Palestinians so well? How many of them had met a Palestinian leader or visited a Palestinian refugee camp? And that patronizing, rather derisive, tone of voice in which they spoke about the Palestinians – where had I heard it before?

The answer to this last question dawned on me at a dinner given by Mrs Golda Meir. I realized that these Israelis were indeed constantly meeting Palestinians, but almost always as gardeners, cleaners, domestic servants and taxi drivers. That was why they felt they understood the Palestinians, and why they misjudged them so dangerously. It explained too the tone of voice in which they talked about them. I remembered now where I had heard it before: at parties given me by British settlers in Kenya and Tanganyika on my BBC tour of Africa. Then it had been the Africans who were at heart sensible and loyal, but not bright, and easily led astray by troublemakers.

I was once asked by an Arab taxi driver in Jerusalem, who knew and trusted me, what he should say to Israeli clients who asked him for his political views. 'When I tell them what I really think, I get a smaller tip,' he said. 'What do you think I ought to say . . . ?'

It was during this visit to Israel that I paid my first penalty for supporting the Palestinians. The Israeli leaders seemed to me so self-righteous and unfeeling about the plight of the refugees that I found myself arguing with them angrily. This led them to forward a complaint about me to their friend and supporter Harold Wilson, and a year later, when forming his government, Wilson ignored my long stint as Labour's deputy spokesman on foreign affairs, and did not appoint me Deputy Foreign Minister. A leading Israeli newspaper reported.

> Gordon Walker, appointed Foreign Minister, apparently wanted Mayhew as his deputy. But Mayhew did not get the post. Why? In London there are rumours that the leaders of the Jewish community in Britain, or Israeli friends of Wilson, brought to the Prime Minister's attention the dangerous misunderstandings that might result from such a nomination. How could a pro-Arab be put in charge of Middle East affairs, while Wilson claims to treat Israel with friendship?*

So I was appointed Navy Minister instead, and this ended for a time my involvement in Palestine. Later, however, when I was again on the back-benches, the Arab-Israeli war of 1967 produced a new flood of Palestinian refugees, and I began campaigning again.

It is hard to convey today the bitterness with which friends of the Palestinians were assailed at that time by their Zionist opponents. The dedication of almost all Jewish people to Israel was then intense and unquestioning, and this led them to assume that her critics must be either mad or bad; they must be anti-semites, or communist crackpots, or in the pay

* Ma'ariv, Jerusalem, 14 July 1964.

of the oil companies. Friends of the Palestinians often had
difficulty in making themselves heard.

> Bitterness came to the surface when Mr Mayhew began to
> speak . . . the interruptions began when he argued that it was
> wrong to talk in terms of racial extermination by the Arab forces
> in their war against Israel . . . he was almost shouted down when
> he went on to claim that the existence of the Palestinian refugees
> was the root of the crisis.*

This was a typical meeting of the Labour Party's Foreign
Affairs Committee. From the moment I stood up, Zionist
MPs did not stop shouting abuse at me. I was given no
protection by the chair, and after struggling on for a few
minutes, gave up.

However, I had many opportunities at this time to state
my views on radio and television. I took what would now
be considered a neutral line, criticizing both Israel and the
Arabs, arguing that Britain should not intervene militarily
except as a member of the UN, demanding justice for the
refugees but insisting that Israel had a right to live in peace
within her own frontiers. Nevertheless, the climate of opinion
was so fiercely and uncritically pro-Israeli that pressure soon
built up among the pro-Israelis to get me off the air. A 'round
robin', signed by twenty-six of my fellow Labour MPs, was
sent to Mr John Silkin, the Chief Government Whip. Mr
Silkin, a strong supporter of Israel, publicly declared his
official support for the petition and forwarded it to the BBC.

The hostility of Jewish supporters of Israel spilled over
into my other work. When I was elected chairman of the
National Association for Mental Health (with the support
of all the executive committee except its two Jewish
members) and we decided to launch a fund-raising appeal to
the City, it was put to me that, to avoid offending possible
Jewish subscribers, my name should not appear in the appeal
literature. I agreed with this readily enough, but afterwards
decided, at the risk of being snubbed, to test the temperature
of the opposition. I called on a well-known, wealthy and

* *Guardian*, 7 June 1967.

influential Zionist businessman, Sir Marcus Sieff,* and
suggested that it was surely incongruous that a charitable
appeal on behalf of the mentally sick and handicapped
should suffer because of its chairman's views on Palestine.
Would it not be a generous gesture, in everyone's interest, if
he were to become a sponsor of the appeal? He replied, with
obvious satisfaction, 'You'll not get a penny from me, and
not a penny from my friends.'

On another occasion, a famous firm of jewellers agreed to
donate to the National Association the proceeds of the sale
of catalogues at one of their exhibitions. Our royal patron,
Princess Alexandra, had agreed to open the exhibition, and
had told me she was hoping to see me there. However,
the days passed and my invitation did not arrive. This was
awkward. Was it simply a mistake? Or had the firm decided
that it was not necessary to invite the chairman? Or could
it be that the firm was Jewish and Zionist, and determined
to have nothing to do with me? It was not easy to decide.
Eventually, I came to the conclusion that the last explanation
was the likeliest and decided, for once, to make a fuss. I
telephoned the head of the firm, thanked him for his firm's
promised donation, and said that my invitation had not
arrived. The reply came back that this was a Zionist firm
and that an invitation to an anti-Zionist like myself had not
therefore seemed appropriate. 'But what would you think',
I objected, 'if our positions were reversed? What would you
think of somebody who refused to have any social or business
dealings with you simply because you were a Zionist?' After
a pause, the jeweller, a man of character, declared that he
had been wrong, and that my invitation would be sent round
immediately. So I went to the exhibition, and was warmly
welcomed by the jeweller and members of his charming
family. But I could not help asking myself, as I wandered
round among the Fabergé and the diamond clusters, from
how many social and political gatherings I had been quietly
excluded because of my support for the Palestinians.

The most effective weapon used against me was the alle-

*Now Lord Sieff of Brimpton.

gation that I was anti-semitic. This was a plausible and colourful invention, easily remembered and passed round, and damaging in many ways. I was therefore much relieved when a Zionist MP made the allegation in actionable terms, in an article in the *Jewish Chronicle*. Now at last – or so I thought – I could clear myself with a court action.

In the prevailing climate of opinion, merely to have proved that there was no evidence that I was anti-semitic would not on balance have been helpful; and if that had been all that a libel action could have established, I would not have issued a writ. Fortunately, however, I had a rather colourful record of active opposition to anti-semitism, and in due course the following statement was read in open court on behalf of the *Jewish Chronicle* and my parliamentary colleague.

> The plaintiff has a long and distinguished record of opposition to anti-semitism and of support and friendship for Jewish people. Before the war he took part in the East End demonstrations in support of Jewish residents against the British Union of Fascists, and in the post war years, as a member of the Inter-government governmental Committee for Refugees and of the International Refugee Organization, he assisted in the resettlement of victims of Nazism, including many Jews. In his writings and broadcasts he has shown sympathy and understanding of Jewish questions, and a television film he made about Judaism has been widely acclaimed by Jewish people in Britain.
>
> The plaintiff has attended many meetings and functions of Jewish organizations and has rendered assistance to the Jewish community in his own constituency, for example by helping them to acquire a site for a new synagogue. He has visited Israel on several occasions, where he has been guest of the Chief Rabbi in Jerusalem and of the Prime Minister and Foreign Secretary . . . the defendants offer their sincere apologies to the plaintiff . . . they wish to pay tribute to his record as a person of liberal opinions, an enemy of intolerance, and a man who has on many occasions manifested friendship to Jews.

I would have liked my counsel to have added one colourful detail: my BBC film on Judaism had pleased some members of the Jewish community so much that they had planted a grove of trees in Israel in my honour – 'The Christopher

Mayhew Grove'. However, the *Jewish Chronicle*'s tribute was handsome enough, and I hoped that I was now in the clear. But this was not to be. Soon afterwards, one of my party leaders was heard to say at a diplomatic dinner, 'Chris Mayhew? A good man really. A pity he hates the Jews.' In the *Sunday Times*, Frederic Raphael referred to me as 'A Judophobe – a significant mutation of the old style anti-Semite'. The editor of the *New Statesman*, Paul Johnson, a strong supporter of Israel, published a defamatory letter from a reader and then mangled my letter of reply. I reported this to the Press Council and they upheld me, but the incident did me no good. Mr Johnson fared better: shortly afterwards he was appointed by Harold Wilson to be a member of the Royal Commission on the Press.

However, though few in number, the Palestinians' friends fought back. Our first step was to organize ourselves. In 1969 we founded the all-party Council for the Advancement of Arab-British Understanding, and in the following year the Labour Middle East Council. These organizations gave us much-needed mutual support and encouragement, and quickly became influential. An experienced printer and publisher, Claud Morris, joined me in launching a magazine, *Middle East International*, which continues successfully to this day. Claud's company had flourished until the late sixties, when in the normal course of business he began printing *Free Palestine*. His rotary press was thereupon destroyed by unknown arsonists, and his local newspapers were badly hit when Jewish traders cancelled their advertising.

However, persecution drew the friends of the Palestinians together. We were a band of brothers, quick to help and defend each other. Among the first activists were Michael Adams, John Reddaway, Betty Collard and Sir Anthony Nutting, and we were helped by a handful of heroic Jewish friends, including Marion Wolfson and Mick Ashley.

Our first targets were not the politicians or the public, but the media. At that time virtually all the newspaper and broadcasting organizations, from ignorance or pressure or both, distorted or disregarded the Palestinians' case. It was their common practice to appoint Jewish supporters of Israel, sometimes actual Israeli citizens, as their Middle East correspondents. This was true of *The Times*, the *Telegraph*, the *Guardian*, the *Observer* and the *Evening Standard* and, worst of all, and to its eternal shame, the BBC.

At the time of the June war in 1967, the media were particularly susceptible to Israeli propaganda designed to show that Nasser and other Arab leaders were anti-semitic and genocidal. In particular, they persisted in reporting that Nasser had threatened to 'drive the Jews into the sea'. I knew and respected Nasser, and after tracking down the source of this and similar propaganda myths, made a public offer on television, repeated in the House of Commons, to pay £5000 to anyone who could produce documentary evidence of a genocidal statement made by a responsible Arab leader. A number of eager claimants wrote in, invariably quoting from familiar propaganda sources, and I would write back explaining that their chosen statement was a misquotation, or mistranslation, or straight invention, as the case might be, but always inviting them, if they disagreed, to take me to court.

Eventually a young Jewish lawyer took up my invitation. Significantly ignoring the alleged statement by Nasser, he sent me a blood-curdling genocidal statement apparently made by Azzam Pasha, a former secretary-general of the Arab League. My lawyers promptly replied with the original text in Arabic, pointing out that the claim was based on a mistranslation. My opponent then tried to withdraw, but I refused to allow this, and had his lawyer declare in open court that after considerable research they had been unable to discover any genocidal remarks by any responsible Arab leader.

However, my victory went largely unreported in the media, which continued feeding the public with Israeli misinformation. The deputy editor of the *Sunday Times*, Frank Giles, solemnly revealed to his readers that Nasser had threatened to drive the Jews into the sea; and as late as January 1986, Israel's ambassador Dimitz, replying to me in an Oxford Union debate, illustrated the baseness of Arab leaders by quoting the very statement by Azzam Pasha I had exposed as fraudulent in the High Court.

Eventually, in exasperation, Michael Adams and I decided to write a book exposing the vulnerability of the media to Zionist pressure. *Publish It Not . . . the Middle East Cover-up* was well reviewed and widely read. However, it led us into deep water. In a review for the Israeli paper *Ma'ariv* a fervent Zionist, Mr Y. Finkelston,* declared that the book 'contains all the viciousness and all the dangerous slander of a Nazi anti-Semitic pamphlet'. He described Michael Adams as 'lost to any sense of decency and all notions of sanity' and myself as 'a vicious and determined Jew hater'.

At that time the Israeli judicial system had not yet been seriously politicized, and Michael and I decided to issue a writ for libel in the Israeli courts. Not even in Jerusalem, we thought, could Mr Finkelston's preposterous allegations be taken seriously. We would visit Israel, explain to the Israeli public the difference between anti-Zionism and anti-semitism, call on our Palestinian friends on the West Bank, and pay our travel expenses out of the damages the court would surely award us.

It was a disastrous misjudgement. I was chiefly to blame. I did not conceive it possible that one distinguished Israeli after another, including the current President of Israel, Mr Chaim Hertzog, could enter the witness box and declare on oath that two elderly members of the British Liberal Party,* both with impeccable records of active opposition to racialism, were 'Jew haters', and that a book that had been reviewed favourably, or at least with respect, by *The Times*, the *Guardian*, the *Sunday Times*, the *Observer*, the *Economist* and the *New Statesman and Nation* could be adjudged, in Hertzog's words, 'plainly anti-Semitic'. I was particularly struck by the imaginative evidence of a Mrs Dinah Porat, presented to the court as an expert on anti-semitism from Tel Aviv University, who drew elaborate parallels between

*Mr Finkelston is now foreign editor of the *Jewish Chronicle*.
†By then I had left the Labour Party and joined the Liberals. See Chapter 15.

our blameless book and the writings of Goebbels and the notorious anti-semitic forgery 'The Protocols of the Elders of Zion'.

How was it possible for such intelligent, civilized and distinguished people to take the oath and talk such nonsense? The answer surely lies in the tragic past of the Jewish people. For historical reasons which every civilized person understands and respects, many Jews – not just Israelis – are haunted by profound feelings of insecurity, and by the darkest, most irrational suspicions of anyone who seems to confront them. Their reason tells them that they must learn to live with such people, but their hearts forbid it. This was plainly true of all the prosecution witnesses. Nor should Judge Bazak be blamed for his involved, emotional, preposterous summing-up against Michael and myself. He had lost all his family in the holocaust: the trained adult lawyer was no match for the anguished and terrified boy.

One of the saddest truths about men and nations is that insecurity breeds aggression. Anti-semitism – Russian, Polish and finally German – drove the Jewish people to seek a state of their own, and fear led that state to reject compromise and seek power by domination. Yet fear and domination have brought safety no nearer. They have made Israel widely hated, and have pitted three million Israeli Jews against a hundred and seventy million Arabs and a thousand million Muslims, in a conflict which, in the long run, Israel cannot win.

14

RESIGNING AS NAVY MINISTER

Thirteen years of Tory rule ended in 1964, with the election of the first Wilson government. I was appointed Navy Minister, and my days at the Admiralty began with a colourful instance of "Yes, Minister".

One of the Labour Party's election pledges had been to end all arms cooperation with South Africa; and within a few days of taking office, a note came round for myself and other Ministers, initialled by the Prime Minister himself, giving instructions in the clearest terms that all arms sales, military training and joint exercises with South Africa were to cease forthwith.

I was surprised at being given instructions directly by the Prime Minister, but impressed by his display of firm leadership. Determined to show similar loyalty to Labour policies and principles, I quickly summoned a meeting of my relevant civil and naval advisers and asked what the Navy was doing in this field. It emerged that we were selling South Africa Buccaneer aircraft, training Buccaneer pilots and conducting joint maritime exercises. I then explained that I had had clear instructions from the Prime Minister that these activities must now cease.

Immediately, grave difficulties were seen. Would this not jeopardize the Simonstown Agreement, which gave us important base facilities, over-flying rights and a broadcast listening post? Was I suggesting that we should simply renege on our commercial contracts? And so on.

So far from being discouraged by these objections, I felt a growing determination to get my way. I had read somewhere that if a Minister is to establish the right relationship with his staff, he must show the greatest firmness at his first encounter with them. This was obviously just such an occasion. I explained that instructions had come from the Prime Minister himself, in the clearest terms, and I would be

glad to receive detailed proposals without delay for carrying
them out. I then dismissed the meeting.

It so happened that that evening there was a big official
reception – tails and decorations – at Lancaster House. In
the midst of it, my Permanent Under-Secretary, Sir Michael
Cary, for whom I developed a great liking and trust,
advanced towards me. Taking me aside, he said he had bad
news for me. He had had a word with the secretary to the
Cabinet about the South Africa business. Apparently the
Prime Minister now felt that the matter should be more
thoroughly discussed, and intended to raise it on the Defence
and Overseas Policy Committee of the Cabinet. I thanked
him politely, and agreed that meanwhile we should continue
sending Buccaneers to South Africa, training South African
pilots, and holding joint training exercises.

Just how long we continued doing this, I cannot now
recall, but we certainly completed the two Buccaneer
contracts. More than a year later the joint exercises were
still continuing, and Ministers were earnestly discussing the
sale to South Africa of military helicopters.

There was nothing I could have done about this: decisions
about the Navy's dealings with South Africa were taken by
the Defence and Overseas Policy Committee, to which I had
no access. This was an early example of the problem that
was to haunt me during my whole time at the Ministry of
Defence. On the one hand I was called 'Navy Minister' –
even, sometimes, 'First Lord of the Admiralty' – and the
Navy looked to me to speak up for it. On the other hand,
the new centralized structure of the Ministry of Defence
meant that I was little more than a junior adviser to the
Secretary of State. All the trappings of power were there: as
Minister-in-Attendance, I accompanied the Queen and Prince
Philip throughout the Royal Review of the Fleet; in the Far
East, I was 'piped' in splendour across Hong Kong harbour;
visiting the US Navy, I was awarded a nineteen-gun salute.
At the same time, even when the most important naval
matters were being decided, I could never attend the relevant
cabinet committee, let alone the Cabinet itself.

And seldom before in its long history had the British Navy so badly needed a powerful spokesman.

In its 1964 general election manifesto, the Labour Party had declared, 'the Navy has been run down to a dangerously low level, and is now pathetically inadequate in number of ships in commission, in manning, and in the most modern types such as nuclear powered tracker submarines'.*

This was perfectly true, and so now we were in government, our duty was plain: we must increase the Navy's resources or reduce its commitments. Yet within two months of taking office, the Government had ruled out both courses. Two high-level decisions had been made which, taken together, were bound to over-stretch the Navy still further and make my position as Navy Minister impossible. On the one hand, the Government had committed itself publicly, in response to left-wing pressure, to cutting defence expenditure by four hundred million pounds to two thousand million pounds a year; and at the same time, Wilson, in response to American pressure, had pledged himself publicly to maintain our defence commitments east of Suez. He declared in the House of Commons, on 16 December 1964, 'I want to make it quite clear that whatever we may do in the field of cost effectiveness, value-for-money and a stringent review of economy, we cannot afford to relinquish our world role – our role which, for shorthand purposes, is sometimes called our "East of Suez" role.'

It was obviously tempting to lay down quickly a 'ceiling' for defence expenditure: quite apart from left-wing pressure, this had to be done before the Government's five-year national economic plan could be worked out and published. It was equally tempting to make an early announcement about staying east of Suez: this would reassure the Americans, whose help we were seeking for propping up the pound.

What was indefensible was the Government's readiness to commit itself to both objectives before making sure they were compatible with each other. Could the task announced

Let's Go with Labour, p. 22.

by the Prime Minister be achieved on the budget planned by
the Chancellor of the Exchequer? An elaborate defence
review was launched in the hope of finding the answer,
and it soon became clear that the two objectives of the
Government were irreconcilable.

By the end of 1964, the danger signals already shone
clearly in the Navy Department. I spent my first month
challenging the naval staff to justify various expensive-
looking items in our budget, especially our aircraft carrier
programme. I visited ships and shore establishments, cross-
examined officers and men about equipment and conditions
of service, pored over tables and graphs showing manpower
requirements and shortages, the ageing of our escort fleet,
the increase of family separation, and similar subjects. The
result of all these inquiries confirmed the soundness of
Labour's conclusion in opposition: the Navy was dangerously over-stretched.

On 6 August 1965, I wrote to Denis Healey, the Secretary
of State for Defence,

> Yesterday's meeting has prompted me to restate the misgivings
> about the defence review which I have been expressing to you
> in recent months. . . . On current prospects the government will
> have taken well over a year before making even provisional
> decisions about commitments. . . . During this period, the ser-
> vices will have continued in a state of strain and uncertainty,
> committed to fulfilling a 'world role' on two thousand million
> pounds and badgered to make still further economies without
> reciprocity. . . . I feel that the time has come when we must
> call a halt. . . . We must accept no further cuts in our defence
> programme without equivalent irrevocable cuts in commitments.

However, Healey not only rejected my views but would not
allow me to express them to the Cabinet, or even to the
Cabinet's defence committee.

Increasingly desperate, I wrote on 8 November 1965

> May I renew my plea to be present at the ministerial meetings
> when the carrier programme is certain to be discussed? . . . If it
> were decided to phase out the carriers, without the Navy having

been able to present its case fully – either on paper or through its chief spokesman – the task of presenting the decision afterwards would of course be made vastly more difficult.

However, Healey was rigidly committed to the doctrine of centralized decision-making in the Ministry of Defence. There were good arguments for this: inter-service rivalry had often wrecked defence planning in the past. But it ran the risk of subordinating to a centralized bureaucracy those who best understood the particular problem to be solved – in this case, the defence of ships against air attack. The Navy, experienced and well-informed, knew that meeting its east of Suez commitments would require seaborne air power: its masters at the centre, inexperienced and inexpert, overrode it and pushed their mistaken views through the Cabinet.

At the last moment, when the decision to scrap the carriers had already been taken, Wilson took advantage of Healey's absence abroad and allowed me to state my case to the Cabinet's Defence and Overseas Policy Committee. I argued at length that carriers were essential to the east of Suez role, that scrapping them could only be defended in the context of a new defence policy, that there were strong political, military and economic reasons for withdrawing from east of Suez, and that we should now do this, and concentrate our resources in Europe.

I had long held doubts about the east of Suez role. Visits to the Persian Gulf and the Far East in the early 1960s had convinced me that our peace-keeping role there was becoming anachronistic and counter-productive. On 11 April 1963, I had sent a memorandum to Labour Party leaders, including Wilson, setting out the case for withdrawal at some length, and concluding, 'All these factors seem to point to a policy of resolute disengagement from our special military and political position in the Gulf.' About the Far East, I wrote,

There is a limit to what Western countries can do to support Asians against Communism; there is a point beyond which further assistance from us defeats its own ends, because it arouses suspicions of 'colonialism' and weakens the will of free Asian peoples to stand up for themselves. In Vietnam since the war, the West has over-stepped this limit many times.

My statement to the Defence Committee received some support, especially from Roy Jenkins. Indeed, one of the Ministers present was reported as saying afterwards, 'I have never heard a case deployed so powerfully before the Cabinet. It visibly impressed Jenkins and a few others, and from that moment the skids were under the Healey policy.'* However, the decision had already been taken to abandon the carrier fleet, and on 2 February 1966, the day after the defence committee meeting, Healey declared to the Press Club in Canberra, 'We intend to remain and shall remain, fully capable of carrying out all the commitments we have at the present time, including those in the Far East, the Middle East, and in Africa and in other parts of the world.'

Obviously I had to resign. I had committed myself publicly to the view that carriers were essential to the east of Suez role, and could not now turn round and recommend the Cabinet's decision to Parliament and the Navy. No one in the Navy Department, from the First Sea Lord to my admirable driver, 'Nobby' Hall, attempted to dissuade me.

My immediate problem was the need to dissuade other members of the Navy Board from resigning too. Fortunately, the precedents were clear and made good sense: only the First Sea Lord, Admiral Sir David Luce, had the right to resign. But I had a busy time urging other outraged admirals to stay at their posts.

Normally the Board of Admiralty held its meetings in the undistinguished Defence Council suite at the Ministry of Defence. On formal occasions, however, we would walk over to Admiralty House and meet in the historic old boardroom. Here I presided over the board for the last time, and formally announced my intention to resign. David Luce, who was to resign two days later, replied. Our language was impeccably

*Geoffrey Williams and Bruce Reed, *Denis Healey and the Politics of Power*, p. 245.

calm, contrasting with the robust expressions of disgust being heard elsewhere throughout the Navy.

Round us on the walls hung portraits of the great figures of Britain's naval history, and I wondered what Pepys, Collingwood, Nelson and Beatty would have made of our proceedings. They would surely have noted with dismay the decline in the powers of the Board of Admiralty since their time, and would have recalled occasions when they too had been given commitments beyond their resources by their political masters. I hoped they would also note that their successors, though hopelessly outgunned, were still firing as they went under.

All of us on the board agreed that seaborne air power was essential to the east of Suez role, but after that we differed. The admirals thought the Government should find the money to keep the carriers afloat, while I thought that we should withdraw from east of Suez.

Ironically, both points of view were soon to be vindicated. Within two years the Cabinet had abandoned Healey's defence policy and decided to withdraw from east of Suez, accepting in every detail the recommendations I had made in my resignation statement.

Then, a few years afterwards, even though we were now withdrawing from east of Suez, the incoming Tory Government acknowledged the importance of seaborne air power and ordered two new carriers, *Invincible* and *Illustrious*. Without *Illustrious*, the Falklands war could never have been fought, let alone won.

In my resignation speech in the House of Commons, I said,

> The basic mistake of the defence review has been the classic crime of peace-time British governments, of giving the armed forces too large tasks and too few resources. The overseas departments have laid down a proud defence role for Britain, the Treasury has laid down a humble defence budget for Britain and the servicemen 'carry the can'. This has all happened before. It happened in 1939. . . .

Memories of the BEF were much in my mind during those

days. In the closing stages of the war, I had written about military unpreparedness in the *Eastern Daily Press*.

> The British Liberation Army has now finally shown us how much the British Expeditionary Force lacked. The convoys now passing through our old haunts are long columns of the finest military MT in the world. . . . Overhead are huge fleets of first-class aircraft. Our tanks can be seen everywhere. . . . Our rations are much better. The mail comes more quickly. We have petrol cans nowadays which you can pour petrol out of. . . . Above all, we are fully trained, and every man knows his job backwards.
>
> It is an astonishing contrast, with an obvious moral – that if, which God forbid, we have to go to war again we must go to war properly prepared. We have got away with it this time, somehow or other. But if ever we are driven to war again we must have a BLA up our sleeve to wage it, not a BEF.

My period as Navy Minister was a time of frustration and stress. Besides the carrier controversy, I also became involved in an unpleasant brush with George Wigg, MP, the Payma-ster-General, Wilson's close and trusted adviser on security matters. 'Never tangle with George Wigg', was the advice we Ministers constantly gave each other, and with good reason. A devious, somewhat paranoid character, Wigg contributed generously to the air of Byzantine intrigue that permeated No. 10 during Wilson's tenancy. One day I learned by chance that he had persuaded Wilson, absurdly, that I was a source of a 'leak' in a Sunday newspaper about the manning of the Polaris fleet. With my security record in SOE and the Foreign Office, it was irritating to be accused of leaking state secrets by these two excessively suspicious people. Nor did Wigg give up easily. It took me several weeks of correspondence to extract from Wilson an admission that there was no evidence against me whatever.

Nor was the Royal Review of the Fleet free from stress. One evening aboard HMY *Britannia*, as I was changing for dinner, into the customary white tie and decorations, a steward knocked on my cabin door and handed me a copy of a cable addressed to the ship's captain. Earlier that day, the royal party, accompanied by myself, had been conducted round *Dreadnought,* a nuclear-powered submarine, all of us wearing radiation badges. The message read:

OPERATIONAL IMMEDIATE. Preliminary development of Dread-nought radiation badges reveals unacceptable dose for holder of Badge No. 303. Immediate decontamination and cleansing should be carried out. Facilities available in Maidstone if re-quired.

My blood froze. Whose badge? Not mine. The Queen's? How big a dose?

I asked my steward for an immediate report from the captain. It was unbelievable. The Navy would never be forgiven. I began rehearsing answers to an imaginary series of devastating parliamentary questions.

The steward came back. 'Captain's apologies, sir. The badge was Princess Anne's, but it was just a joke of Admiral Mountbatten's.'

15
LAST DAYS WITH LABOUR

Before becoming Navy Minister, during the long spell of Conservative Government, from 1951 to 1964, I had done little work in Parliament. From time to time I would ask a question or make a speech, usually as a 'shadow' spokesman, on broadcasting, or the Army, or public information or, as deputy spokesman, on foreign affairs; but the counter-attraction of television, radio and the press was irresistible. Far more PMs and Ministers − let alone members of the public − would listen to me on the air or read my weekly column in the *Star** than would dream of staying to hear me speak in the Commons. There, I might spend days preparing a speech and then fail to get called by the Speaker, or might deliver the speech to an audience of a dozen MPs and win a single paragraph of press coverage. On the other hand, provided I avoided partisanship, which I was happy to do, my BBC contract allowed me to broadcast regularly and at length on current affairs to an audience of many millions. Paradoxically, moreover, this non-partisan broadcasting made me a likelier choice as a party spokesman on other programmes.

However, as the 1950s ended, things began changing. Current affairs television became more complex and sophisticated, and the role of commentators declined. No longer able to handle research, script-writing and presentation by themselves, they gradually became mere interviewers and presenters, a role that held few attractions for me. At the same time, Hugh Gaitskell, as party leader, was coming under increasing pressure from the left, and in 1960 asked me to put in more work in Parliament. He pointed out, fairly enough, that otherwise there would be opposition to his giving me a senior post in a Labour Government.

*An admirable London evening paper, now defunct.

I needed little persuasion. It was not that I wanted a job in a future Cabinet. Indeed, I now affirm – in the full knowledge that the same claim is made, insincerely, by almost every politician – that I have never wanted or sought high office. The reason does me little credit: it is simply that, like my Paget forebears, I have a well-hidden streak of timidity and diffidence. The robustness of my fellow-politicians often fills me with admiration. How do they endure humiliating public criticism with such apparent indifference, and then come back for more?

Not that, in my television days, I minded being famous. Indeed, I rather liked being recognized and accosted by strangers. But at that time I already felt quite famous enough. I agreed to help Gaitskell because I shared his wish to reform the party's image and reverse the growing influence of unilateralism and the left. The Crossman diaries record a contribution I made on 21 October 1959 to a post-mortem debate in the parliamentary party after our 1959 election defeat.

> Far the best speech came from Christopher Mayhew, who said that the image of the Labour Party at present was that it is the party of the working class, of the underdog and of nationalization. This was an image that would get us an ever-declining number of votes. We must dissociate the Labour Party from this narrow class connection. I was struck by the way the trade unionists were willing to receive this speech in silence ... the speeches made by Mayhew and Jenkins were very well delivered and thoughtful and were received thoughtfully. It was the highest level of debate that I had heard for a long time.

Knowing that Gaitskell held the same views, I happily wound up my BBC contract and wrote to him offering my services. He replied by asking me to be deputy to Harold Wilson, then 'shadow' Foreign Minister. He explained candidly that he wanted me to 'keep an eye on Harold'.

Gaitskell and Wilson had several characteristics in common. Both were kindly, civilized and polite, and both were prodigiously able and intelligent. Yet their ambitions were widely different.

Politicians tend to be either 'be-ers' or 'doers'. That is to say, some of them want to *be* something – a Minister or a peer, or a Whip, or a social success; and some want to *do* something – to abolish nuclear weapons, or unify Europe, or reform the electoral system. Famous 'be-ers' of the past include Richard Nixon, Josef Stalin and the Vicar of Bray. Famous 'doers' include Abraham Lincoln, V. I. Lenin, Martin Luther King and Don Quixote. Gaitskell was a single-minded 'doer' and Wilson a single-minded 'be-er'. Gaitskell was committed to social democracy and the Atlantic Alliance. Wilson – witness the famous photograph of the short-trous-ered schoolboy in Downing Street – was committed to taking up residence at No. 10 and staying there as long as possible.

At that time, supporting social democracy and the Atlantic Alliance called for a confrontation with the party's Marxists and unilateralists. Getting to No. 10, on the other hand, called for courting all sections of the party – moderate and Marxist, pro-Nato and anti-Nato, multilateralist and unilat-eralist, loyal and disloyal – with a view to becoming party leader.

During his short time as leader, Gaitskell rallied the moder-ates, confronted the left, and won. Then in 1963, suddenly and tragically, he died.

This was a major turning-point for the Labour movement. From this moment, its fortunes and integrity began their long decline.

When Wilson became leader, most Gaitskellites made their peace with him, some of them actually issuing public state-ments to this effect. I could not do this myself. Wilson's industry, intelligence and ability were unquestionable, and we had worked together amicably enough from time to time; but I distrusted his political style. My misgivings had been deepened by his handling of the defence review and our relations in Israel.

After resigning as Navy Minister in 1966, my first thought had been to get the Government's defence policy changed. I helped to forge a strange alliance between pro-Europeans and the left, and with the help of an acute sterling crisis we quickly achieved our aim.

After this, life began to feel rather empty. Awkward questions began presenting themselves. How much enthusiasm did I still feel for the Labour Party? Could I risk spending the rest of my life working for a cause in which, at best, I only half-believed? Uncertain about the answers, I decided to write a candid book about the party and make up my mind in the process.

I began by visiting some of my old Labour colleagues of pre-war days. What did they feel about the party now?

I visited Dowlais, to consult my old mining friend, Llew Davies. He looked so much smarter and fitter than thirty years before that he seemed scarcely to have aged at all. The inside of his terraced miner's house was unrecognizable, with bright new furniture and decorations, a television set and indoor lavatory and bathroom. The war had brought work to Dowlais, and Llew, retrained as a fitter, had taken a job in a new ICI plant. 'If all employers were like ICI, we would have no problems,' he said. He praised the system of bonus shares for employees. 'We all used to look on profits as a dirty word: we know differently now.' He was proud of the Labour Party's achievements, but said that because their needs had been met, few people now bothered to work for the party or the unions. 'If you took twelve active men away from the unions in Merthyr and Dowlais, there'd be nothing left.'

I heard the same story from old Labour colleagues in South Norfolk, mostly roadmen and farm workers. They too were enthusiastic about the party's achievements, but gloomy about its future. 'There was a different spirit in the party in those days, wasn't there? I mean, we were all out for something big then, as a regular crusade.' 'And there was a better kind of person in the party then.' 'They're not interested now, Chris. We simply can't hold trade union or party meetings – people don't come.'

I revisited the Oxford Union, invited to defend the Labour Government's foreign policy against a leftist resolution. Sitting on the familiar bench near the president, waiting my turn to speak, I surveyed the new generation of student left-wingers on their crowded benches. How did they compare with ourselves thirty years earlier? They seemed even scruffier than we had been, and, as their heckling began, even more self-righteous, dogmatic and partisan. Their passion seemed to spring more from temperament and less from intellectual conviction: at one point in my speech, amid the expected tumult, I turned round to see several of them standing on their seats shouting 'Balls!' repeatedly in unison at the top of their voices.

In due course, after much investigation and research, I reached clear and depressing conclusions about the Labour movement. My book *Party Games*, published in 1969, declared:

> The overwhelming majority of Trade Union and Party members never attend a meeting or vote for their officers or committees. Leadership at local level – and sometimes at national level – tends to fall into the hands of leftists whose views are wildly unrepresentative of their members. Since these extremists tend to dominate or scare away the rest, the process is cumulative.
>
> Hundreds, perhaps thousands, of Trades Councils, Shop Stewards' Committees, Trade Union and Co-op Branches and Constituency Labour Parties throughout the country, churning out resolutions in support of leftist political and industrial campaigns, constitute a kind of stage army of the British working class.*

About nationalization *Party Games* concluded:

> However unfairly, the practice of nationalization has discredited the theory of socialism. In communist as well as non-communist countries, experience has shown that centralization and monopoly normally produce inefficiency and complacency, and arrogance towards the consumers.**

Logically, it might be thought, these depressing conclusions should have led me to leave the party without delay. Instead, paradoxically, they encouraged me to stay in and fight. The leftists had surely overreached themselves and were completely out of touch with the mass of party members. A

*p. 87
**p. 75

determined revolt by moderates could regain control of the
unions and the party and then drastically reform them. By
the end of 1967, before finishing the book, I had decided
not only to work for a reformed party but for a subsequent
alliance of moderate members of all three parties. *Party
Games* declared:

> This alliance could and would present itself as a revolution of
> the centre against the extremes . . . it would be a revolution of
> classless citizens against all the classes – the working class, the
> middle class and the upper class. In some respects, it would be
> a revolt of the consumer against the producer. Its formation
> would shake up and invigorate our political life.*

These aims seemed absurdly ambitious and distant at the
time. But what had I to lose by pursuing them? What more
useful and challenging work could I hope to be doing during
the coming years?

The first need was to find a leader for the new crusade.
He must be a committed moderate, imaginative, articulate,
not tied to the past. Obviously, the best candidate was the
Chancellor of the Exchequer, Roy Jenkins.

At that time, Jenkins was wrestling with the consequences
of the 1967 sterling devaluation. Our relations were frank
and friendly. A diary note of mine dated 19 December 1967,
records:

> Saw Roy Jenkins at his request. He asked me how I saw the
> future. I said there were two objectives, to make devaluation
> work and to restore the morale of the party, which involved
> replacing Harold with him. I thought the two essential things
> were for the anti-Wilson, anti-left Cabinet Ministers to stick
> together, and for them to be supported by a very discreet group
> of militant back-benchers, having no overt contact with himself.
> He agreed with this. He said that he did not think there was
> much possibility of getting rid of Harold immediately. I agreed,
> and said it seemed to me that there were two issues on which
> he might come unstuck – party discipline and the major national
> problem of trade unions and wage restraint. On the latter

*p. 134

problem, a really brave line would be needed which would be bitterly resisted by the left.

The obvious base from which to organize the moderate group was the '1963 Club', a dining club of old supporters of Hugh Gaitskell. My diary records a dinner held on the same day as my meeting with Roy Jenkins.

> Twelve members present, including six Junior Ministers – Jack Diamond, Dick Taverne, Neil McDermott, Dennis Howell, Bill Rodgers and Dickson Mabon. All declared themselves utterly opposed to Harold. Most – not including Dick and myself – thought it impossible to get rid of him. I put forward the view that the back-bench members of the club should for the coming months form themselves into an action group to resist the left in the Parliamentary Labour Party ... we must keep in touch, with extreme discretion, with Roy ... My ideas got a good deal of support.

On 22 January, I had another talk with Jenkins.

> He explained that though a number of Cabinet Ministers wished to get rid of Harold, they couldn't agree on any successor. . . . He thought Jim (Callaghan) was a bit jealous of himself. . . . Unfortunately it was no good looking to the anti-Wilson members of the Cabinet for any help. If Wilson went, the push must come from the parliamentary party.

I was not discouraged, and went ahead with bringing together a discreet group of ten militant back-benchers – Patrick Gordon-Walker, Bill Rodgers, Austen Albu, Dick Taverne, Ivor Richard, David Marquand, Carol Johnson, David Ginsburg and Will Howie.

Five of these old colleagues later became leading members of the Social Democratic Party. Sadly, two others, Patrick Gordon-Walker and Carol Johnson, did not live to see the breakaway, which they would surely have joined.

Our first meeting was held in Roy Hattersley's house in Gayfere Street. Afterwards, we met regularly in Ivor Richard's chambers in Middle Temple. I was elected chairman.

Aware that we might be in for a long haul, we decided to organize carefully and to follow rigorous rules of security. We divided up between us the hundred-odd back-bench MPs who seemed most likely to be sympathetic, and agreed to canvass personally each member of our group, making sure that the names of supporters were known only to ourselves. We classified as a supporter any back-bench MP who would be willing, as part of a concerted move, to write to the chairman of the Parliamentary Labour Party, Douglas Houghton, requesting a party meeting to discuss the leadership. Within a few weeks, our list showed 35 'certainties' (including ourselves), 39 'probables', 63 'possibles' and 17 unknown. Among the better-known 'certainties' were David Owen, Bob McLennan, Brian Walden, Douglas Jay and Woodrow Wyatt.

At the end of May, I went through our list with Roy Jenkins, who added and subtracted one or two names. We agreed that although a majority of back-benchers might be in favour of a change of leadership, we should wait for some precipitating event before our group took action. I said that before long he might well find himself leader, but that the problem that increasingly worried me was what happened thereafter. Even if we had a change of leadership, with an economic upturn, I did not think we would win (the election) in 1970. Roy Jenkins agreed with this. My diary continues:

I put it to him that simply to take over the leadership and to struggle on trying to maintain unity and morale would at best allow him two years as Prime Minister before a shattering election defeat. . . . The only hope would be to continue the takeover of the leadership with an entirely fresh revolutionary political approach. We should embrace the biggest political issue of all – far-reaching constitutional reform, aimed at ending the farce of the present party struggle. He most warmly agreed. 'I would not agree to lead without getting out of this appalling nonsense' – he nodded in the direction of the Chamber. 'We must break loose from the present political strait-jacket.' I said that action along these lines would mean the loss of the left. This was right and indeed overdue. Roy entirely agreed. We both agreed that no plans should assume any defection from the Tory Party. We also agreed that we could pick up the Liberals for the asking. 'But I don't intend to do a Ramsay MacDonald' said Roy. 'I must have a substantial part of the Party with me.' '50/50?' I queried. '70/30' he replied.

At this stage, I felt quite hopeful. If an issue were to arise, perhaps connected with Europe, or unilateralism, or party discipline, on which the Labour moderates felt strongly, but on which Wilson again equivocated or sided with the left, I thought the moderates could take action and win.

However, no such issue arose. On the contrary, Wilson disconcerted the left and reassured some moderates by supporting (at least up to the last moment) the far-reaching proposals for trade union reform contained in the government's White Paper *In Place of Strife*. In this he was naturally supported by Roy Jenkins. At the same time, these proposals were vigorously opposed by James Callaghan, and a gap thus opened up between his supporters and Jenkins'.

By chance, in December 1968, I found myself sitting next to Callaghan on a Glasgow–London flight. Though our political views were far apart, our talk turned naturally to the leadership question. I made a note of what was said at the time.

The question was, Jim said, whether or not we could win next time under Harold, and whether or not we could do any better under anyone else. I said that I thought there was also the question as to whether we would lose worse under Harold than under anyone else and he agreed. We quickly agreed that there could be no question of a change of leadership at the present time and the issue was dead. We also agreed that the next ratings would show a sharp fall in Harold's and the party's standing and the next by-election would be a bad one. I said that as Jim well knew there were members of the parliamentary party who wanted Jim to be Prime Minister and other members who wanted Roy to be. He said that last June thirteen Labour MPs came – apparently separately – to urge him to take over from Harold. He asked me whether I was a Callaghan man or a Jenkins man. I said I always had been and was still a Jenkins man, and my friends knew this, but this was an operation that had to be conducted in two stages. First, one removed Harold, and then the Parliamentary Labour Party, at the second stage, chose between Roy and Jim. Anyone who was seriously concerned about the first stage would be foolish – indeed dishonourable – to canvass for a particular candidate until Harold was gone. Jim took this point and remarked that he and Roy had always got on very well and that he would happily serve with or under him. He went on to say that he was now fifty-six, had been Chancellor and Home Secretary and had bought 150 acres in Sussex he was now passionately enthusiastic about – he showed me his copy of the *Farmers' Weekly* – and felt no personal inclination to try to go further. But he was proposing to think about the problem seriously over Christmas. He thought that a decision would have to be taken one way or the other before the end of March – after the Easter recess we should be too near the general election to consider changing horses. He then went on to say that the future leader must be well in with the trade unions and the party and people told him that Roy carried no weight in these circles. I said that wasn't the question we had to decide at this point – that was the second stage of the operation. If we started backing particular horses before the first stage was over, the whole operation was bound to be a complete cock-up. He readily agreed with this, but obviously thinks his claims are much better than Roy's.

The conversation was very easy and pleasant. I gave the gist of it to the group, which happened to be meeting the following day. Jim undertook when we parted to ensure that if he decided after Christmas that something ought to be done he would let Roy or me know.

Christmas passed, and no word came either to Roy Jenkins or myself. I guessed that Callaghan had decided on a different course, that he would win substantial union and party support by vigorously opposing trade union reform and in due course go for the party leadership against both Wilson and Jenkins. This decision, I feared, would effectively wreck all our plans.

Nevertheless, by the beginning of May 1969, Wilson had lost further ground in the party. He had forfeited the confidence of his own supporters by supporting trade union reform, and had run into difficulties over party discipline and a change of Chief Whip. Moreover the party's public opinion ratings were extremely low. My diary records:

> The 1963 dinner was crowded. Tony Crosland* opened the discussion with a very frank statement to the effect that at the proper time Harold must be got rid of. What was the use of just meeting for dinner and moaning? Not knowing anything about our group, he criticized the lack of intelligence work, planning and organization. But he said we should on no account move without consulting Roy, and that we could not assume that the precise moment had come to strike. Every single member of the group – about sixteen in all – agreed that a move must be made against Harold. Dick Taverne said that the move should be made on Friday week, after the local government elections, Bill Rodgers made an impassioned speech about saving the Party . . . I said Tony's comments about planning and organization were a tribute to the capacity of the 1963 Club activists to keep their mouths shut. No action should be taken until the activists had updated their lists. My guess was that fewer people today would be willing to strike against Harold, because of the confusion over the Industrial Relations Bill and the lack of a clear successor.

The next day I contacted all the activists individually, and asked them to update their lists. The fact that canvassing was taking place leaked out and stories of plots against the leadership dominated the press and television for three whole days. Nevertheless our security stood the strain. Wilson himself plainly underrated us. Some years afterwards he was still writing:

> There were rumours of a plot to change the tenancy of No. 10. There was never anything in them, apart from the idle tea-room gossip of a few who could always be counted on to suborn support on behalf of this or that possible candidature, without any support from their favoured putative leader. . . . The lobby, such as it was, consisted almost exclusively of a few ex-ministers I had dropped and an equally small number of others who were

*Then President of the Board of Trade.

aggrieved by the fact that I had failed to bring them into the Government in 1964 or subsequently.*

By good luck Roy Jenkins was away in Washington during this period and was not linked even in press speculation with any plot. When he got back, I rang him at East Hendred and then went to see him at 11 Downing Street. My diary records:

> He was in very good form and was completely open with me. I said I could not estimate the strength of the anti-Wilson forces until our group had met to pool our canvassing returns, but I thought there was a good chance of getting Harold out over the weekend. If the figures justified it, I was proposing to recommend that Sunday morning's papers should publish a letter to Douglas Houghton calling for a party meeting to elect a new leader, signed by three respected middle-rank back-benchers. We would then invite all our contacts to write in in support of the letter. But the main problem might well be not to get rid of Harold but to prevent Jim taking over with the support of the left and the old-fashioned trade union types. I thought Jim was the front-runner over Roy at the moment, but this again was only a guess until our group had met. It seemed to me that while back-benchers could and should be responsible for getting rid of Harold, the Cabinet should be responsible for stopping Jim.
>
> Roy listened with the utmost attention. He said there was no hope for the party under the kind of backward-looking traditional leadership Jim would provide. We had to break out with a fresh image or we were lost.

Sadly, our canvassing returns were disappointing. Some of Callaghan's supporters were now against an immediate challenge to Wilson. Some of Roy's supporters feared he would not win an election. We went through 138 selected names without being able to list more than 48 we could rely on absolutely to come out against Wilson.

Some members of our group still argued that we ought to stick to our plans. There would never be a better time, and failure would lose us very little. But David Marquand and

*Harold Wilson, *The Labour Government 1964–70*, pp. 459 and 543.

Bill Rodgers were sceptical. They simply did not think we had enough troops behind us, and they were probably right. On the other hand, a resolute move by the moderates, even if defeated, might have encouraged more Labour MPs to leave the party when the social democratic breakaway eventually took place.

Be that as it may, the move against Wilson petered out. He survived as leader, and the decline in the party's fortunes and integrity continued.

My moderate colleagues, sensibly enough, now kept their heads down and bided their time. In my own case, however, perhaps because I was older and had less to lose, I kept to the same course. This was now a lonely, uphill road and often led me into trouble with my constituency party and the Whips.

When the Tories won the 1970 election they brought in a Bill to reform the trade unions, very similar to the Labour Government's Industrial Relations Bill, which had been withdrawn in face of trade union pressure. When I refused to oppose the principle of the Tory Bill, not a single member of the Parliamentary Labour Party supported me. The *Daily Telegraph* reported:

Mr. Christopher Mayhew made a courageous one-man stand yesterday against the Parliamentary Labour Party's plan for total opposition to the Government's Industrial Relations Bill.

He said at the Party's meeting in the Commons that he thought Mr. Wilson and Mrs. Castle were right when they published 'In Place of Strife'. He had told his constituents so, and he could not just turn round now and say the opposite.

Mr. Mayhew was heard generally in silence but with occasional murmurs of anger and dissent. The biggest demonstration against him at the meeting of about a hundred MPs came when he alleged that the leadership of a number of Trade Unions was no longer in the hands of people whom the public trusted. Public opinion – and many people in the Unions – believed that the Unions were gaining too much power. If the gap widened between what the Unions were demanding and what the Party stood for, it would destroy the Party.

I was the sole Labour abstainer on the second reading of the Bill. During the debate, I said:

> I find it difficult to understand the extreme attitude of my Right Honourable friends. This attitude contrasts so sharply with their attitude quite recently, when they were the Ministers responsible. We all know that from time to time politicians have to eat their words. It is one of the drawbacks of our profession. It is no great disgrace to eat one's words on a small matter, or even on a big matter, provided a decent interval of time had elapsed between one's avowal of conviction in one direction and one's avowal of conviction in the other direction. But when one eats one's words on a major matter of national importance with a minimal interval, the politician concerned loses credibility.
>
> At that time I thought – and I am sure that I was right – that my Right Honourable friends were facing up to a very serious national problem with great courage and complete conviction. I agreed with what they said. I spoke in my constituency and on television in favour of the stand which they were taking. Now tonight they invite me with a 3-line whip to change my mind.
>
> But I have not changed my mind. Why should we change our minds compared with the position a year ago? Has the problem got better? On the contrary it has got worse.

Quite apart from the Parliamentary Labour Party, most of which was outraged, this was too much for many members of my constituency party, already upset enough by *Party Games*. Woolwich was still at that time one of the largest and best constituency Labour parties. Leftist infiltration had only just begun, and I could rely on the support of many traditional, moderate party members, including a number of stalwart friends. Nevertheless, without waiting to give me a hearing, the Executive Committee publicly dissociated itself from my views, and ten delegates to my General Management Committee, part of the new influx of leftists, circulated an emotive leaflet demanding my de-selection as Labour candidate.

I wrote to the executive:

> I was of course well aware that by urging the Party to try to improve the Industrial Relations Bill instead of destroying it, I

would arouse strong hostility from some of our left-wing and
Trade Union colleagues, and that some of them would not only
try to get my views changed but to oust me as MP for East
Woolwich. As the Executive knows, this process has now begun;
and I feel I should state frankly that since I feel I am acting in my
constituents' interests and with their support, I do not propose to
yield to this pressure at all, but to stick to my position, and in
all circumstances to stand again in East Woolwich at the next
Election.

This threat seemed to work, and the campaign to de-select
me subsided. However, worse troubles lay ahead. In 1972,
the Heath Government brought forward the European
Communities Bill, providing for Britain's entry into the
Common Market. The vote on second reading would be of
immense importance. If the Government lost, Britain would
remain outside the community, perhaps for ever. Yet a
government defeat was perfectly possible: a number of Tory
MPs led by Enoch Powell, would either vote against or
abstain, while the Labour Opposition, scenting a devastating
defeat of the Government, had imposed the strongest possible
three-line whip.

Labour supporters of British entry were thus placed in an
acutely difficult position. They had already shown political
courage some months previously in a White Paper debate,
voting with the government for entry against the bulk of their
colleagues and in many cases against the fervent demand of
their constituency parties. Could they now go further and
abstain in a vote which might bring down the government?
Eventually they agreed on a desperate stratagem. They
decided to vote against the Government − against their
deepest convictions on this historic issue of principle − while
at the same time quietly organizing sufficient Labour abstentions − ten was thought to be enough − to ensure the passage
of the Bill. I was asked to organize these abstentions.

Had it not been so worrying, this task would have been
entertaining. Abstention meant serious trouble, quite possibly de-selection, and in canvassing potential abstainers I was
treated to a fascinating series of agonized and implausible

excuses. The straightest reply came from an old friend and colleague who was not only a dedicated European but actually a former president of the Council of Europe. 'Chris,' he said, 'I know you'll think I'm a shit. But the chairman of my party's a Trot, and two of my ward parties are entirely run by Trots.'

In the end, seven Labour MPs abstained (none of them, except myself, proposing to stand again at the next election) and Britain's entry into the Common Market was approved by a majority of eight votes.

When the result of the division was announced, the Labour Chief Whip cornered me outside the Chamber. I have always liked Bob Mellish, but he had his job to do. 'Who the bloody hell do you think you are?' he cried. 'Roy Jenkins, George Thomson, all of them, all a bloody sight better Europeans than you, they all voted. Too big for your boots, that's your trouble, mate'. – and so it went on.

I dislike four-letter words, but they have their time and place. 'Fuck off, Bob!' I said, and the Opposition Chief Whip departed.

I had greater difficulty with my constituency party. Three votes of no confidence were moved against me. I survived them all – on the Executive Committee by 3 votes to 2, with some abstentions, on the General Management Committee by 23 to 15, and at the Annual General Meeting by 45 to 39. I owed everything to hard-tried, stout-hearted friends and supporters – John Keys, John Cartwright, Terry Malone, Marie and Sid Kingwell, Ethel Brooks and others. These were the kind of people who had built the fine old Woolwich Labour Party. Most of them are now members of the SDP, including John Cartwright, my former agent and my successor as MP. So that we are still political allies more than fifteen years later.

16
ALL-PARTY CAMPAIGNING

By 1972 I was thoroughly disillusioned with the Labour Party and seriously doubted whether it could be reformed from within. So I began spending more time and energy on all-party campaigning, especially for the Palestinians and the National Association for Mental Health, of which I was Chairman. The Association's newly launched MIND campaign was going well. I was kept busy attending committees, conferences and public meetings, and visiting hospitals, day centres and branches of the National Association. Meeting psychiatrists and mental nurses was particularly stimulating. I admired their patience and cheerfulness, and their cool familiarity with the uglier sides of insanity – hostility, incontinence, sometimes violence. They were as keen to talk as I was to listen. Questions poured out of me: answers poured out of them.

By contrast, I usually found meeting the patients dispiriting. Almost by definition, people who are mentally ill have much to ask and little to give, and a lay visitor to a mental hospital, however well-disposed, can soon find his reserves of compassion draining away. This, at least, was my experience. It had been different visiting prisons, borstals and approved schools some years earlier, for my TV series on crime. Here, many of the inmates – especially offenders against property, such as burglars, thieves and forgers – had been outgoing, communicative and sometimes very funny, and I would emerge positively refreshed. Yet I seldom left a mental hospital without feeling drained.

I was kept going by two convictions. First, that the mentally sick were deprived of normal human relationships only by an illness for which a cure would be found. The wall that kept us apart was high but brittle. Research could and would break it down.

I was also now convinced that although poverty, unemployment and housing were still grave social problems, mental disorder in its many varied forms, and with all the social ills it brought in its train, had become the biggest cause of misery in contemporary Britain. This was shown by the number of hospital in-patients and out-patients, the prevalence of stress illnesses, the widespread use of sedatives and stimulants, the acuteness of mental suffering and the heart-breaking problems it presented to the sufferers' families.

Further evidence came, for me, in the long-term change in the nature of my constituency casebook. In South Norfolk, with the farm workers' wage at 35s. 6d. and the old-age pension at 10s., most of the problems brought to me had been the natural consequences of poverty. How could this child get some shoes? How could that cottage get piped water or electricity? But in East Woolwich in the seventies, far more cases involved personality problems – a son 'in trouble', noisy neighbours, inability to hold down a job. A society that was better-fed, better-clothed, better-housed and better-educated was producing more crime, violence, loneliness, anxiety and depression. I warmly supported MIND's demand for more priority for mental health over material advance.

As part of our campaign, the leading officers of MIND spent some days as 'patients' in different mental hospitals, reporting afterwards to the Health Minister, Sir Keith Joseph. I chose to stay again in the hospital – Warlingham Park in Surrey – where I had stayed for the 'Hurt Mind' TV programme twelve years earlier. I was curious to see how much had changed.

Some things, sadly, were much the same, but in the most important respect – the degree of suffering of the patients – there had plainly been an improvement. The patients were less disturbed and depressed, and the hospital quieter. This seemed to be due partly to the better use of medication, but partly also to less overcrowding in the wards. Patients had more privacy, more room to move and more individual attention from nurses. My MIND colleagues and I began campaigning vigorously – too vigorously, I now think – for lessening the pressure on hospitals by discharging patients into community care. This was the right policy but was carried too far too fast. The provision of care in the community was inadequate, and I fear that many patients were discharged who would have been happier in hospital and would have improved more quickly there.

I was struck in Warlingham Park by the patients' tolerance of each other. They were a great deal in each others' company, with little or no privacy, and the behaviour of some of them, because of their illness, was irritating and disturbing. But conduct that would have aroused resentment in the community outside aroused much less disapproval from fellow-patients. If a patient was disturbed and noisy, someone might comment, 'Dick's bad this morning,' but this would be a medical, not a moral, judgement. Mental patients in hospital enjoy a strange freedom – freedom to say or do outrageous things without arousing moral disapproval. For people who are not responsible for their actions, this must be a great blessing.

Besides my work for MIND, I was campaigning actively during these years for the Palestinians. This was then a two-way campaign – to persuade the West of the right of the Palestinians to a homeland of their own, and at the same time to persuade the Palestinians of Israel's right to live in peace within her recognized frontiers. At a conference in London in 1969, I lost friends among the Palestinians by arguing that their idea of a united Jewish–Arab Palestine, which would involve the dismantling of the Zionist state of Israel, was unrealistic, and that they should settle for a 'two Palestines' solution. Today, the Palestinians would gladly accept this, while Israel now insists, foolishly, on a united Jewish Palestine. But after the 1967 war a compromise seemed possible, and I made several visits to the Arab world, always urging the 'two Palestines' solution.

Western friends of the Palestinians were then still a rarity, and since the Arabs believed, with some reason, that we were paying a heavy penalty for our opinions, they treated us with respect and trust. I found myself attending a meeting of the Jordanian Cabinet, and being pressed for my advice on matters of high policy. Once I mediated informally between the two famous rivals in the Gulf, Sheikh Zayed of Abu

Dhabi and Sheikh Raschid of Dubai. A talk with President Nasser lasted so long that eventually I had to tell him that I was due at the airport. Where was I going to? he asked. Libya, I replied. He laughed delightedly. I would find a real mess there. Had I any experience of government by revolutionary committee? No agenda, no minutes, no follow-up! Total chaos! Still laughing, he reached for a telephone, ordered my plane to be held back and went on with the conversation.

Of all the famous people I have met, General Gamal Abdel Nasser was the most shamelessly misrepresented by the western media. Contrary to repeated allegations, he was neither anti-semitic nor genocidal, and did not start, or want, the wars of 1956 or 1967. His vision of a united Arab world was unrealistic but by no means ignoble. At all times he was readier than the Israelis for a compromise peace. He wielded autocratic power for eighteen years without becoming corrupt, cruel or paranoid.

He was also a candid and amusing conversationalist, often admitting, and laughing at, his own mistakes. At our last meeting, in 1970, I asked him what he thought would happen in the Middle East if he were to die. 'I think that at this moment', he replied, 'I am the only Arab who could arrange a just and peaceful settlement. But it is strange how, while the No. 1s are about, nobody notices the No. 2s; but as soon as the No. 1s disappear, the No. 2s emerge and people see in them qualities which were always there but which they had not noticed before.'

This was an uncannily accurate prediction about his successor. When Anwar Sadat came to power, he was generally regarded as a nonentity, yet when he died a few years later, at the hands of assassins, he was widely acclaimed as one of the great men of his age.

To meet, Sadat was unlike Nasser in every way – small in stature, pipe-smoking, seemingly diffident. One thought of Churchill's succession by Attlee. This comparison should have warned me not to underrate Sadat, but in fact I did so, grossly, and with a curious result. When I met him in April 1973, when the Israelis were still entrenched in Sinai and on the Suez Canal, he told me that he had now tried all possible peaceful ways of getting them out. To please the Americans, he had thrown the Russians out of Egypt and had accepted every one of the UN's resolutions on the Arab–Israeli conflict. Yet there had been no American pressure whatever on the Israelis to leave. He was therefore now compelled to fall back on the military option. He proposed to attack the Israelis and cross the Suez Canal.

I was astounded. He could not mean it. The Egyptian armed forces could not possibly cross the Suez Canal. And why was he saying this to me? He must be hoping that I would report his statement to the British Government, who would relay it to the Americans and thus increase the pressure on Israel. I felt disappointed at being used in this way.

On my return, I duly reported Sadat's remarks to the Foreign Secretary, Alec Douglas-Home, adding that in my opinion he was bluffing and did not intend military action. Seven months later, however, Sadat gave the signal, and in a brilliant feat of arms Egypt's armed forces crossed the canal.

With Yasser Arafat I failed to establish a personal relationship. At the time of our only meeting, in 1971 in Beirut, he was being hunted equally by Israeli-backed and Syrian-backed assassins, and was moving his place of residence every twenty-four hours. My interview, arranged without notice in the small hours of the morning, was also handicapped by Arafat's poor command of English. He gave his views in a series of short, elliptical, apparently witty sentences which I could not fully understand. I probably made things worse by insisting too much on my own opinions – about the need for clear PLO statements against terrorism and in favour of the 'two Palestines' solution. Arafat was already committed more deeply in this direction than I had realized, and must have found my exhortations irritating.

Like Nasser, Arafat has been unfairly treated by the western media, but unlike Nasser is partly to blame for it himself. On western television, he would be wise to speak

Arabic, with an interpreter, and to adapt his personal appearance more closely to western expectations of a peace-loving statesman.

A particularly brave and effective spokesman for the Palestinians was Said Hammami, the PLO's representative in London during the early seventies. Like other outspoken Palestinian moderates, supporters of a negotiated settlement, he paid for his courage with his life. In 1975, two Abu Nidal terrorists walked into his Mayfair office and shot him dead, subsequently escaping. Said had discussed this precise danger with me a few months earlier. I asked him what protection he was being given, and he replied that if he was going to be killed he was going to be killed, and the Special Branch could not prevent it. Nevertheless, I wrote to the Home Secretary, expressing my anxiety, but was told that special protection had not been asked for.

I spoke at Said's memorial service and ended with these words:

> He demanded justice for his people, but insisted that justice should go hand-in-hand with reconciliation and peace.
> This was also the message of the most famous Palestinian peacemaker of all, who was a Jew.
> The reward of the greatest of men of peace is not the Nobel Prize, but the bullet and the cross.

If Israelis and Palestinians one day agree to live together in peace – hopefully in neighbouring states in Palestine – the lion's share of credit will belong to the select band of Jews and Palestinians who have acknowledged in public the elements of justice on the other side. They include PLO representatives like Said Hammami, Naim Khader and Izzeddin Kalak who, because they openly worked for peaceful settlement, were murdered. Among Israeli peacemakers should be numbered Uri Avneri, Israel Shahak, Nahum Goldmann, Marion Wolfson, Moshe Menuhin, Elmer Berger and many others. These brave Jews already have a unique achievement to their credit: they have proved to the Arabs that their adversary is not an ethnic group, the Jews, but a political movement, Zionism. They have strengthened the possibility that as the world comes to understand the true nature of Zionism, its anger will turn against the Zionists and not against the Jewish people.

At this time, the British friends of the Palestinians were better organized and more influential than their colleagues in other western countries, who often looked to us for leadership. In 1974 I met an enterprising and experienced French Gaullist Deputy, a former ambassador, Raymond Offroy, and we agreed to summon a conference of pro-Palestinian European MPs in Paris. This conference gave birth to the Parliamentary Association for Euro-Arab Cooperation, which now has 650 European MPs as members.

Financing this campaigning presented a challenge. A number of wealthy and far-sighted Arabs were willing to help us, but we were anxious to guard against outside interference, possibly complicated by inter-Arab rivalry, and to keep our work orientated towards European as well as Arab interests. We solved the problem by establishing a foundation in Switzerland, wholly controlled by European trustees, to raise and distribute funds for promoting friendship between the Arabs and the West.

During the 1970s, I spoke about Palestine at some difficult meetings in the USA. After one of these, Senator Fulbright, then chairman of the Senate Foreign Affairs Committee, came up to me. 'Mr Mayhew, I agree with 80 per cent of what you said, and wouldn't mind saying it myself; but I don't know any of my colleagues in the Senate who would dare to say any of it at all.' I asked him about the pressures on senators. He replied,

The voters don't matter, unless you have an East Coast constituency. But if we speak as you do, the media will turn against us over the whole range of our activities, and I judge that the majority of my colleagues in the Senate get a decisive proportion of their campaign funds from the Jewish lobby.

My most memorable meeting in the USA took place in Washington Cathedral. This was the first big public assembly of

American friends of the Palestinians, and the huge building was crowded. The previous evening a group of intruders had been spotted and the police told us to expect trouble. Soon after my address, which I delivered from the pulpit, just as we were kneeling to pray, some shouts of protest rang out. It was amusing to see the speed and expertise with which a number of plain-clothed worshippers rose from their knees and evicted the protesters.

Back in Britain, the Labour Middle East Council was making good progress in detaching the party from its unbalanced support for Zionism. Our main obstacle was the party leader, Harold Wilson. His unqualified commitment to Israel reflected the one-sidedness of his contacts. Jewish supporters of Israel enjoyed easy access to him as members of the Parliamentary Labour Party, the Labour Friends of Israel, the Jewish Board of Deputies and the Israeli Knesset, and as his Ministers, legal advisers, publishers, press officers and personal friends. He had no equivalent Arab contacts at all. I learnt at this time that he was also receiving, secretly, substantial subsidies for his political work from a trust composed almost entirely of Jewish supporters of Israel.*

However, Palestine was far from being my main source of concern over Wilson's leadership. Much more disturbing was his tolerance of irresponsible trade union power and left-wing infiltration. Even Trotskyism was now becoming a problem. In December 1968, I complained to the national organizer of the party, Harry Nicholas, about a weekend school I had addressed, organized for Scottish young socialists.

The fact that about half of the forty scholars were Trotskyists, or under Trotskyist influence, meant that the weekend did far more harm than good to the Party. In particular, the 'study groups' into which the school was divided became simply indoctrination classes, in which the leading Trotskyists asserted them-

*According to the *Daily Mail* (18 Feb 1977) the trustees were Lord Wilfrid Brown, Sir Samuel Fisher (later Lord Fisher), Sir Rudi Sternberg (later Lord Plurenden) Lord Goodman and Mr Arieh L. Handler.

selves over the twenty or so young and inexperienced Party supporters.

It is plaintly contrary to the interests of the Party that any more weekend schools of this type should be held, and I hope that you can assure me that the Executive will be taking the appropriate action.

The reply, from the assistant national organizer, typified the complacency of the National Executive: 'Although there are often dissidents in attendance at them the general report is that these schools are most useful, and at those which I have attended it has been found possible to avoid any minority faction "taking over" the school.'

In 1973, the National Executive Committee abolished the 'proscribed list' which had hitherto prevented Labour Party members from joining communist or fellow-travelling organizations. This was a further helpful concession to the Marxists, and reinforced my growing conviction that the party was beyond reform.

One of the last trade union meetings I addressed in Woolwich was organized by a branch of the National Graphical Association. This branch contributed two delegates to my management committee, which would decide whether or not I would be re-selected as Labour candidate – that is, whether or not I would remain MP for East Woolwich. There were about twenty-five members present. At the back of the hall were about ten older men who took no part in the proceedings. The meeting was dominated by younger men, some of them sprawling back with their legs up on the seat in front. They supported and passed resolutions backing a communist-led dock strike, further widespread nationalization and the establishment of a republican form of government in Britain.

It was not the presence of these extremists but the absence of active moderates that was so disturbing. The cause of common sense rested with ten silent, unorganized, useless old men at the back of the hall.

How different it had been in the old days, when moderates could be rallied against the extremists. I remembered my first trade union meeting in Woolwich, in 1951, called by the Woolwich Trades Council. Owing to a muddle over dates (the fault of the council's secretary) I failed to turn up on the expected day and the council passed, and issued to the local press, a resolution deploring my absence. Annoyed and suspicious, I attended the next meeting. It began with the unanimous passage of a number of communist-type resolutions. Observing the forty delegates carefully, I came to a conclusion that about thirty-five of them were good Labour Party people and that the remaining five, who were in effect running the meeting, were probably communists. When called on to speak, I started to explain why I had missed the previous meeting, but the chairman refused to let me go on about this, and when I insisted, called for a vote. The vote went my way, and I could see that the majority of the meeting was on my side. So I continued, 'After long service in the Labour movement, I think I can size up this meeting fairly. What I see is thirty-five good Labour people being taken for a ride by five communists.' At this there was uproar – that is to say, five delegates jumped to their feet, creating an uproar. But the other delegates smiled broadly. Their faces told me plainly that I had said something they had been longing to hear said for years. Ignoring the chairman's bell, I therefore spoke about the techniques of communist infiltration, with special reference to trades councils, and advised the delegates either to dismiss their chairman, secretary and other members of the executive or else to dis-affiliate from the Trades Council and form a new council 'worthy of the Labour movement in Woolwich'. My advice was promptly taken and a new Trades Council was organized.

But that was 1951. What could I do now about this NGA meeting? Those ten old men could never regain control of the branch. Nor was there any point in trying to influence the branch under its present leadership.

The final straw, for me, was Tony Benn's chairmanship of an official party committee on the media. The committee's membership was grotesquely unrepresentative – a few democratic socialists pitted against a small army of immature Marxists, led by Alan Sapper, the powerful, fellow-travelling general secretary of the Association of Cinematographic and Allied Technicians.

Benn's proposal was that the BBC and ITV should be broken down into small independent broadcasting units and that 'the controlling body of each broadcasting production unit should be elected by the workers engaged in the enterprise, based on the trade union structure'.

I wrote to Benn:

This proposal constitutes, in view of the political orientation of the main trade union concerned, a serious threat to democratic freedom. As you will know, six of the eight officers of ACAT are either Communist or Trotskyist, and the General Secretary has long supported organizations which were until recently proscribed by our Party as pro-Communist.

Benn replied coolly that I could always raise this matter on the committee. He was chairman of the Labour Party's Home Policy Committee at the time, and his wild left-wing views on the media finally decided me to abandon all hope of reforming the party, and instead to leave it and denounce it.

17
'JOHN THE BAPTIST'

'Don't go yet. Wait for the rest of us,' said Roy Jenkins. This
was the advice of all my friends. What would be achieved
by my leaving the Labour Party – this was July 1974 – all
by myself? It would produce a nine-days' media wonder and
after that, nothing. As a Liberal, I would never get back to
the House and my political career would be at an end. I
should stay in the Labour Party and try to change it from
the inside, and if that failed, leave as one of a group.

But I catechized myself. How long had I been trying to
change the party from the inside? Eleven years. What had I
achieved? Nothing. How long had I been trying to organize
a breakaway of Labour moderates? Six years. With what
results? None. If I were not already a member of the Labour
Party, would I join it now? Certainly not. Would the return
of a Labour Government be in the national interest?
Certainly not. So ought I to fight the forthcoming election
as a Labour candidate? Certainly not.

My views on political realignment and other major issues
had long been close to those of the Liberals. I decided to
join them.

I knew and liked the Liberal leader, Jeremy Thorpe. Our
fathers had been friends, and our families had occasionally
visited each other. One afternoon, he was striding in my
direction down a corridor in the House of Commons. 'Why
not now?' I thought, and stopped him.

'Jeremy, I can't take the Labour Party any longer. I want
to join your lot.'

At first he was unable to grasp what I was saying. It had
been a long time since an MP, let alone an ex-Minister, had
asked to join the Liberal Party. Finally, realizing that I was
in earnest, he led me off jubilantly to his office, where we
were joined by David Steel, then Liberal Chief Whip. I
remember little of the subsequent conversation, except that

it was conducted in the highest spirits and with much celebratory consumption of Scotch. It was agreed – a shade too confidently – that sooner or later other Labour MPs would leave the Party, and that political realignment was bound to come.

We called a press conference, and I issued this statement.

> The Labour Party has done immense service to the country over the years. I am proud to have belonged to it and fought for it since before the war, and feel sad at parting company with so many good colleagues in Woolwich and Westminster.
>
> But as these colleagues know, I have for some years been very concerned at the way the party has been developing. In particular it has become too vulnerable to the extreme left and too dependent on the unions. Time and again in the past, moderate members, including myself, have tried to change this and to broaden the basis of the party, but with declining success, especially since Hugh Gaitskell's death. I can no longer feel genuinely convinced that a clear Labour majority at the next election will be in the country's best interest, so I have resigned.
>
> Like other moderate Labour MPs, I have long shared many convictions with the Liberals, for example on Europe, east of Suez, industrial relations and the re-distribution of wealth. But at the present time, I particularly support their campaign for political realignment. We need a revolt of the centre against the extremes. We must break away from the old Tory–Labour confrontation which sets one half of the country against the other. It is not impossible if enough people vote Liberal. I believe it will happen.

All this got very good media coverage. Possibly the most perceptive comment appeared in a *Times* leader:

> Mr. Mayhew's defection is symptomatic of the unease of many on the right wing of the Labour Party at this time. There will not be a stampede in Parliament to join him, but a good many Labour people, as well as those of other Parties, will echo his sentiments. . . . The tragedy of the Labour Party is that while many within its ranks accept his diagnosis, too few have been prepared to do anything about it.

Mr. Mayhew has given Labour not a body-blow but a warning.*

I was warmly welcomed into the Liberal Party. However, I had a foretaste of the otherworldliness of some of its activists when objections were made to my having been admitted to the Parliamentary Liberal Party without reference to the Liberal Party Council or the Annual Assembly. Another surprise for me, which I should have foreseen, was the departure from the party in disgust of a substantial number of its pro-Israeli Jewish members. At Jeremy's request, I hastily produced large numbers of copies of what we called my 'health certificate', consisting largely of the *Jewish Chronicle*'s public tribute to me in the High Court. Even so, some Jewish Liberals challenged my statement that there was a grove of trees in Israel called 'The Christopher Mayhew Grove'. They simply could not believe this. However, my filing system was equal to the occasion, and I was able to produce, for Jeremy's inspection, the certificate of planting.

But how could I get back to the Commons in the coming general election? I ruled out standing again in East Woolwich, not because I might lose, though this would be likely, but because so many Labour members there had been loyal to me. I felt sure that they too would break away in due course – and in fact, as I have recorded, many of them did so – but they were not ready to leave yet, and I did not want to campaign against them.

I then received a noble offer from the Liberal candidate for Bath, Peter Downey. He said he agreed so strongly with my views on realignment that he would stand down in my favour and act as my election agent. I agreed immediately.

Bath was strongly Conservative. The MP, Sir Edward Brown, a Tory trade unionist, was sitting on a majority of 5,000.

In previous elections, I had established quite friendly relations with the opposing candidates; but with Sir Edward

*The Times, 10 July 1974.

I failed to do this by a considerable margin. He began his campaign by informing a group of supporters that I was anti-semitic, and ended it, at the count, as my defeat became known, by remarking to the mayor, in the presence of my loyal and indefatigable wife, that it was 'good to see a turn-coat biting the dust'.

However, the campaign had compensations. I had a message in which I passionately believed and which got wide publicity. A huge crowd in the Victoria Gardens watched Jeremy and Marion Thorpe descending from the clouds by helicopter to support me. Jeremy described me as 'John the Baptist, the prophet and forerunner of great events', which was gratifying and, as it turned out, not wildly mistaken.

Bath is a difficult city to canvass: too many front doors are set back from the road by too many steep stone steps. Few constituencies, however, contain so many beautiful old houses, and one of these I remember with particular warmth. It was freshly painted, late Georgian, and with a blue plaque proclaiming that the poet Walter Savage Landor had lived there. The door was opened by a well-dressed, elderly lady, whom I took to be the householder. 'Good morning, madam.' I said, ' "Nature I loved, and next to nature, art. I warmed both hands before the fire of life. It sinks, and I am ready to depart." ' 'Mr Mayhew, you have my vote,' she replied, and we both had a good laugh.

We only just lost, and the margin might have been smaller but for a successful pro-Israeli propaganda stunt. The High Court case about my £5000 challenge had not yet been heard and won, and my Zionist opponents circulated 15,000 leaflets round the constituency declaring that I had promised to pay £5000 for certain evidence about Arab leaders, had been given this evidence, and was now refusing to pay up. Was this, they asked, a man the Bath electors could trust?

I was now back in the political wilderness, and this time my prospects of returning to the Commons were bleak. Other worries crowded in. Jeremy Thorpe became involved in a sensational scandal. He stood trial for conspiring to murder a homosexual, Norman Scott, and was acquitted after declining to give evidence. Soon after joining the Liberals, I had asked him, casually and innocently, what lay behind the absurd rumour that he had had a dog shot on Bodmin Moor. He replied that he was being persecuted by a madman called Norman Scott, and proceeded to relate a long and involved story, in which I soon lost interest. I believed him, but had business to discuss and wished he would stop.

Jeremy's downfall makes it easy to forget his fine qualities. He was brave, human, witty, a fine speaker and a devastating mimic. He was also a tireless and inspired political canvasser. I remember a particular day's campaigning during the 1974 election. Jeremy's plan was characteristically colourful and ambitious: after staying the night on the Isle of Wight with the local MP, our colleague Steve Ross, we would hold an early morning outdoor meeting in Ryde, cross to the south coast by hovercraft, and call in at the main seaside resorts, landing each time dramatically from the sea, to preach the gospel of realignment.

From start to finish, the day was a disaster. It was cold and windy and never stopped raining. The hovercraft broke down immediately, and had to be abandoned on a beach, a target for the world's press photographers. We commandeered cars but were late for all the meetings, and most of our audiences had left before we arrived. Throughout this long-drawn-out shambles, Jeremy never lost his enthusiasm and good humour. Finally, in the evening, as we walked towards the Devonshire Hall in Eastbourne for our last meeting – myself cold, wet, exhausted and miserable – Jeremy spotted two elderly ladies waiting at a bus stop. Advancing on them with a smile, he held out one hand above each lady's head and declared, to their astonishment and delight, 'My dears, I *do* like Eastbourne hats.'

In the leadership contest that followed Jeremy's resignation, I strongly supported David Steel: but no sooner had he been elected than he made – as I saw it – a rare but disastrous mistake. At that time Labour's poll ratings were spectacularly low, and the Labour Government could only maintain itself in office with Liberal support. At the same time, an issue of critical importance to the Liberal Party was before Parliament – should there be a proportional electoral system for the forthcoming European elections? I was chairman of the party's electoral reform campaign at the time, and author of a booklet on proportional representation, and my fellow-campaigners and I resorted to every available means, including the summoning of a special Liberal Party Assembly, to try to persuade the party leadership to seize this opportunity. From my long experience of Parliamentary Labour Party I felt certain that if confronted the with the stark choice between proportional representation for Europe and a disastrous general election, enough of its members could be browbeaten by the Prime Minister, Callaghan, into voting for PR.

However, David thought otherwise, and accepted Callaghan's plea that he could not deliver the back-bench Labour vote. So the Liberal Party saved the Labour Party from disaster while allowing Labour Ministers and back-benchers to vote against it on a popular issue vital to its future. It remains my view that this was a historic mistake.

I began a spell of dutiful service to my new party, getting elected to the executive and standing committees, speaking at innumerable meetings, standing – unwisely and unsuccessfully – for the presidency, and helping to form the Liberal Middle East Council, which quickly ended the party's one-sided commitment to the Zionist cause. But all the time my eyes were fixed, impatiently now, on my old colleagues in the Labour Party. Why did they not make a move? I could see no reason except lack of courage. I began criticizing them publicly.

> The role of the Labour moderates has been ignominious for years: now it has become discreditable. They neither reform the Labour Party nor leave it. Instead, they go through the motions of revolt and then stay in, giving an air of democratic respectability to political elements which they themselves deeply and rightly distrust.*

*Speech to Surrey Liberal Assembly, Dorking, 14 June 1980.

However, the likelihood of a breakaway steadily increased, and in October 1980 I sent David Steel a prediction of the problems it would bring:—

'The first impossible outcome of a Labour split would be the creation of a centre party. This would be ruled out by the opposition, for understandable reasons, of leading Social Democratic and Liberal activists. To get re-elected the Social Democratic MPs would want to keep as much as possible of the moderate Labour vote which elected them in the first place; and this would mean stressing the continuity of their political attitudes, presenting themselves as the heirs of the Attlee/Gaitskell tradition. Much as they would like to win Liberal and non-committed votes and to avoid being opposed by a Liberal candidate, they would shrink from the abrupt loss of Social Democratic credibility which would follow merging with the Liberal Party.

Many Liberal activists would also oppose the centre party idea. They believe, with good reason, that the cause of Liberalism for which many of them have slaved for years without reward is at last coming into its own as the fortunes of [the Labour Party] collapse. They have a national organization, a substantial and growing membership and a credit balance in the bank. The identity of the Liberal Party is precious to them and they will not surrender it.

Moreover, even if both sides liked the idea, creating a single, unified party would involve protracted negotiations on many delicate constitutional issues. . . .

The second impossible outcome of the split would be the adherence of the Social Democrats as a block to the Liberal Party. . . .

But the third impossible outcome is conflict between the two groups. Not even the most sectarian activist in either camp would want to gratify Mrs. Thatcher and Benn by putting up Social Democratic candidates against Steel and Beith, or Liberal candidates against Shirley Williams or Rodgers. . . .

With these impossible scenarios discarded, it must follow that the relationship between the Social Democrats and the

Liberals will take the form of an alliance between two auton-
omous groups. . . .'

Not being an MP or peer at this time, and holding no
official position in the Liberal Party, I was an onlooker rather
than a participant in the negotiations leading to the
formation of the Alliance. However, in 1981 David Steel sent
me to the House of Lords and made me Liberal spokesman on
defence, and I was able to play some part in the long-drawn-
out struggle to reconcile the two parties' defence policies.

My elevation to the House of Lords did not go unopposed.
The Liberal leadership there, strongly committed to Israel,
were susceptible, to their shame, to the old, malign whispers
that I was anti-semitic, or at least *thought* to be anti-semitic
by other people. At David's request, I sent him, resentfully,
an updated version of my well-worn 'health certificate', together with proof of my support for what had now become
the party's policy on Palestine.

The pro-Israeli *Sun* commented on my elevation:

What, you may ask, has this rather nasty little man ever done
in public life to deserve the accolade in the Honours List? . . .
   Apart from his own self-advancement, Mr Mayhew has
displayed only one passion.
   A zeal for the cause of the Arabs.
   His blinkered attitude has led him to insult the Israeli Prime
Minister, Mr. Begin . . .
   *All that David Steel has accomplished is to bring discredit on
the whole Honours system and deny a place to someone who
deserves it.*

These were familiar zionist insults, and did little to spoil my
pleasure at being back at Westminster. It was a kind of
homecoming. The House of Lords contained so many old
friends and acquaintances – Labour, Liberal and Tory – that
I felt I was re-joining the House of Commons of bygone
years. We might be frailer, balder, less upright and harder
of hearing, but our political attitudes and the style of our
speeches – and their brevity or length – were remarkably
unchanged.

My appointment as defence spokesman was also a kind

of homecoming. The Liberal Party was riven between unilat-
erists and multilaterists almost as badly as the Labour Party
had been in Gaitskell's day. Should Britain have its own
nuclear deterrent? Was nuclear deterrence moral or immoral,
practicable or an illusion? I blew the dust off my twenty-
year-old speech notes and re-entered the fray. If the Alliance
was to succeed, Liberal unilateralists had to be defeated.

Liberal supporters of CND proved to be no less active and
enthusiastic, and a good deal less ill-natured, than their left-
wing predecessors of the early sixties. But they had no leaders
to compare with Nye Bevan, Bertrand Russell and Michael
Foot. Our debates were conducted in a more civilized manner
but at a lower political and intellectual level.

In 1982, the unilateralists defeated the leadership on the
issue of cruise missiles. This was partly due to their eloquence
and enthusiasm, but the tone, briefing and organization of
their campaign carried unmistakable marks of communist
inspiration, and I guessed that CND's official liaison officer
with Liberal CND, Dr John Cox, must be a communist. I
put this to CND's director, Monsignor Bruce Kent, and he
confirmed it. It was just like old times. My feelings of 'déjà
vu' deepened when, on making my discovery public, I was
denounced as a 'McCarthyite' by a leading Liberal activist.

Very slowly, and with some sharp setbacks – notably at
the Liberal Assembly at Eastbourne in 1986 – the defence
policies of the two parties converged, until finally the Alliance
reached agreement on a single comprehensive statement
which made good sense.

On 12 June, 1985, as a 70th birthday present, Cicely threw
a party for me in the House of Lords. Nearly a hundred
friends and relations came. It was a strange sensation, seeing
so many familiar faces at the same place and time. It was as
though my seventy years had been a play, and all the actors
had suddenly appeared together on the stage to take a bow.

My brother Pat was there, who had asked our governess
over nursery tea what would happen to God if he was under
the clouds when it started raining. I noted the small chip in
one of his front teeth which I had made in the twenties with
a fast leg-break.

I saw my cousins Stephen and David Howarth, who had
been at the Manor House, Horsham with me, and whose
reassuring presence had eased the pain of homesickness. They
had been valued contributors to our book 'One Family's
War'.

The sight of my brother-in-law George Heywood brought
back football and music at Haileybury, and of Frank Longford, tutorials and anti-fascist demonstrations at Oxford.
Alastair Sedgwick was a reminder of the invasion of Sicily,
Norman Reddaway of 'Phantom' and the Foreign Office,
Michael Adams – who has done more for the Palestinian
cause, for less reward, than anyone else I know – of our
disastrous libel action in Jerusalem.

Many old political colleagues came. John Cartwright was
there, formerly my incomparable agent in East Woolwich,
now the Alliance spokesman on defence; also Marianna
Clarke, friend, guide and hostess in Bath, and my Party
leader David Steel, fellow-campaigner for a Liberal–Social
Democratic Alliance from the earliest days.

In the place of honour, alert and beaming, sat my stepmother Beryl. Not long before, *The Times* had reported
admiringly that in a regatta off Lowestoft, sailing her much-
loved Norfolk brown boat 'Pochard', Beryl had won a third
place *at the age of 83*.

A toast was proposed by my elder son David, with the
fluency to be expected from a lay preacher and
Liberal–Alliance parliamentary candidate.

The most beautiful of the guests, in my eyes at least, were
my daughters Tess and Judy. Tess, a busy and successful
solicitor, is much in demand in the family for free legal
advice, while Judy, a first violin in the Royal Opera House
orchestra, helps to sharpen our appreciation of music. Like
David, Judy does her kindly best from time to time to remove
my doubts about the authenticity of the Bible.

The party's most stylishly and inexpensively dressed couple
were my younger son David and his wife Debbie. Besides
their regular jobs, they run an embryo antiques business, and
have no scruples about valuing, and offering to sell, their
parents' modest possessions.

Masterminding large parties is child's play to Cicely, and this birthday present of hers reminded me that if I had not abducted her from the foreign service, she would certainly have become an ambassador. As it is, she is a member of the Parole Board, and of the police and prison service selection boards, and a long-standing chairman in the Civil Service Selection Board. She has supported me, right or wrong, in all my numerous and varied battles, usually with much more passion than I could ever summon up in my own cause.

18
THE VERDICT

I have written most of this book at home in Wimbledon. My study overlooks our garden and a small stream and belt of trees that separate it from the sixteenth fairway of the Royal Wimbledon Golf Club. If I looked out now, through the trees, I would probably see golfers moving slowly, by stages, towards the difficult, sloping green; and if I opened the window wider and leant out, I might well hear distant cries of frustration: 'Oh, no!', 'Not *again*!', 'Hell!', and so on. This is music in my ears. For over fifty years I have been hearing it, and adding my voice to it, on golf courses all over Britain, and occasionally abroad.

It is strange that we golfers, of all people, should be such poor judges of our talents. Usually we overrate them: a good shot reflects our natural form, a bad shot is a strange aberration, and our 'normal' round is a round of exceptional merit such as we seldom if ever achieve.

Yet we all have official handicaps, which measure our capacities quite accurately. Before the war I played to six, nowadays to nineteen, which shows that I was once quite a good golfer and am now a poor one. It is a useful piece of self-knowledge. It tells me where I stand, and helps me to chart the progress or (over the last fifty years) the decline in my prowess.

Unfortunately there is no system of handicapping in politics, or diplomacy, or personal relations or in life itself. We can only guess, or accept other people's guesses, as to our proper ranking. My guess is that as a politician I have been a medium-handicap player, a cut above the rabbits but no match for the scratch players.

Perhaps if I had been more single-minded, I might have gone further. But what is the point of this kind of speculation? Obviously, if I had acted differently, my career would have been different, but then I would have been a different person. More than we realize, I think, we are prisoners of our nature and nurture, loaded down with baggage from our genetic and environmental past.

Studying crime for one of my TV series, I was impressed by the techniques used by criminologists for predicting the future conduct of offenders. They would compute a number of the offenders' known attributes – family background, history of mental disorder, previous offences, intelligence, number of previous jobs and so on – and then forecast which offenders would, and which would not, commit new offences within a given period of time. The accuracy of their predictions was striking.

The same techniques, I believe, could in theory predict the conduct of law-abiding people, among whom I include myself. Though blessed throughout my life with a great measure of freedom, I have a strong sense that my decisions, like those of convicted offenders, have been predictable. The decisions were free because it was I who made them; but they were predictable because a computer fed with sufficient information about me – my physique, IQ, Christian upbringing, Paget forebears, public school education and so on – could in theory have foretold them. I am free to be myself, but not to change myself, or be changed by outside forces, beyond the limits of my nature. I cannot add a cubit to my stature, or ten points to my IQ, or even, at my age, thirty yards to my tee-shots.

When we compare ourselves with others, we should feel neither proud nor humbled by what we find: their talents and opportunities are not the same as ours. I have visited too many hospitals for the mentally handicapped to believe that men are equal or can have equal opportunities. All men are unequal, but equal respect is due to people of unequal abilities.

In personal relations, my guess is that I have been a long-handicap player. Not unkind, but inattentive and clumsy. At Oxford, I once confessed to Frank Longford that I could never summon up any interest in human beings in units of less than a million. He replied, with typical charity, that the fact that I was aware of this was a sign of grace. But failure

to be considerate towards individuals is a serious shortcoming, and I am sadly aware of having received more kindness during my life than I have given. Campaigning for
anonymous groups of people – the Palestinians, the mentally
sick – is no substitute for personal acts of charity. The two
things conflict to some extent, since there is a limit to everyone's time, but they can never replace each other. Kind
people need to support good causes: without kindness,
campaigners become mere do-gooders.

Before the war, my fellow-socialists and I preferred ideas
of human betterment to acts of charity. Campaigning for
socialism and peace is a worthy activity, but so is visiting
the sick. A balance has to be struck and we did not strike
it.

Preoccupation with ideas also undermines human
relations. It produces bad listeners, impatient of small cour-
tesies. It also presents special dangers to politicians. My
life has been full of strong convictions – about socialism,
Stalinism, political realignment, commercial television,
mysticism, mental health, Palestine, East of Suez and, most
recently, disengagement* – and almost all of them have
either been irrelevant to my career or have gripped me too
strongly, or too soon, for my political good. Roy Jenkins
once offered me some friendly advice – 'In politics it doesn't
always pay to be right.' This is undoubtedly true. Skilled
politicians are careful not to put forward the right idea at
the wrong time, or out of turn. But such self-discipline has
always been beyond me. Ideas have carried me away. They
have used me, not I them.

Ideas about religion and mysticism have influenced me
most. Yet I still find the question, 'Do you believe in the
existence of God?' unanswerable. Because I perceive colours,
shapes and sounds, do I believe in the existence of things
called Colour, Shape and Sound? It does not follow, and I

---

*Long-term changes in East–West relations in Europe are making
it possible to revive the idea, widely supported in the fifties, of a
mutual withdrawal of American and Soviet forces and the reunifi-
cation of Germany

am not sure. The Hindu spokesman in my religious TV series, Swami Lokeswaranda, told viewers the story of three sons who returned from a scripture lesson. When asked to describe God, two of them gave lengthy answers, but one remained silent. It was this third son, said the Swami, who understood God best.

It was a great Christian mystic, Meister Eckhardt, who said, 'Why do you prate about God? Whatever you say about God is untrue.'

But what then are we left with?

We are left with the perceptions and guidance of the founders, saints and mystics of the world's religions, and of the great poets and writers. And this is enough. We do not need to go further and accept their interpretations of what they perceived, most of which, taken literally, contradict each other, defy science and logic, and produce dissension.

What cannot be challenged is the importance of the perceptions and the good sense of the guidance; and here there is a consensus. The perceptions are essentially the same, and they lead to the same message: that we should distrust worldly values and put first the things of the spirit, trying to be truthful, loving, peaceable and selfless.

Even for saints and mystics – let alone for ourselves – attainment of the spiritual heights is a rare achievement. The spiritual summit is not a place to live in or even a place for recreation. It is more like a lighthouse, visited occasionally by a lonely specialist, showing the rest of us with occasional flashes how to avoid the rocks and get home safely.

There are peaceful moments in the countryside when we feel strangely at one with our surroundings, when the grass seems unusually green, and the trees are outlined against each other and the sky with particular sharpness.

There are moments at meetings when the speaker says something brave and true from personal experience, and the audience sits quite still, with their eyes on his face.

On fine mornings in Cambridge, a moment comes when the sun lights up the pinnacles of King's College Chapel.

There is the moment of entry of the ripieno choir in the opening chorus of Bach's St Matthew Passion.

I once watched a nurse playing patiently and affectionately with a three-year-old girl who was deaf, dumb and blind.

I once heard the closing lines of Shaw's *Saint Joan* spoken by Sybil Thorndike, kneeling, spotlighted in a darkened theatre: 'Oh God, who madest this beautiful earth, when will it be ready to receive thy Saints? How long, O Lord, how long?'

Such things, for me, are brief, faint gleams from the distant lighthouse; and they remind me of the traditional words of my governess, which I quoted at the beginning of this book: 'Wherever people are, all over the world, God is in their hearts, and in everything beautiful and good, like flowers and the sea and sunsets and music.'

I feel then that I understand these lines of T. S. Eliot:

> We shall not cease from exploration
> And the end of all our exploring
> Will be to arrive where we started
> And know the place for the first time.

INDEX